THE TITANIC
AND
SILENT CINEMA

Stephen Bottomore

Number nine in a series of monographs
on pre-cinema and early film

**THE
PROJECTION BOX**

No. 13 (handwritten)

of an edition of 500

© Stephen Bottomore, 2000

ISBN 1 903000 00 9

A CIP catalogue record for this publication is available from the British Library

Published by The Projection Box
12 High Street Hastings East Sussex TN34 3EY
s-herbert@easynet.co.uk

Printed by Windmill Press, Uckfield, East Sussex
Typeset by David Brown, Maynards Green, East Sussex

CONTENTS

Introduction 5
Acknowledgements 12
Film People on the Titanic 14
William H. Harbeck 26
The Titanic and the Lantern 48
Titanic News Films 69
Exhibiting Titanic News Films 90
Dramas out of a Crisis 105
Helping the Victims .130
Conclusion 139
Appendix: Extant contemporary
 films of or about the Titanic 142
Appendix: the Lusitania and
 Early Cinema 149
Notes and References 164
Index 185

To my sisters
Kate and Eleanor

Introduction

> And as the smart ship grew
> In stature, grace, and hue,
> In shadowy silent distance grew the Iceberg too.
>
> Thomas Hardy, 'The Convergence of the Twain'
> (a poem to commemorate the *Titanic* disaster)[1]

Prelude to disaster

The *Titanic* was the largest ship of her day, a veritable floating palace, and was said to be practically unsinkable. Yet on 15th April 1912 on her maiden voyage from Southampton to New York City, she did indeed sink after striking an iceberg, and 1517 passengers and crew members lost their lives. Only 706 survived. The loss of *Titanic* was the greatest ever peace-time marine disaster, and the biggest news story of 1912.

The Bishop of Winchester described the sinking of the *Titanic* in 1912 as 'a monument to human presumption', and perhaps this is one reason for the continuing fascination of this story of maritime disaster.[2] A ship that everyone thought was unsinkable, one of the great technological achievements of the age, and yet on her maiden voyage this vast, apparently immortal liner proved as vulnerable to the forces of nature as any other human endeavour might be.

This book is devoted to the various relationships between the *Titanic* and the silent cinema. But well before this greatest of all ship disasters, the seas and oceans had attracted the attention of filmmakers. When people first saw films in the 1890s, they found the portrayal of seas and wave motion enormously impressive, and this flirtation of moving pictures with the sea also extended to its grimmer aspects. Long before the *Titanic* disaster, shipwrecks had been a staple subject for panoramas and magic lantern shows and were also to be a regular theme in the early days of film. But filmmakers were not only interested in ships when they were in trouble, for these vast liners had an interest all of their own.

(1) Cover of one of the leading American film trade journals published just after the sinking of the Titanic, Moving Picture News *20 April 1912*

The early twentieth century was the heyday of large passenger liners, especially on the North Atlantic route. Record numbers of emigrants to the New World filled the cheaper accommodations: between 1900 and 1914, over 12 million people crossed the Atlantic in 3rd class and steerage. At the same time, rising disposable incomes meant that increasing numbers of the middle and upper classes wanted to travel. To fill this demand, the great shipping lines, including White Star, Cunard, and Norddeutscher-Lloyd vied with one another to build bigger, faster and more luxurious liners. The film companies had an interest in these liners, for these mammoth ships were hugely impressive on screen, and were big news when being built or arriving at port, and most of all when floated down the slipway for the first time.[3]

It is worth reminding ourselves of the sheer ambition of the design of these vast ships. The *Titanic*, for example, had a length of 882 feet and a gross tonnage of 46,328. The ship was fitted out with every luxury and modern convenience, including a gymnasium, Turkish bath, swimming pool (the one on the *Olympic* was the first ever to go to sea), squash racquet court, lending library, barber's shop, hospital with operating room, grill and palm garden, and dark room for photographers.[4] These in addition to all the fabulous fittings – from chandeliers to hardwood paneling – in the dining and reception rooms. And the entertainments included at least one small orchestra. Perhaps the only modern luxury that the *Titanic* lacked was a cinema![5]

The *Titanic* missed out on things cinematic in another sense too. Sadly only a few shots were ever taken of this ship, whereas some of the other floating palaces of this era of great liners were the subject of several films. This is ironic considering a proposal that had come from filmmaker Charles Urban before the *Titanic* was even built. The order for the sister ships, *Olympic* and *Titanic* was placed with Harland and Wolff on 1st July 1907. On 26th September 1907 Urban wrote to the company requesting permission to film the two ships during construction. It seems that the filming was to be undertaken 'free of cost to the firm', so the resulting film would effectively be free publicity for the shipbuilder. The Harland and Wolff representative wrote back the following day to give a general welcome to the proposal. He did, however, suggest that it would be better to postpone filming until a previous ship order had been completed by Harland and Wolff. He added helpfully that no problem of industrial secrecy would arise during the filming, as, with such a large workforce in the shipyard, secrecy was practically impossible anyway! The Urban cameramen, he said, would be allowed to film the initial work on the *Olympic* and *Titanic*, to include the initial construction of the slipways and gantries.[6]

TELEGRAMS:
"Harland, Belfast."

Shipbuilding & Engineering Works

Belfast, 27th. Sept., 1907.

2/10/07

Refer to the
"Titanic"
& "Olympic"

Dear Mr. Urban,

I am in receipt of yours of yesterday's date, along with the Catalogue, for which I am much obliged; and I am quite sure the firm will have much pleasure in complying with your request. I will put the matter before Lord Pirrie on his return here next month, and write you more fully; and the next time I am up in London I will try to arrange an interview with you at the firm's offices, 1a, Cockspur Street.

So far as I know there would be practically little or nothing that would require absolute secrecy, as, in a big place employing so many, this is practically impossible. Lord Pirrie, however, I know will be much interested in your proposals, and I am sure will further your wishes as far as practicable.

I notice that the whole thing will be done free of cost to the firm.

I presume your reason for writing is on account of the many notices appearing lately in the press regarding the construction of a couple of large ships that we are likely to build in the future, and the preparations which are being made. I do not, however,

(2) Letter from shipbuilders Harland and Wolff 27th September 1907, responding to Charles Urban's proposal to film the Titanic *and* Olympic *during construction (Science Museum)*

(2).

think it would be necessary for you to commence taking any photographs or films until after we have launched two ships from the North End of our yard: when no doubt two or three interesting films might be made of the starting of the slip-ways, the foundations for the gantries, and the erecting of the two gantries which the firm have ordered from Sir Wm. Arrol & Co., of Glasgow. with their numerous cranes, etc..

Yours very truly,

[signature: A.M. Carlisle]

Charles Urban, Esq.,
LONDON

For some reason the *Titanic* was not filmed, and instead Urban's cameramen filmed the construction of the sister ship, *Olympic*, and her launch on 20th October 1910: this was screened the day after the launching ceremony.[7] The *Olympic* was filmed not only in black-and-white but also in the Kinemacolor process, the films being shown at the Scala Theatre, London in September 1911.[8] The monochrome version survives in the NFTVA with German titles, and is a superb record of the construction of the *Titanic*'s sister ship in 400 feet. The film begins by showing us the dry dock where it will be built. The process includes the laying down of the keel and the positioning and riveting of sheet metal onto the ship. We see the entire superstructure and steam cranes in operation, and a sign on the dock confirms the identity: 'White Star Royal Mail Ship Olympic'. We see the ship being launched down the slipway and the crowds dispersing afterwards.[9] (Kinemacolor footage purporting to be the launch of the *Titanic* was shown in the USA, but may have been film of the *Olympic*).

We do not know why the *Titanic* was not filmed under construction, but perhaps it was a compromise, with Harland and Wolff deciding to let Urban's men film just one of the ships, so avoiding the disruptive presence of a film cameraman around both ships. Or perhaps it was Urban himself who decided to restrict the filming to one ship, in which case he must have been kicking himself in April 1912 for having chosen the 'wrong' ship. As we shall see, at the time of the sinking of the *Titanic*, newsreel men were desperate to find any footage which was in any way related to the *Titanic*, but there was practically none available of the liner.

Interestingly, the third of the sister ships to *Titanic*, named the *Britannic*, built in 1914, was also filmed during construction. The film survives in the British Pathé archive, and seems to have been shot (presumably by the Pathé Gazette) on a day when one of the funnels was being put in place. And it seems that the launch was also filmed – by the Topical Budget newsreel. The *Britannic* was employed as a hospital ship in 1915, but was blown up by a torpedo in 1916, at which point the newsreel companies dusted off the earlier films.[10]

Cinema's response to the disaster

In recent years there has been increasing interest in the *Titanic*, especially with the rediscovery of the wreck of the ship, and an apparently unending stream of publications has appeared, examining every aspect of the infamous disaster of 1912.[11] Interest has been further stimulated by the successful release of the feature film by James Cameron. But Cameron's film is only the latest of several fiction films and documentaries that have been produced, and the *Titanic* disaster has had an extremely close relationship with the moving image for many decades. In fact there were links between the infamous shipwreck and the screen even at the time of the event itself and in the months that followed, and this is what will chiefly concern me in this small book.

My interest in the relationship between the *Titanic* and early cinema began several years ago as I worked my way through the cinema trade journals of the pre-First World War era, in search of material on a number of topics, especially non-fiction film. In the pages of periodicals like *The Bioscope* and *The Moving Picture World* I noticed a considerable amount about the *Titanic* disaster (and about films related to the sea in general), and it seemed worth pursuing this as a separate research project. As my research progressed it became clear that the *Titanic* disaster offers an interesting case study of various aspects of the cinema in this early period of the medium's evolution. While this book focuses on the *Titanic*, I have tried to draw out from these events some more general points about film and media history.[12]

To start with, it is worth reminding ourselves of the sheer 'newness' of the cinema at the turn of the century, for the first public film shows were given in the mid 1890s. But moving pictures immediately attracted large audiences, and the medium rapidly developed in terms of technique and commercial organisation. By the time of the *Titanic*'s maiden and only voyage in April 1912, the cinema was going through an unprecedented period of activity and growth. The three years before the First World War were, in terms of exhibition, the height of the cinema building boom in Britain and elsewhere; and in terms of film production, dozens of one-reel dramas and comedies were appearing on the market every month, and newsreels and feature films were also getting into their stride. So at the time of the *Titanic* sinking, a variety of film genres already existed, and a large number of exhibition venues were in place, to splash versions of the disaster before millions of eager spectators.

A news story could be presented at this time in a number of screen genres, including newsreels, reconstructed news, dramas, lantern slides, as well as various mixtures of these formats. The news coverage was especially interesting, because, with so little genuine footage available of the *Titanic* (and of course none of the sinking itself), producers and exhibitors were sometimes tempted to screen fraudulent moving images purporting to be of the *Titanic*. Such distortions of the truth are often of great interest to film historians.

My research has also made clear that, perhaps surprisingly, the lantern slide business was still in robust health in this period, and slide sets depicting the disaster were available from many distributors. The *Titanic* disaster also spawned a number of dramatised film versions, and the first of these was rushed into production within days of the events, starring a real participant in the tragedy, Dorothy Gibson, who re-enacted her ordeal for the cameras.

It is clear from contemporary reports that screenings of these films – notably the newsreels – often had a deep emotional impact on audiences, and benefit screenings raised a good deal of money for the hundreds of victims' families. These victims, incidentally, included several people connected with the film business who were travelling on the *Titanic* – a reminder of the importance of the transatlantic film trade at this time, in films, equipment and personnel. In this sense the sinking had a very direct effect on the cinema industry. The deceased included William Harbeck, today a forgotten name in film history, but in the early teen years one of the leading documentary cameramen in the world.

I hope that this book will have some appeal both for people primarily interested in the *Titanic* and shipping, who may not have realised the close connections between the disaster and the early movies, as well as for those more preoccupied with the subject of film. The *Titanic* disaster offers a fascinating case study of the cinema at one moment in its pioneering period, and demonstrates that even at this early date producers, cameramen and others could react with imagination and vigour to the challenge of presenting a major news story in moving images.

Stephen Bottomore
July, 2000

NB. In what follows I will refer to the length or running time of films. In 1912 films were measured in feet in the anglophone world, and in meters on the European Continent. A reel of film was about 1000 ft (300 meters), which at 16 frames per second would last about 16 minutes. I should add that just because I list or describe a particular film does not mean that it survives – sadly, the majority of early films have in fact been lost.

Acknowledgements

In researching and writing this small book, I have been assisted by many individuals and institutions. First and foremost I would like to thank Stephen Herbert and Mo Heard for having the confidence to commission this work, which at the time they agreed to it, was little more than a long essay and a pile of notes.

In my researches I have extensively mined from the work of John P. Eaton, both for general background history and for detailed information. For French early cinema sources on the *Titanic* I have been advised by Jean-Jacques Meusy. For German sources I have relied on the suggestions of Deac Rossell, who also very generously translated articles by Michael Wedel and his colleagues into English. These articles originally appeared in the journal *Filmblatt*, whose editors have kindly allowed extracts to be published here in translation. I should like to thank lantern experts Richard Crangle, Hans-Danklev Hansen, Peter Jewell and Lester Smith for allowing me to reproduce items from their collections, and further information on lantern sources has come from David Francis and Stephen Herbert.

I am indebted to several sources for information about William Harbeck: the National Archives of Canada, the British Columbia Provincial Archives and Colin Browne; the researchers at the Cripple Creek web site; George Behe and Don Lynch, respectively past and present vice presidents of the Titanic Historical Society; and to the researchers at the website Encyclopedia Titanica. Ned Comstock and Michele Lowery of the University of Southern California, and Madeline Matz of the Library of Congress and Paul Spehr provided copies of pictures from the *Moving Picture News*. In my researches on Arne Fahlström I relied on the Norwegian Film Archive, who alerted me to the work of Per Kristian Sebak.

Frank Thompson's detailed research on the film *Saved from the Titanic* has been invaluable, as has Hans J. Wollstein's research in a number of areas of film and Titanica. Simon Mills' book, *The Titanic in Pictures*, has helped in a number of areas. As ever I have done much research at the British Film Institute library, and many thanks to David Sharp who kindly allowed me to photograph from the *Bioscope*. Bryony Dixon of the BFI helpfully provided facilities to view copies of extant *Titanic* films; frames from Pathé and Gaumont productions are the copyright of those respective companies. The Cinema Museum also helped with the illustrations. And no tribute would be complete without mentioning Luke

McKernan of the British Universities Film and Video Council in London, on whose expertise and good judgment I have increasingly come to rely in recent research projects, and Simon Brown of the National Film and Television Archive, an expert *Titanic* scholar in his own right.

Thanks also to Nick Hiley for several useful tips; to Tony Fletcher and Vittorio Martinelli for information on Rita Jolivet and the *Lusitania*, and to Ivo Blom for generously translating the Italian sources. Ivo also provided unique information from the Netherlands concerning the exhibition and distribution of *Titanic* films.

I have made use of the published researches of a number of regional British film historians, and have been greatly helped by Linda Greenwood of Belfast Public Libraries, who kindly checked through newspapers of that city to find details of screenings of *Titanic* newsreels. Finally, my thanks to various libraries and collections in the United States, France, Germany and elsewhere in which I have found interesting details about the *Titanic* story.

Stephen Bottomore

The author and publishers gratefully acknowledge the kind permissions of the many libraries, film archives and and picture libraries that have provided illustrations for this publication. These are reproduced for purposes of historical review, and the copyright and reproduction rights remain with the respective sources. Some uncredited illustrations are from private collections, or from unattributed copies in research files.

Film People on the *Titanic*

The film industry in 1912 was booming on both sides of the Atlantic, and there was a constant exchange between the two continents in moving picture films and personnel. It is symptomatic of this important trade that a considerable number of people on the *Titanic* were connected with the film business. Several of these people died when the ship sank in the early hours of April 15th, and the disaster had a direct effect on the infant industry. To the general public the best known of these film folk travelling on the *Titanic* was movie starlet, Dorothy Gibson, who survived the sinking, and who within weeks was starring in a film version of the *Titanic* events. There is more on her story in my chapter on film dramatisations of the *Titanic* story.

Daniel Marvin
After Dorothy, the best known of the movie people on the liner was 19 year old Daniel Warner Marvin, from New York. He was from a very well established 'film family', being the nephew of the pioneering Biograph cameraman Arthur Marvin (who'd worked with film pioneer David Wark Griffith), and son of Henry Norton Marvin, co-founder and President of the American Mutoscope and Biograph Company and President of the Patents Company of America.[1] Depending which source one follows, at this point in his life Daniel had either been training to be an engineer or planned to follow his father into the film business. Daniel was travelling on the *Titanic* with his 18 year old wife – another wealthy American, Mary Graham Carmichael Farquarson, whom he had just married in England on 12th March. They followed their wedding with a three-week honeymoon tour of Europe.[2]

The young couple seem to have made a hit in England: in the wake of the disaster, Mr Aron Hamburger, a director of the Dover-street studios in London (which had once been the Biograph studio) said of young Marvin:

'He was a splendid specimen of American youth – strong, athletic, and well-set-up. Mrs. Marvin is an extremely pretty and vivacious girl. They were both of them full of the joy of life and affection for each other, and when in England behaved just like two happy school children on a holiday. They spent most of their time sight-seeing and going to parties, dances, and the like. Everyone made much of them. The girl's parents are wealthy, and she had received £2,000 from her mother as a wedding present.'[3]

*(3) Mr and Mrs
Daniel Marvin*
Daily Sketch
17 April 1912

Interestingly, their wedding was filmed – the 1912 equivalent of today's 'wedding video'. The ceremony was in fact performed twice, the second time being restaged for the camera.[4] After the loss of the *Titanic* and the realisation of Daniel's death, frames from this film were reproduced on the front page of the *Daily Mirror* (on 15th May, 1912), which reported it to be the very first wedding ever to be 'cinematographed'. (It was in fact not the first).[5] Apparently the couple had received a film camera as a wedding present, which may have been used for filming the 'wedding video'. The fact that the quotation above comes from the director of Dover-street studios implies that this company may have assisted in the filming, for they were especially used to immortalising the rich and famous on film.[6]

Daniel and Mary boarded the *Titanic* at Southampton as first class passengers, final destination New York City. *Titanic* researchers have worked out that they occupied cabin D-30. On the night of the collision, as the ship was sinking, Daniel fought his way through the crowd, carrying his wife to the lifeboats, and promising to follow her later by jumping from the ship with a life preserver.[7] Mrs Marvin recalled how Daniel had called out:

'"It's alright, little girl. You go. I will stay." As our boat shoved off he threw me a kiss, and that was the last I saw of him.'[8]

(4) Images from the film of Mr. and Mrs. Marvin's wedding. Daily Mirror, 15 May 1912

Daniel died in the sinking: his body, if recovered, was never identified. But Mrs Marvin was picked up by the *Carpathia*, the ship which, too late for most of the passengers, came to the rescue of the *Titanic*.[9] Among the crowds which gathered at the New York offices of White Star on 15th April 1912 were relatives of both Daniel and Mary Marvin: Mrs Frank Farquarson and Mrs W. H. Marvin learnt that Mary had been saved but there was no word of Daniel Marvin.

Mrs Marvin was pregnant at the time of the sinking, and gave birth to a baby girl, Peggy, but for a long time did not tell the girl about what happened to her father. She destroyed all the cinema pictures of the wedding. For many years she lived happily with her second husband, Horace DeCamp, and had two other children.[10]

William Thomas Stead

Another passenger on the ship who had been immortalised on film shortly before the voyage was veteran journalist, William Thomas Stead. A few days before his departure on the *Titanic* Stead visited the London studios of the Biofix company, at 56 The Strand, to have his image ('living likeness') taken. The Biofix system became available to the British public in 1911, and, at the low cost of a shilling provided the sitter with a professional flick book made from the film taken at the sitting.[11] The book could be flicked to show the sitter in motion: a moving portrait in effect.[12]

After his session in the studio the Biofix pictures 'were bound and sent to Mr. Stead within a quarter of an hour'. They were the last photographs taken of the famous journalist, and were to be used in an article he planned to write on novel systems of photography. In the circumstances the pictures ended up being reproduced in the *Daily Sketch* as an obituary tribute to him.[13] The pictures show Stead's face in medium close up, as he turns through 360 degrees. Perhaps he was placed on a rotating platform to accomplish this? This rotation might have been a normal Biofix technique, though this is not evident from an article on the system in the *Royal Magazine* in 1912, which reproduces a picture of the studio, showing an ordinary, non-rotating chair.[14] Or perhaps he simply turned around as he was being 'biofixed'.

This was not the first evidence of Stead's interest in photographic, projected and moving images. As early as 1890 he wrote an article on 'The mission of the magic lantern' in the *Review of Reviews*, a journal which he edited. He became very interested in the lantern for religious propaganda, and he edited a magazine called *Help*, (scarcely known today, even among lantern scholars) which aimed

Last Portrait of Mr. Stead Before He Sailed to His Death on the Titanic

(5) William T. Stead
Daily Sketch, 20 April 1912

(6) William T. Stead filmed by the Biofix process
Daily Sketch, 23 April 1912

HOW MR. STEAD MET HIS DEATH.

Mr. W. T. Stead died as he lived—courageous and fearing nothing. He was foremost in the work of helping to get the women and children into the boats, and when the last boat had pushed off Mr. Stead jumped into the sea. During the dinner he talked much of Spiritualism, thought transference and the occult.

specifically to promote the use of the magic lantern as a means for social and religious improvement.[15] Later, in around 1901, he advocated a similar educational and social agenda for cinematography in an article with a title, 'The mission of the cinematograph' which harked back to his lantern statement. He wrote:

18

"Biofix" Series of the Famous Veteran Journalist in Characteristic Gestures.

'The living picture, which has long been one of the most popular turns in the music-hall entertainment, must now take its place as one of the potent weapons with which the well-equipped educationist goes forth to combat the hosts of ignorance.'[16]

Stead's interest in cinema seems to have waned over the years, and his journal, *Review of Reviews*, later devoted little space to the cinema, in contrast to the American *Monthly Review of Reviews* which published several articles on film.[17] In truth Stead had many interests aside from visual instruction: he was an editor of the *Pall Mall Gazette* at one time, and was a vigorous advocate for international peace. Ironically, given his death in mid-Atlantic, he was also a great 'trans-Atlanticist', and even had a combination of the British and American flags in his office to demonstrate his belief in the 'Americanisation of the world'.[18] His trip to America in 1912 was partly to lecture for the Men and Religion movement, along with his colleague the Rev. Dr. J. Stuart Hodden(?) of Glasgow. Both men were friends of Alfred H. Saunders, the editor of the *Moving Picture News*, one of the major film trade journals at this time. They had been friends since the time of Stead's lantern enthusiasm in the 1890s, and Saunders wrote an obituary tribute to him.[19]

Jacques Futrelle

Another literary figure with film connections who drowned in the *Titanic* disaster was popular novelist Jacques Futrelle (1875-1912)[20]. Known as 'the American Conan Doyle' he first gained a wide popularity with his short detective stories, eventually published in book form in 1907 as *The Thinking Machine*. His career also included work as a newspaper man and as a theatrical manager.[21] He was a passenger on the *Titanic* with his wife, May (also a novelist), they having changed their plans and decided to return to the USA after becoming homesick in Europe.

(7) Jacques Futrelle
Daily Sketch 17 April 1912

While Futrelle may not have had any concrete connections with the film industry during his life, at least eight films were produced from his works after his death, in the period from 1914 to 1920. For example, his novel, The Diamond Master, which had originally appeared in the *Saturday Evening Post*, was released as a 3-reel film in 1914 by the Eclair film company. His wife was also a novelist in her own right, and a film was made based on one of her works in 1915.[22] During the *Titanic* disaster Futrelle proved himself something of a hero, steadfastly refusing to accept a place in a lifeboat, and begging his wife repeatedly to go alone. But she would not leave him, and only after his plea – 'Remember the children' – decided to enter a lifeboat for the sake of their children at home, who, if both parents died would have been orphaned.[23]

Noel Malachard
Two film cameramen also went down with the *Titanic*: William Harbeck and Noel Malachard. Harbeck is sufficiently important a figure in early film history to deserve a chapter to himself (see following chapter). But there is considerably less information on Malachard. We know that he worked as a cameraman for the newsreel Pathé-Journal in France.[24] But there is no further information on him from French sources on the Pathé company, nor in French Canadian film history sources.[25] (There is a French actress, Delphine Malachard, and one wonders if she could be a relative?)

But thanks to a number of tireless *Titanic* researchers more information has come to light. Malachard travelled from Paris, France, and boarded the *Titanic* at Cherbourg as a second class passenger. He held second class ticket number 237735, price: £15 0s 11d. On board the *Titanic* he shared a cabin on D-Deck with René Lévy and an unknown man.

At the beginning of the voyage Malachard made the acquaintance of Mrs. Marie Jerwan, who occupied the cabin opposite. On 14th April, after lunch, he was on deck together with Jerwan and René Lévy who was pointing out the drawbacks of the lifeboats and the equipment to lower them. This was ironic, for it was the very night of the collision with the iceberg, when the lack of lifeboats became tragically apparent and many drowned who could have been saved. When, later that night, the *Titanic* struck and began to sink, Mrs. Jerwan went to B-Deck and suddenly heard her name being called. Noel Malachard, René Levy and their room-mate were there and Malachard said: 'We'll take care of you'. She entered lifeboat 11 helped by Malachard, and he and the others shouted: 'Good bye!' as the boat was lowered, and waved their hands. That was the last time Malachard was seen. He died in the sinking, and his body, if recovered, was never identified.[26]

Malachard was on his way to work for the Pathé Weekly newsreel in North America, and according to one source he had a film camera with him and 'secured negatives of the sailing of the ship' (how did they know this, one wonders?) all of which were of course lost.[27] An obituary was published in the French film periodical *Ciné Journal* on 20th April 1912, which noted (giving his name as Malachart):

'The tearful mother and the friends of Mr. Malachart, one of the valiant cameramen of Pathé frères, are going through some agonising moments, for Malachart was one of the passengers on the *Titanic*. Our friend was on his way to Canada to run a branch of the company, but did he manage to survive? We ardently wish for this, but without any real hope. Malachart was 26 years old, he came from Lyon and was a film enthusiast from an early age. His name is associated with many travel films which were especially well-made. Let us hope he has not become a victim of his great profession.'[28]

Malachard seems to have been a genial fellow, one journal describing him as our 'sympathique confrère'. This was not the only journal to report his possible demise, and an item appeared about Malachard in *l'Echo du Cinema* (of the 19th April). Interestingly, if one scans the text just above this report there is an item

A bord du "TITANIC"

Cruelle Angoisse

La mère éplorée et les amis de Monsieur Malachart, un des vaillants opérateurs de la maison Pathé frères, traversent en ce moment de cruelles minutes. Malachart était, en effet, parmi les passagers du *Titanic*. Notre ami, qui se rendait au Canada pour y diriger une succursale, est-il parmi les rescapés ? Nous le souhaitons ardemment mais, hélas, sans un espoir bien ferme.

Malachart a vingt six ans. D'origine lyonnaise, il s'était de bonne heure passionné pour la Cinématographie et son nom demeure attaché à maints films de voyage d'une exécution supérieure. Puisse-t-il n'avoir pas été victime de sa glorieuse profession ?

(8) Item about cameraman Noel Malachard (misspelled Malachart) Ciné-Journal, 20 April 1912

about the head of the Eclair film company, M. Jourgeon, setting off for America to visit his new branch there – further witness to the constant comings and goings across the Atlantic of numerous film personnel in this period of early cinema.[29]

Arne Fahlström

Another man who had a connection with the early movies was on board the *Titanic*: 18 year old Arne Joma Fahlström (anglicised to Fahlstroem). Arne, from Slemdal, Christiania (as Oslo was called up to 1925) was born on 5th July 1893, the only child of Alma and Johan Fahlström. Fahlström's parents were a prominent couple in Christiania in the late 1800s and early 1900s, being well known actors and theatre proprietors, and Johan was a recognised artist (and painted several portraits of his son Arne). They owned two theatres in Christiania (Centralteatret and Fahlström Theatre), and were very much involved with many aspects of the theatre business in the capital and other towns in Norway for over 30 years, before they decided to semi retire in 1911.

*(9) Arne Fahlström,
as a student*
To norske
skuespillares
liv, 1927

Meanwhile, Arne was finishing his studies at Royal Fredrik's University in Christiania, and after doing very well in his exams, his parents offered to send him on a trip to America where he intended to study acting and cinematography. They wanted Arne to get a thorough training in film and theatre. As well as being a generous and public spirited youth, (his motto was 'go out and do good amongst people') Arne had shown an interest in the performing arts from an early age, and in this period the movies were an obvious opportunity for a young man.

Arne started off from Christiania on 3rd April on board the Wilson Line steamship *Oslo* bound for Hull. He paid 320 NKr for his first class ticket. His final destination was to be a family contact, the father of a good friend: Minister Edvard Hagerup Bull, of 33 Linden Street, in Bayonne, New Jersey. Arne boarded the *Titanic* at Southampton on 10th April as a second class passenger. Nothing is known of his activities aboard the *Titanic*, and his whereabouts during the fateful evening are also unknown. His body was never recovered.

A few days after the disaster an item appeared in the *New York Times*, noting that Fahlström's father had asked E. H. Bull to meet his son from the *Titanic* and to look after him while in America.[30] Bull now feared that Fahlström (misprinted as 'Salstrom') had drowned, and he planned to put an ad for him in the **Lost and Found** column of the *New York Times* (but I cannot find this ad on that day).

Arne's parents, who heard about the disaster during a holiday in Copenhagen, never recovered from the loss of their son, and later created a fund in his name for poor theatre artists.[31] To help to avoid further shipping disasters, they donated nearly all their fortune to the Norwegian Lifeboat Association (NSSR). In return the association agreed to build a lifeboat named after Arne so that he would never be forgotten. Two Arne Fahlströms were built, the first completed in 1913. During its 33 year long service it saved 32 people from a certain death and assisted nearly 1800 ships. The second one was launched in 1967.[32]

Further losses
In the aftermath of the tragedy it emerged that there had been a number of other people with more tenuous film connections on the *Titanic*. It seems that one unnamed sailor who went down with the *Titanic* was a regular performer in the 'Lieutenant Daring' series of naval-based action films and 'had many times been depicted by the kine-camera in numerous adventures.' This series, produced by the British and Colonial Kinematograph Co., was one of the most successful products of the British cinema in this era. Another cinematic link with British seafarers was through J. Fred Watson, the manager of a picture palace in Hoxton, (in east London, near Shoreditch) who lost a personal friend in E.J. Smith the famous Captain of the *Titanic*, while one of the patrons of this cinema lost eight relatives on the ill-fated liner.[33] Quite possibly there were others on the *Titanic* with links to the film industry.[34]

But in addition to the several people mentioned above who worked in or were connected with the early film industry, the *Titanic* also carried a considerable number of films. It was claimed in May that about 1 million feet of film had gone down with the ship, '...the Sales Company, the Ambrosia, and Great Northern Company being among the losers.'[35] There is official backing for the existence of film prints on the *Titanic*, as several cases of film are listed on the ship's cargo manifest (with, alas, no titles given for the films they contained) as follows: the New York Motion Picture Company consigned one case of film on the *Titanic*, and C.B. Richard also consigned one case of films, the latter shipped by the European xxx Company (the middle name cannot be made out) and said to be 1 ft. 7 inches in size. The American Express Company consigned six cases of film, and also three cameras and camera stands, though it is not clear if this camera equipment was for movie or for stills work.[36] There were definitely some photographic supplies on board, for the Halifax Photographic Company placed an advertisement after the sinking to announce that a number of their parcels had gone down with the *Titanic*, and that any of their American or Pacific Island customers who had not received their orders as a result would receive replacements free of charge.[37]

It was claimed initially that the film version of Max Reinhardt's mystery play, *The Miracle* had been lost in the *Titanic* sinking. This was apparently being taken to America by Mr Henry Birkhardt Harris, an important theatrical manager based in New York, who'd acquired it for £10,000 plus a royalty.[38] Some claimed that about 1000 meters of the original negative was lost, but this was later admitted not to be the case.[39] There is some confusion here, as it seems the film had not even been shot when the *Titanic* sank, though it had been copyrighted in the USA as early as January: possibly as an advance warning against piracy![40] Notices in the British trade press later in the year say *The Miracle* was being filmed in May 1912 and would be released in mid-August.[41] Perhaps the film on the *Titanic* was an earlier version, or perhaps Harris was only taking the rights in the future film to New York, not an actual film?

In any case Harris (aged 45) was not to survive the voyage. He had boarded the *Titanic* at Southampton with his wife Irene Harris. As the *Titanic* foundered he escorted his wife to lifeboat D, and on being told that he couldn't go any further, said: 'Yes, I know. I will stay'.[42] He died in the disaster, while his wife was rescued.[43] Harris was by any standards a major figure in the theatrical world. He owned the Hudson and the Harris theatres and had an interest in two other show houses in New York. He also owned three theatres in Chicago, one in Syracuse and one in Philadelphia.[44] His interests extended beyond the performing arts: one British newspaper claimed that he was a former Mayor of Chelsea and much interested in art matters, and that he was involved in discussions over the King Edward memorial.[45]

Films on board might also have included William Harbeck's films (see following chapter for more on Harbeck). As far as I know none of these films or cameras has ever been salvaged from the *Titanic*, but I live in hope! After all, a film was recovered from the wreck of the *Lusitania*, and while this film was badly decomposed, the title could still be made out and a few feet saved. (See Appendix 2). The recovery of Marvin's or Malachard's or Harbeck's film camera or films would be a particularly fine discovery.

William H. Harbeck

(10) William Harbeck with film camera somewhere in the western United States
Moving Picture News
27 April 1912

Of all the people connected with the film industry who were on board the *Titanic* for her maiden voyage, none had had a longer or more distinguished career in the industry than William H. Harbeck, and at the time he drowned he was on the verge of further achievements in the film business. In the early years of the cinema, documentary films such as travelogues were one of the more popular genres, and Harbeck was a leading exponent of this type of film-making.

Starting Out

Harbeck has been an unknown and unacknowledged figure in film history for many years, and even now there are a number of unanswered questions. Indeed his life begins with a mystery, for while we know that the place of his birth and early life was Toledo, Ohio, we are not so sure of the date: a 1900 census claims it was in December 1866, though more recent family contacts suggest it was in September of 1863.[1] William was an only son. His father, John S. Harbeck was from New York and his mother, Ida, from Pennsylvania.[2] William married Catherine (Katie) L. Stetter sometime in the 1880s, with whom he had two sons, John S. and Stanley.

Prior to embarking on work in the nascent film industry Harbeck had a varied and colourful career: he was successively a bookkeeper, journalist, inventor, travelling book agent, baker, and owner of a steam laundry.[3] He even worked at one time as 'a Lucas county deputy sheriff'.[4] (Lucas county is in northwestern Ohio, at the southwestern tip of Lake Erie.) But Harbeck was soon to venture much further from home, when he moved far west, to Anaconda, Colorado, a town in Cripple Creek's mining district. The town grew up during the gold rush in the region in the 1890s, when it was home to several mines and many miners. In late 1899 and early 1900 Harbeck was the editor of the local newspaper, the *Anaconda Examiner*, and lived on Main Street in the newspaper's offices.[5] Though he was married during the time he served as editor in Anaconda, Harbeck is listed as living alone here in 1900: perhaps, like most miners and gold rush pioneers he left his wife at home while he went to work in the gold fields. But in about 1904 his wife Catherine also came west from Ohio, and the couple lived briefly in California before settling in Seattle.

It is not certain when Harbeck began to work in motion pictures. According to some sources, he commenced his film career in 1897 when he worked as an assistant for the film business of Miles Brothers in San Francisco. But this seems unlikely, because, as we have seen, in the late 90s he was working as a journalist in Cripple Creek. He was almost certainly working as a cameraman by 1906 though, for in that year it is said he was the first cinematographer in San Francisco after the great earthquake in April, and shot a film about the aftermath of the quake.[6] According to the *Moving Picture News*, his association with Miles Brothers dates from this period rather than the 1890s, and that would make sense, as Miles was of course based in San Francisco.[7]

At about this time Harbeck started filming for the Selig Polyscope Company of Chicago. Perhaps his connection with Selig began in Cripple Creek, where, in 1904 the Selig company had shot what is now considered to be the earliest

American narrative film: *Tracked By Bloodhounds*, or *Lynching At Cripple Creek*. Selig had a western agent and cameraman based in Denver, one H. H. Buckwalter, who shot many of their Colorado films. Harbeck may have either come into contact with the Selig company as they were filming the Cripple Creek story, or through meeting Buckwalter elsewhere.

In 1906 Harbeck was at work in Yellowstone Park, on behalf of the Selig Company. According to one witness who saw him there he was filming scenes including 'the Geysers, the Falls and other scenery'.[8] The company's 1907 catalogue offered several films which are probably the result of this trip by Harbeck. *Scenes in Yellowstone Park: the Land of Geysers* was a compilation of 660 feet, with views of 'Old Faithful' geyser and the Grand Canyon and Falls, buffalo and elk in the wild, and a coach full of tourists visiting the park.[9]

(11) A Hale's Tours 'carriage' (in London)
Kinematograph and Lantern Weekly 1 October 1908

Many of Selig's films of this period shot in the West were intended for the so-called 'Hale's Tours', a popular form of moving picture exhibition from about 1905 in which films, often taken from the fronts of moving vehicles, were shown in theatres built to resemble railway carriages.[10] Much of Harbeck's work for Selig was probably for Hale's screenings. His Yellowstone films were shot as part of a major filming trip he undertook at this time. He told a trade journal that he had been filming in 'Oregon, Idaho, Utah and Colorado, where I exposed 8,000 feet of moving picture negative, mainly railroad scenery, including 1,000 feet made over the Midland Terminal Railway through the Cripple Creek mining district.'[11] Selig's August 1906 catalogue supplement lists a Hale's production of 600 feet, *Trip over Cripple Creek Short Line* which may be the film referred to. According to the description of the film it began in Cripple Creek, showing the mines, but quickly came to beautiful scenery of 'snowcapped mountains, grassy valleys and monster rock formations'. The catalogue enthused:

'This is one of the most wonderful and realistic views of Mountain railroading ever made. A special train over the famous Cripple Creek Short Line is in the picture constantly and on the rear platform is a group of pretty girls in summer dress. Their smiling faces and actions add much to the picture and give a touch of novelty never before attempted. The engine ahead is seen to puff and pant up the heavy grades and around the short curves, dashing into black tunnels and along narrow shelves hewn out of the solid rock.'[12]

Clearly part of Harbeck's skill in this film (if it was indeed his) was to combine the typical Hale's moving scenic view with the group of girls in the foreground. This more complex image, with two layers of depth, would have been a refreshing novelty. By early 1907 Harbeck was solidifying his business as a cameraman. He owned two film cameras, and a specially constructed studio at 1223 Third Avenue, Seattle. Here he had installed a printing and developing plant capable of handling 10,000 feet of film per week, 'where I have already turned out considerable special film for the local trade.'[13] His location assignments continued, and in February 1907 he was about to leave on another trip, this time to Mexico:

'...where I will again expose 10,000 feet of negative on railroad scenery and Mexican attractions. These films will be used to supply the demand of tour cars [ie. Hale's shows] in this section during the early spring and summer. The subjects will be all new and very choice for this purpose.'[14]

But this work was not to be as simple as he implied, and a journalist later noted of Harbeck's Mexican assignment:

'...he had some hair-raising experiences in taking pictures from railway trains hanging over cliffs 3,000 feet in height. He even ventured into the arena while a bull fight was on, and almost came to conclusions with the bull.'[15]

The Canadian Pacific Railway

Just a few months later, in May 1907, Harbeck was off on another filming trip, this time just across the border from Seattle in British Columbia, Canada. A 1907 *Victoria Daily Colonist* newspaper article outlines his trip, and notes that Harbeck was working for the 'Hale's Tourist Association of Portland, Oregon'.[16] In fact this assignment was probably sponsored by the Canadian Pacific Railway (C.P.R.), though the films might well have been shown in Hale's Tours outlets. Thanks to the *Colonist* article we have a detailed account of some of Harbeck's work in B.C. Film-making was still an utter novelty in this era and the writer of the article noted his strange film camera, as a '...queer box-like piece of apparatus', and described Harbeck bent over this device,

'...turning a crank and adjusting it so that the powerful lenses situated at the front could command the best views that could be had.'

(12) Vancouver's Hale's Tours (Scenes of the World) establishment at 131 Cordova Street, known as the Edison Grand Theatre. Frame from Harbeck's only surviving film, taken in British Columbia in 1907 (National Archives of Canada)

(13) The Johnson Street Bridge in Victoria's harbour, from the same film (National Archives of Canada)

Harbeck spent one day, 4th May, in Victoria where he shot 600 feet of film of local scenes, working with the support of the local Tourist Association. Some shots were filmed from a streetcar which took him along Victoria's main streets, ending up in James Bay where he stepped off and filmed a long pan of the Empress and Parliament Buildings. He also filmed several other local sights: the sealing fleet at Point Ellice Bridge, the 'reversing falls' at the Gorge, the Island of the Dead in the Harbour, and the local saw mills.

The *Colonist* article reported Harbeck's plans for his next bout of filming. On the 5th May he planned to travel to Nanaimo, stopping off at Shawnigan Lake. Then he would cross the water to shoot in Vancouver, and, travelling on the C.P.R. would film some 1000 feet of negative of the Fraser Canyon. For his on-train filming he planned to use an interesting technique. Hale's-type films, earlier known as 'phantom rides', were often taken by the cameraman perched on the front of a train, often from the cowcatcher. But presumably it was not possible to film from such a position on this trip, as Harbeck described a trick technique he planned to use. He would position himself on the last carriage of the train, filming the view looking backwards along the track. His film was then to be projected in reverse, thus creating the illusion of moving forwards. He added, however, that:

'The only trouble...is that if you happen to pass a man on the tracks he appears to be walking backwards. Otherwise the illusion is perfect.'

The article claimed a hundred copies of Harbeck's B.C. film would be made and screened in 'half a hundred' sites in the world, so presumably quite a number of prints would have been made. At least one of them ended up in Australia, and in 1994 Australia's National Film and Sound Archive returned 70 rolls of Canadian-made nitrate film to Canada, among which was an unidentified 12-minute film of British Columbia. It turned out to be this film of Harbeck's. The restored film was 'premiered' in Vancouver at the Ridge Theatre in November 1996. It is probably the only surviving film made by Harbeck.

Harbeck's link to C.P.R. is clearly reflected in this film, as he has included C.P.R. piers, ferries and a C.P.R. station in several shots. The Victoria segment closely follows the description from the *Colonist* article. On the other hand no shots of the Fraser Canyon line are on the surviving print, so perhaps he didn't actually go ahead with this planned part of the trip. Also, it seems that more was shot in the city of Vancouver than he had anticipated, much of it taken from a moving vehicle, possibly, as in Victoria, from a streetcar. Interestingly, at one point the

(14) The Empress Hotel in Victoria. From the same film (National Archives of Canada)

camera reveals Vancouver's Hale's Tours establishment at 131 Cordova Street, known as the Edison Grand Theatre.[17]

Harbeck's next plan was to cross Canada (possibly filming some more for the C.P.R.), and in June 1907 was due to make scenic films in Britain and continental Europe. It is not known if he actually took this trip. But his film work was on a firm foundation by this point in his life. He had become an established resident of Seattle by 1908, listed as a 'manufacturer of moving pictures'.[18] His links with the Canadian Pacific Railway were becoming more and more solid, and in 1909 he went back to western Canada as official photographer for the company to film locations along their railway line from Victoria to Calgary. The project was conceived and developed by J.S. Dennis, assistant to the 2nd vice president of the C. P. R. Harbeck was given every facility to accomplish the project, and he left Vancouver on a special train with instructions which would be the dream of any dedicated photographer:

'Proceed on special train, June 17th, 10.40, go where you want, stay as long as you like, return with the best set of motion pictures ever made.'[19]

The film Harbeck eventually came back with was well up to expectations, and was screened at the end of 1909 in a coloured (ie.tinted) version 4,000 feet in length. The venue was in a special C.P.R. theatre at the Alaska-Yukon-Pacific Exposition in Seattle.[20] Screenings six times a day, were free of charge accompanied by a yarn-filled lecture by an old C.P.R. man, Kit Carson. The film was exceedingly popular with the visitors to the exposition, and apparently there was standing room only in the theatre. It included views of beautiful mountains and other attractive scenery, from the Pacific to the Rockies, some filmed from the front of the train. There were scenes of trout fishing in Banff, views of the Selkirk Mountains, Laughing Falls, Twin Falls and Takakkaw Falls in Yoho Valley, BC, and even light relief with a sequence of a runaway surrey team. A trade journal commented:

'The diversity of subjects embraced in the film is beyond description, it covered so much of intense interest that one surprise followed another in such rapid succession there was always an argument after the performance as to which part of the film was the best.'[21]

After the exposition screenings there were plans to show the film in several venues in the United States, while Harbeck himself exhibited it in Canada, for which territory he had obtained the rights.[22] As publicity he distributed a photograph of himself in the process of filming at Takakkaw Falls. This was labeled 'Compliments of W. H. Harbeck, official motion picture photo-grapher, C. P. R. ' which confirms that he had indeed established an official position for himself with the company.[23] Harbeck spent the year end break of 1909 in his former city of Toledo, and early in January 1910 he gave a private screening of his C.P.R. film with an amusing publicity dodge, in which invitations were printed as rail tickets.[24]

(15) Harbeck filming for the CPR at Takakkaw Falls in Yoho Valley, British Columbia in 1909
Moving Picture News 11 Dec 1909

34

While filming at Lake Louise in Alberta it seems that Harbeck had met Lord Northcliffe, the great British press baron, who promised to publicise Harbeck's film. He also invited the cameraman to visit him in London, and in late January 1910 Harbeck did indeed make the trip to Britain, sailing on the *Lusitania*, to screen his C.P.R. film and other films he had made in Canada.[25] It is not known if he did meet Northcliffe again, but Harbeck's larger ambitions in motion pictures were also becoming clear by now, and he planned to visit most of the principal manufacturers in Britain.[26] On a rapid visit to London (and then Paris) he did meet some of the British film fraternity, and seems to have got on well with them, being impressed with their enterprise and business methods.[27] In future visits he would renew some of these acquaintances.

In mid 1910 C.P.R. again entrusted Harbeck to film Canadian scenes, of farming and ranching, from a special train that they had laid on. He was by now an assistant to the company's second vice president.[28] In February the following year he was back in Europe again, visiting Paris and Berlin, and in London he met Will Day, one of the leading cinema equipment dealers in Britain at this time, and a prominent booster and historian for the industry.[29] Day showed Harbeck the new hand-held Proszynski film camera which ran on compressed air, 'and he immediately bought the second that will be produced, so smitten was he with its practicability'.[30] It seems Harbeck had come to Europe partly in order to film several thousand feet of views of the continent, to be used by the C.P.R. 'on its theaterette cars.' (presumably meaning it would be shown in cinema-wagons on trains). Interestingly during his Atlantic crossing on the *Empress of Ireland* he gave the sea-sick passengers a screening of his films of the Canadian Rockies to take their minds off their sickness.[31] Harbeck completed a two-year contract with C.P.R. in July of 1911.[32]

His work for C.P.R. in showcasing Canada for potential immigrants had made its mark, and other organisations and town boosters were having similar thoughts about the effectiveness of film in attracting business and tourism to their regions. There are any number of paragraphs in the trade press at this time about towns in America (and even in Britain) commissioning films to advertise their particular part of the world. In the spring of 1911 the Western State Illustrating Company of Seattle took on Harbeck to film Yakima County – the films were to be shown free of charge back east to attract interest in the region.[33] It is not clear if this project actually took shape, but in an age when the West was in expansive mode, there was a developing market to produce advertising films.

Harbeck soon found himself back in British Columbia again, this time employed by the Grand Truck(?) Steamship Company to film the inauguration of their northern steamship service. His helper on this trip was Archie Wills, who seventy years later recalled this expedition in company with Harbeck, whom he called 'the first and only movie-cameraman on the Pacific coast'. He remembered in particular that the cameraman's equipment, compared to modern gear, 'looked insignificant'.[34] The idea behind this project was to film two of the company's ships, and to this end the group set off from Vancouver on one of the ships, the *Prince Rupert*. Harbeck and Wills were landed at an outcrop of land, from which point they were to film the *Prince Rupert* and her sister ship, the *Prince George* – both head on as they steamed towards camera. 'A great promotional shot,' said the Captain. But at the last moment the currents in Seymour Narrows turned one of the ships so that it was hidden behind the other, and the shot was not nearly as impressive as planned. They couldn't do a retake, and while the pictures were useable, 'the glamor was gone'. One suspects that many such filming projects in this era had a similar outcome.

Alaska

In July of 1911 Harbeck went to southern Alaska and spent two months filming there. It was an arduous assignment – on one occasion he had to wait for eight hours in front of Child's glacier to film an avalanche of ice. He was very impressed with the landscape and animals, but there were surely other reasons for going there at this time.

This was a crucial moment in the history of Alaska. During the Klondike gold rush, the richest source of copper ore in the United States was discovered in southern Alaska in the region of Controller Bay, as well as silver. This discovery set into motion events that would change American political history. J. P. Morgan and financier Meyer Guggenheim formed the Alaska Syndicate and purchased the claims. This led to accusations of political wrong doings at the federal level, and inflamed by this and for other reasons Theodore Roosevelt split from the Republican Party, forming the Bull Moose Party, and ran against William Howard Taft for President. Alaska was given territorial status in 1912.

Thus, when Harbeck's Alaska film was screened at the Eden Musee in New York on 7th February 1912, presented by Harbeck himself, it must have raised considerable interest. In addition to natural scenery of mountains and glaciers, the film showed industrial operations including mining and the Copper River Railroad, a major construction achievement in itself which transported the copper ore to the coast for shipment. There were also scenes of the only oil

(16) Notice concerning Harbeck's controversial film about Alaska
Moving Picture News
10 Feb 1912

MOVING PICTURES OF SOUTHERN ALASKA

On Wednesday afternoon, February 7th, there were shown at the Eden Musee, some excellent and interesting moving pictures of Southern Alaska.

Alaska is a portion of the Union but little understood except by the meagre few who have thought well enough of this rich Northern possession to explore its inner recesses, and one or two large capitalists who are quietly gripping the throat of the country, and who are endeavoring to crush out of existence the small enterprise.

Mr. Harbeck, of Seattle, to whom we are indebted for this animated pictorial display, explained step by step the story of beauty and virgin wealth set forth upon the screen. Only one thing Mr. Harbeck neglected to impress upon the minds of unitiated Easterners, in Alaska, although half of the year darkness prevails with the exception of a short time each day, the other half has perpetual sunshine, and Alaska is not by any means the land of ice and snow which Easterners are inclined to think it is. As was demonstrated not long ago at the land show at Madison Square Garden, some of the finest agricultural produce that was exhibited there was grown in Alaska.

Nevertheless, Mr. Harbeck's remarks on Alaska were intensely interesting, and the films shown, of exceptional beauty and true to life. The scenes along the Copper River Railroad, the mountains and glaciers, mining operations, the only oil refinery in Alaska, and many other scenes of interest.

A unique manner of describing the topography of the Katalla and Controller Bay district, showing the location of the coal lands over which there has been so much controversy. Previous to the Alaskan display an interesting film was shown demonstrating the beauty of the scenery through which the Canadian Pacific R. R. passes.

Perhaps one of the most interesting films among Mr. Harbeck's collection is the one giving illustrations of the fishing industry in Alaska. In this film one of the interesting points is the return of fish up stream after an absence of considerable length where they actually make ascents in the river by jumping upward distances of several feet. The fishing industry is one of the largest in Alaska and is capable of creating intense interest in the film.

---

refinery in Alaska and the major fishing industry in the territory. The final film was more than just actuality shots strung together, and included animated maps of Alaska, showing the positions of towns, rivers and railways, which '...appeared and disappeared on the map as the lecturer described them.' This film was copyrighted in the Library of Congress as *Alaska (Panoramic Views of) in animated maps*, submitted in January 1912.[35]

Some kind of political motive may have been behind the making and screening of the film, though it is difficult to work out exactly what. Among the audience at the Eden Musee were prominent Wall Street investors with interests in Alaskan railway and mining developments. There were also plans for the film to be shown to President Taft and members of the cabinet in Washington.[36] The Taft administration were in favour of turning Alaskan lands in the public domain over to private ownership. On the other hand, one report noted that the film showed 'the Guggenheim interests' and that it was screened in the home of Gifford N. Pinchot in Washington.[37] Pinchot (1865-1946), as Chief of the Forest Service and a key mover in the conservation movement of the early 1900s, opposed Taft's plans and Taft eventually fired him.[38]

The film was also destined for more general screening, and it would inevitably have packed a political punch at this time. One trade journal, the *Moving Picture News*, noted that the film would serve to educate more people about a territory in which 'one or two large capitalists ... are quietly gripping the throat of the country, and who are endeavoring to crush out of existence the small enterprise.'[39] It is not at all clear what Harbeck's attitude to this issue was. He apparently went to Alaska on his own account, believing that the territory had 'wonderful possibilities for agriculture' and that when Canada had run out of land, immigrants would look north.[40] But immigration was scarcely a burning issue in the Alaska of 1912, and Harbeck was not so naïve that he could have ignored the current issues. Indeed a more critical attitude is revealed in the text printed on headed paper apparently belonging to Harbeck:

'Watch for Harbeck's latest motion pictures exposing the Guggenheim interests in Alaska and the Controller Bay grab. Films that will worry Congress and startle the whole United States and probably change the present political map.'[41]

Perhaps the real motives behind this film would become clearer through consulting government papers. In the meantime it remains something of a mystery. In any case, Harbeck also undertook other, less controversial projects at this time, filming the *Round-Up* at Pendleton, Oregon, copyrighted in the Autumn of 1911; and also films of or for the Winnipeg Exposition in Manitoba and the San Francisco Exposition.[42] By 1912 Harbeck had become an established member of the film industry, well-liked on both sides of the Atlantic because of his trustworthy character, and known to his friends as 'Willie'.[43] But his was a career about to be drastically cut short on the *Titanic*.

The *Titanic*
William Harbeck left Seattle in January of 1912 and sailed for Europe on 27th February. During the trip he visited London, Brussels, Paris and Berlin, and filmed in these cities, including Easter scenes and spring fashions in Paris, for later presentation in American theatres.[44] While in Europe he also sold prints of several of his films that he had brought with him (including *Lumber Industry* and *Mountain Climbing in the State of Washington*).[45] But in addition to this relatively small-scale business, Harbeck had a major newsreel project in the offing:

'Mr. Harbeck had been working for a number of months to establish a complete chain of representatives throughout Europe and America to cover all events of interest with the moving picture camera, and to collect and concentrate the film thus acquired into a periodical release.'[46]

By the time of his death, his preparations had been so complete in contacting a line of cameramen that the scheme was continued, and the releases were to be under the title of the Argus Weekly, based in Los Angeles. The Argus Weekly did start up, but was a short-lived concern.[47]

Harbeck wrote a letter to his wife from Berlin on April 1st saying that he had completed his business and was returning by way of Amsterdam and London, staying at the Strand Palace hotel (this was a relatively new hotel on The Strand in 1912, and is still there). He would be sailing home on the *Titanic* on April 10th. He asked his wife to forward his mail to the Hotel Cadillac in New York.[48] While in London he appears to have transacted most of his film business with his old colleague Will Day at Jury's Kine Supplies Ltd. Day supplied Harbeck with five different cameras, including two model 'A' Ernemann and two Jury's Kine 'Popular' cameras. Harbeck also brought 110,000 feet of film with him on the *Titanic*: that is over a hundred reels.[49]

One source claims that Harbeck had been engaged to film the *Titanic*'s first voyage. The *Moving Picture News* noted that he 'was under a $10,000 contract with the White Star line to take moving pictures of the giant vessel on her maiden trip to America.'[50] His wife later claimed he had actually filmed the *Titanic* leaving Southampton, and planned to take pictures of the ship arriving in harbour in New York.[51] Plans were elaborate – in addition to filming on board, he was to have been taken off the *Titanic* by a tug at Sandy Hook, New Jersey, in order to beat the ship into shore and so be in position to film the liner's arrival at the dock in New York.[52] A British trade journal claimed that the cameraman 'elected to return by the *"Titanic"* with the idea that as it was the first voyage, some interesting pictures might be secured, little expecting that he would find himself in the centre of such a serious calamity.' One of the five new film cameras that he had bought from Will Day was loaded by Day himself, for Harbeck to use on the voyage, '...so that should anything happen worth recording he might be equipped ready. Certainly if he has secured a picture it will be of the greatest wreck in history.'[53] Harbeck may have been, in Day's words 'ready for eventualities' but needless to say any film that he took was never shown, for his films went down with the ship.

Harbeck's Companion

A few days after the disaster Will Day received a letter from Harbeck, dated 10th April (the day of the *Titanic*'s departure) 'on board R.M.S.*Titanic*', and postmarked 'Transatlantic Post Office'.[54] It read:

> 'Dear Will, – We are away at 6 a.m. and are now proceeding eastward. As agreed I left a small tripod in the care of the operator at the Strand Palace, which bears a tag with your name thereon and they will take pleasure in handing same to you. With kind regards and best wishes from Mrs. Harbeck and
> Yours truly,
> W.H. Harbeck.'[55]

Perhaps the most intriguing part of this letter is the phrase, 'from Mrs. Harbeck'. It would seem strange, though not out of the question, to write this if one's wife were back in the United States (and it is certain that Catherine was in the United States at the time of the *Titanic*'s voyage, as she was contacted in Toledo after the sinking). Perhaps, I thought when I read this, that it was just a habitual phrase which Harbeck used whether or not his wife, Catherine, was actually accompanying him. But then I came across a trade journal report of his arrival in Britain in early March, which stated:

'Mr. W.H. Harbeck (accompanied by his wife), motion picture photographer to Canadian Pacific Railroad, arrived from America last week.'[56]

Then again, at the time of Harbeck's departure on the *Titanic* the same trade journal noted that he was returning to New York 'with his wife'.[57] This is surely more than a stock phrase, and suggests that the reporter really had some evidence that Harbeck's wife was with him. It now seems to me likely that Harbeck was accompanied on his trip by a mistress travelling as his wife. Perhaps he had introduced her to Day and others as such, and this is how the trade journals heard of it. There are several pieces of evidence, located thanks to the recent researches of a number of *Titanic* scholars, which support the existence of this mistress.

Harbeck boarded the *Titanic* at Southampton as a second class passenger. His ticket number was 248746. A Mlle. Henriette Yvois, aged 24, from Paris, France, also boarded the *Titanic* at Southampton as a second class passenger. Her ticket, though bought under her own name, was number 248747 – consecutive with Harbeck's (both tickets cost £13), suggesting that they bought them together. The last 'place of abode' for both of them was given as London.[58]

Confirming a connection between the two people is the fact that among other items found on Harbeck's body after the sinking was a lady's handbag, which was later identified as belonging to Miss Yvois, in a letter to the Canadian authorities from a certain Brownie Harbeck in Seattle. She wrote:

'Referring to lady's articles among W.H. Harbeck's effects, I knew the lady well. I understand she was also lost on the *Titanic*. Her name was Henriette Yvois. Do you know if such Person's body ever been picket(?) up and being brought to Halifax.'[59]

In a published account of the *Titanic* disaster, one of the survivors gives what is probably a description of Harbeck and Yvois on board the ship. As the *Titanic* left Southampton it narrowly avoided a collision with another ship, and Lawrence Beesley noticed someone filming this incident:

'...a young American kinematograph photographer, who, with his wife, followed the whole scene with eager eyes, turning the handle of his camera with the most evident pleasure as he recorded the unexpected incident on his films. It was obviously quite a windfall for him to have been on board at such a time. But neither the film nor those who exposed it reached the other side, and the record of the accident from the *Titanic*'s deck has never been thrown on the screen.'[60]

When I first read this account I assumed that it must refer to young Daniel Marvin, who, as we learned in the previous chapter, owned a film camera. But a few pages later Beesley describes seeing the same couple again, in the library:

'In the opposite corner are the young American kinematograph photographer and his young wife, evidently French, very fond of playing patience, which she is doing now, while he sits back in his chair watching the game and interposing from time to time with suggestions. I did not see them again.'[61]

Because this woman is described as French, the Marvins are ruled out, as we know that Marvin's wife was American.[62] There was another cameraman aboard, also mentioned in my previous chapter, Noel Malachard. But Malachard was French, while Beesley clearly refers to the cameraman he saw as American. So, even though Harbeck was in his forties at this time – scarcely young – he and Yvois best fit the nationalities in Beesley's description, and I believe they are the people he is referring to.[63] Probably we shall never know for sure.

Equally we do not have any further details of how Harbeck spent his time on the *Titanic* or how exactly he came to his end. But there was one other person on board with whom he may have made contact. Before the *Titanic* sank Harbeck may have been negotiating with the US Government and with the Guggenheims for the purchase of his Alaskan films, and coincidentally, one of the Guggenheim family, the banker and smelting baron Benjamin Guggenheim was on the *Titanic*.[64] Perhaps Harbeck had discussions with Guggenheim during the voyage? No-one will ever know, but there is one rumour that can be dismissed. It has been claimed that as the *Titanic* went down, Harbeck, Guggenheim and his secretary changed into evening attire, to meet their maker, as Guggenheim said, 'like gentlemen'.[65] But Harbeck's name is a spurious addition to this story, which was originally related by a surviving steward, who only mentions Guggenheim and his secretary (a Mr Giglio) changing their clothes. He does not mention a third man, certainly not Harbeck.[66]

Interestingly though, Guggenheim and Harbeck may have shared one secret. If it is likely that Harbeck was travelling illicitly with a young French woman, it is even more likely that Benjamin Guggenheim was. He was known as something of a playboy, and had been away from his wife and children for eight months in Europe. He'd had affairs with a couple of women while in Paris, including a 'young blond singer' with whom he was travelling back to America on the *Titanic*. When disaster struck, Guggenheim went down heroically with the ship, but the blond survived – she was later seen coming down the gangplank in New York, introduced as Mrs Benjamin Guggenheim, but was never heard from again.[67]

The Aftermath
After the sinking, it was initially thought that Harbeck had changed his plans and had not sailed on the *Titanic*. But on 18th April his sons, John and Stanley, received a telegram in Toledo from the White Star line confirming that Harbeck had indeed boarded the ship at Southampton but was not among the survivors. The horrible truth became indisputable after his body, dressed in a black coat, grey trousers and vest and red tie, was recovered from the sea by the cable ship, *Mackay-Bennett*, one of well over 300 bodies found in the ocean after the sinking, and landed at Halifax, Nova Scotia.[68]

A detailed list of Harbeck's clothes and personal items was drawn up, (the document gives his name as 'Herbeck') and included about £30 in cash, and such items as a diary, false teeth, a union card for the Moving Picture and Projecting Machine Operators' Union, and, as mentioned above, a woman's bag and

Harbeck's body

In the wake of the *Titanic* disaster, the rescuers on board the *Mackay-Bennett* found Harbeck's body – assigned body number 35, estimated as around 40 years old – clad in a black coat; gray mixture tweed trousers and vest; red tie; black boots. He had these effects: – cheque books; travellers cheques; lady's bag; gold watch and chain; two gold lockets; time meter; fountain pen; diary; false teeth; pencil; knife; diamond ring; union card for the Moving Picture and Projecting Machine Operators' Union; £15 in gold, £15 6s in silver, 10s in purse in lady's bag; wedding ring in bag; pearl and diamond pin. He was identified as W.H. Herbeck [sic], of 114, 24th Avenue. (no city given)

BODY RECOVERED FROM TITANIC DISASTER SAID TO BE SEATTLE MAN'S

Name of William H. Harbeck, Manufacturer of Moving Pictures, Is In First List of 27 Sent by Cable Ship Mackay-Bennett—Another May Be George D. Widener, of Philadelphia.

Most May Be Members of Crew

NEW YORK, April 22.—The first list of names of bodies recovered from the Titanic disaster by the cable-ship Mackay-Bennett was received here tonight through wireless messages to the White Star line offices.

In the list is the name of William H. Harbeck, a manufacturer of moving pictures, of Seattle.

The list of twenty-seven names contains none of the most prominent men who perished, unless it be that "George W. Widen," as sent by wireless, refers to George D. Widener, of Philadelphia.

(17) Headline about the discovery of Harbeck's body
Seattle Post-Intelligencer
23 April 1912

purse.[69] On 4th May his body was forwarded to Mrs Catherine Harbeck at 733 Michigan Street, Toledo, Ohio. Miss Yvois' body, if recovered, was never identified. Later in May Catherine Harbeck, (declared administratrix on 25th April), wrote to the Provincial Secretary's office, Halifax requesting his effects be sent to her, which they were.[70] William Harbeck was said by one source to be aged 45 at death, though other sources would give his age at anywhere from 44 to 48.[71] There is a memorial stone to him in Woodlawn Cemetary, Toledo, where his wife, Catherine, and their two sons are also buried.[72]

(18) Part of a letter from Harbeck's son, John, September 1912 on letterhead publicising William's Round Up *film
(Provincial Secretary's Office, Halifax)*

W. H. Harbeck's Moving Pictures
OF THE ROUND UP
PENDLETON, ORE.

BEST FILM EVER MADE DEPICTING WILD WESTERN LIFE, DARE DEVIL STEER BULLDOGGING and SPECTACULAR BRONCHO BUSTING.

---TWO---

issue. This so-called Brownie Harbeck, as I have said, is no relative and any correspondence relative to the recovery of the effects and body of Mr. Harbeck has been and should be carried on with my mother, Mrs. Catherine Harbeck, of Toledo.

I ask you to notify me, and, all of this will be in confidence, as to the relationship this woman, of Seattle, claimed to you, in her letters, as to Mr. Harbeck.

Whatever you send me, I assure you, will be kept in the strictest of confidence, and it will never be used for other than information for my mother who resides with me here.

Please let me hear from you soon.

I thank you in advance for copies of the Harbeck-Provincial Secretary letters, and again will promise they will be kept secret.

Very respectfully Yours,

John S. Harbeck
733 Michigan St.
Toledo, O.

44

In British film circles the news of Harbeck's death was greeted by sadness. One gets the impression that he had been genuinely liked and admired by his friends and colleagues.[73] With his friendly manner and sporting his red tie Harbeck would have been a welcome visitor wherever he went. As a tribute to the late cameraman, Will Day arranged for a film which had been shot by Harbeck at Day's residence on the previous Good Friday to be screened at two cinemas in north London. The proceeds would go to benefit the *Titanic* Fund:[74]

'The film was a homely series of pictures of a cat and a monkey, taken in Mr. W. Day's garden at Pellat Grove. The monkey was present at the matinee, and added a pathetic touch to the picture. The performance was under distinguished local patronage, and the entire takings will be handed over to the Fund.'[75]

After Harbeck's death there were a number of claims on his property and business. The strangest was from Brownie Harbeck of Seattle, who wrote to the American Consul in Halifax in July requesting Harbeck's effects, evidently not realising that these had already been delivered to Catherine.[76] Brownie eventually received this information from the Provincial Secretary's office in Halifax, and wrote back on 31st August requesting clarification about the money, apparently having misread the amount of £15.0.0 in gold (approximately $75) as $1500. A gold-digger indeed ! (As mentioned earlier, she also revealed information about Yvois in this letter).

It is unclear what relationship Brownie had to William Harbeck, but there was certainly some direct connection, because Brownie's address of 1311 E. Marion St., Seattle, was the same as appears in January 1912 on a copyright form for William.[77] Also Brownie's letter of 31st August was written on notepaper with a printed advertisement for Harbeck's Alaska films. But Harbeck's family in Toledo wished to deny any connection, and in September Catherine's son, John S. Harbeck wrote to advise the Halifax authorities that this 'so-called' Brownie was 'no relative' of his family and he asked for copies of correspondence with her.[78] So who was this 'Brownie'? To judge from her writing style, she had little education. Perhaps someone who worked for Harbeck and invented the name Brownie Harbeck to try to cash in on his estate?

This was not the only dispute following Harbeck's death. One trade paper outlining Harbeck's recent film work, noted that a certain Dr L.M. Slocum of Seattle 'was associated with Mr. Harbeck in this work and will continue it.'[79] Slocum's name is not mentioned again in trade sources that I have seen, and other sources state that Harbeck's business partner was a Mrs Katherine George of Seattle. This is presumably a confusion for Harbeck's wife, Catherine, who put in a claim of $11,000 for two motion picture cameras and equipment, and $41,000 for film prints that were lost with Harbeck, including the Pendleton Roundup Pictures, which she valued at $25,000.[80] It was also claimed that Harbeck's Alaskan film was lost 'negative and all,' though this was untrue, as this film and the Pendleton one were about to become the subject of litigation.[81]

Mrs Harbeck had assumed that her husband's films had sunk on the *Titanic* with their maker until warned by a Washington exhibitor, Tom Moore, that Charles Wynard was exploiting the films. In May of 1912 Mrs Harbeck commenced legal action in the New York courts against three men: Wynard, George H. Hamilton and C.B. Clements for the return of her husband's Pendleton Roundup film and the Alaskan film. William Harbeck had left all his films with Wynard before going to Europe, and Wynard claimed that Harbeck had given him rights to exhibit these, which he and his associates had started to do.[82] Mrs Harbeck maintained that the rights her husband had assigned to Wynard were only for certain territories.[83] I haven't traced what transpired in this case, but Catherine Harbeck probably won. For a while, following the loss of her husband, Mrs Harbeck took over his movie business, but eventually she moved back to Toledo to live with her sons, John and Stanley.[84]

Conclusion
Following the death of William H. Harbeck, in amongst all the news of threatened legal action, there was still room for tributes to the character and talents of this pioneer cameraman. One trade paper mourned the loss of this 'comparatively young' film professional, and called him 'One of the ablest moving picture men in the world...'[85] His friend, Alfred H. Saunders of the *Moving Picture News*, who claimed to have known him for some 15 years added: 'He was always a cheery, jovial, progressive sort of a man, a man whom we could all appreciate for his sterling uprightness and integrity in business.'[86] The *Moving Picture World*'s obituary read:

'In ordinary parlance he might be called a cameraman. But he was an independent cameraman. He did not work by the week for an ordinary salary. He usually was financially interested in the pictures he was taking. He was accustomed to carrying out expeditions that required much capital, and, as a rule, he was a partner in the enterprise. Financially, Mr. Harbeck was successful. He was just getting to a point where he could enjoy life and carry out large projects that suited his fancy, when he met with his untimely end.'[87]

Harbeck deserved such an accolade. He was one of that breed of highly enterprising travelling cameramen who were so important in the early period of the movies, and often celebrated at the time, yet almost forgotten today. Harbeck is scarcely mentioned, if at all, in any of the standard film reference works. Yet the kind of films that he made – scenic, industrial and educational subjects – were a mainstay of the early film business, and the direct ancestors of modern non-fiction film and television. It is one of the great myths of cinema history that the documentary was born with *Nanook of the North* in the early 1920s. While Flaherty's film was a highly influential production, principally for its personal style, it was not a 'first' in non-fiction filmmaking. Documentaries in every sense of the word were being produced from the turn of the century, and it was people like Harbeck who were pioneering the genre.

The *Titanic* and the Lantern

By 1912, though the cinema was well established as a news medium – and increasingly so through the regularly-released newsreels – this does not mean that earlier forms of visually presented news had died out. Newspapers and periodicals were the main competition, but lantern slides were also widely used for portraying news stories. In this chapter we will see how the lantern slide business reacted to the *Titanic* disaster. By studying the lantern companies in question, and the form and content of their lantern slide sequences about the *Titanic*, we can gain something of an overview of the lantern news industry in this era.[1]

News slides
In the late 19th and early 20th centuries news events were brought to life in a number of visually arresting ways: probably, in fact, in a greater variety of forms than exist today, when newspapers and television are virtually the only ways in which we receive our news. In this earlier era major news events, such as natural disasters or military victories might be served up as magic lantern displays, postcards, and theatrical productions, and were even celebrated in pageants and firework displays. The Boer War, for example, was interpreted in most of these forms, perhaps the most bizarre being its presentation as a pageant battle in the United States several years after the war had ended, featuring troops who had fought in the real war (including General Cronje). All this suggests that news in this era had more of an epic quality than it has these days, and was not so concerned with topicality or with literal truth.

Of course some forms of visual news from this period are still familiar today, including illustrated accounts in periodicals, but even these were written with a rather freer hand of interpretation than is true these days. For example, many articles in the periodical press of the early 20th century were illustrated with drawings and artists' impressions rather than, or as well as, with photographs, though the latter slowly rose in prominence after the 1890s. This gradual move from artists' impressions to photographs was an important symptom of a change affecting news presentation in this period, which would ultimately lead to the more literal style of today.

This contrast was also to some extent apparent between two forms of projected image which were current in the early years of this century: film and lantern. The magic lantern was the major form of projected image in the late 19th century, and was still a medium of considerable importance up to the First World War. Right through the Edwardian period and beyond, many companies produced lantern equipment and slides and several journals were published which catered to this lantern market. These included Britain's *Kinematograph and Lantern Weekly*, which retained the *lantern* in its title until 1919; and in America too the importance of the 'views' (slides) market was reflected in the titles of what are nowadays usually considered to be purely film journals: such as *Moving Picture World and View Photographer*, and *Views and Films Index*.

By the early 20th century the lantern industry was a well-established and mature visual medium. In the United States lantern slides were often in the form of 'song slides' – picture stories with actors, projected to accompany popular songs – and 'life model' slides were also a popular product in Britain. These were photographic images which had been coloured and sometimes retouched, and even more complex effects were possible by montaging several photographs together or incorporating printed words into the slide image. Thus lantern slides could go through a considerable modification from the original, naturalistic photographic image.

On the other hand, to 'doctor' a film in the same way was much more difficult, certainly in this period. This is because a film is made up of many frames, and thus many individual images would need to be worked on.[2] This could be done to some extent, as the many hand-coloured films from the early cinema prove, but it was a far more complex and expensive task. Of course some manipulation can take place at the time of filming – with artificially-created sets and double exposure. But in general the film was, in this early period, more difficult and expensive to manipulate than the slide. Thus the film medium was more reliant than the lantern medium on 'what is out there that can be filmed'. (Perhaps it was partly because of this somewhat greater flexibility that the lantern slide medium lasted so well as it did into the film era.)

To some extent slides should have had a similar advantage over film when it came to news, for a more easily manipulated image could be useful when no dramatic and genuine images of a news event were available. But in fact many news slides were surprisingly banal. The news slides that I have seen in no sense match the imaginative use of montaging and colour – and have little of the sheer artistry – that one finds in fictional, song slide subjects.

Untergang der „Titanic"

wahrheitsgetreue Wiedergabe nach
Originalzeichnung eines berühmten
Marinemalers. 4708

Diapostive 8½ × 8½ cm gross, sofort lieferbar.

Filmhaus Th. Scherff

Telephon 12369. Leipzig-Lindenau Angerstr. 1.

(19) The first advertisement to appear for a lantern slide about the Titanic *disaster*
Der Kinematograph
24 April 1912

The coverage of the *Titanic* disaster seems to indicate a news slide industry that was somewhat 'backward' when compared to either the periodical press or, more to the point, the nascent news film medium. Let us take the question of speed, for a start. In theory a slide producer could have a slide or series of slides on the market within hours. But in practice the potential of the news slide industry to generate its images faster than the film industry, remained purely theoretical. In the case of the *Titanic*, film seems to have been at least as fast.

While the Topical Film Company released their first *Titanic* newsreel on 17th April, a mere two days after the disaster (see Titanic News Films chapter), the first advertisement for a *Titanic* slide that I have found appeared on 24th April. This was for a painted rather than a photographic image released by the Leipzig firm, Filmhaus Th. Scherff, which advertised in a German trade journal: 'The Sinking of the *Titanic*, realistic depiction – from an original by a famous marine painter'.[3] It is not clear if this slide was from an original painting, created specially after the disaster, or from an existing painting. But in any case, it was clearly an artificial image, an artist's impression.

By contrast, many of the subsequent *Titanic* slide releases, especially in the United States, were photographic, an indication of how news values especially in that country were shifting towards the desire for greater 'authenticity' which I have discussed above. Indeed several of the American slide dealers emphasise that theirs are genuine, not 'fake', pictures. It would seem that as far as slides were concerned, most Americans wanted (or were offered) reality rather than drama. Artists' impressions of the disaster were available, but they apparently made up a minority of lantern slides, despite having the advantage over photographs that they could depict the actual sinking and other events which happened out of view of the cameras.

American Titanic slides

While they might not have been quite as fast as some of the film newsreels, it seems that in terms of quantity American lantern slide dealers pulled out all the stops to provide news images of the *Titanic*. A few slides of the *Titanic* had been available before the ship sank, from the W. H. Rau Corporation of Philadelphia, but the fateful accident really galvanised the lantern slide manufacturers.[4] Photographic news slides of this story of disaster were being advertised in the United States from the 27th April by three companies. The Levi Company issued 21 slides taken from photographs by the American Press Association, under the title, *The Wreck of the Titanic*, costing $10 for the set.[5] At the same time the Excelsior Slide Company advertised a set of 15 or 16 'beautifully colored' slides, including views of the rescue ship *Carpathia* and the crowds at White Star's New York office. The company's main attraction, however, was images of the *Titanic* herself and her late Captain, which were described as:

'...positively the last photographs taken of Captain Smith and the ill fated steamship "Titanic" previous to starting on her maiden voyage'.[6]

(20) Advertisements for the Excelsior Slide Company and Levi Co.
Moving Picture World 27 April 1912

The set of slides cost $8, which was presumably a purchase rather than rental, and Excelsior also offered 25 posters free with every slide set, indicating how important publicity was in attracting an audience to news features such as this.

Most enterprising of all the *Titanic* slide merchants was Charles A. Pryor of Pryor and Claire, 46 East 14th Street, New York City, associated with the Western Vaudeville Association. Soon after the news arrived of the *Titanic*'s sinking Pryor rushed to New York to meet his cousin, who was one of the survivors of the wreck.[7] Pryor then turned from being a concerned relative into a keen newshound: he chartered a tug, and he, along with Mr. M.M. Robinson, a moving picture cameraman for Gaumont, were the first camera operators to board the rescue ship *Carpathia*. Once on board Pryor took photographs of Captain Rostron, and with the latter's permission, recorded many other scenes of survivors and crew:

'...and they are GREAT, showing all notable persons connected with the tragedy, the lifeboats, the life preservers, and have [sic] the last bill of fare that was served on the *Titanic*.'[8]

A selection of these photographs, along with some taken by the crew and survivors on the rescue ship themselves, were turned into a set of 30 lantern slides, and were advertised from 27th April by Pryor as 'the biggest sensation of the age'. The *Great Titanic Disaster* slide set could be rented for $15 for three days or $25 for a week, along with a set of 11" x 14" lobby pictures and a list of the slides and an accompanying lecture. The issue of fake images of the disaster had

(21) Advertisement for Charles A. Pryor
New York Clipper 27 April 1912

arisen by this stage, and Pryor's ad assured customers that these were 'Not fakes, but thirty original, genuine pictures...'. This set proved to be of 'great interest' to audiences, and orders came into Pryor and Claire so fast that a trade journal reported that 'the staff has been enlarged and is working overtime'.[9]

Linked to Pryor was J. De Commerce, based at the same New York address, whose motto was 'The only man who guarantees slides against heat'. He advertised his *Titanic* slides from late April in the *Moving Picture News* and in June and July in the newly established *Photoplay* magazine, offering a 40 slide set about the disaster, and 8 lobby photos as advertising material. He also offered what were presumably existing song slide sets, to illustrate two appropriate songs, 'Just as the ship went down' and 'Nearer my God to Thee'.[10]

A week after these four slide companies had put their product on the market, no fewer than five other American slide companies advertised their own lantern versions of the *Titanic* story. At the beginning of May the American Slide Company based in Columbus, Ohio also offered slides made from photographs taken on the *Carpathia* while at the scene of the disaster. These photographs had been obtained from the International News Association, but it is not clear if these were the same slides taken by Prior on the *Carpathia*. The set of 20 slides could be had for $10 sale, or $5 for rental per day.[11]

(22) Advertisement for J. De Commerce Photoplay June 1912

The Only Man Who Guarantees Slides Against Heat
Original photos of Titanic Disaster—40 slides—including eight 11 x 14 lobby photos. Illustrated song, "Just as the Ship Went Down." 18 slides $5.00.
The band played "Nearer My God to Thee." 16 slides, illustrated, $5.00

47 E. 13th St., New York

53

Write, Wire or Telephone
Horrible Titanic Disaster

20 slides made from photographic views taken on board the rescue ship Carpathia on the scene of disaster. We positively guarantee these to be actual scenes and are copyrighted by the International News Association. Rental price $5.00 per day, with lobby display furnished. Sale price $10.00 per set, cash with order. These sets are ready for shipment. Most complete on the market. Remember, these slides are not made from newspaper clippings.

American Slide Co., 165½ N. High St., Columbus, O.

(23) Advertisement for the American Slide Company Moving Picture World 4 May 1912

NOW READY
THE
Titanic Disaster

Produced from original copyrighted photographs by the National Press Assn. from whom we obtained the exclusive rights.

We have produced an interesting lecture showing the ship, her commander, the notables among her passengers, the icefields, the arrival of the rescue ship, officers and survivors.

A graphic, pictorial description of the disaster.

No. 1—10 slides	Plain		$2.50
No. 2—10	"	Colored	$5.00
No. 3—20	"	Plain	$5.00
No. 4—20	"	Colored	$10.00
No. 5—40	"	Plain	$10.00
No. 6—40	"	Colored	$20.00

FREE SPECIAL ADVERTISING MATTER

With Set No. 1—2—1 Sheets
" " No. 2—5—1 Sheets
" " No. 3—3—1 Sheets
" " No. 4—3—1 Sheets
" " No. 5—5—1 Sheets   1—3 Sheet
                        1 M Heralds
" " No. 6—5—1 Sheets   2—3 Sheets
                        2 M Heralds

SPECIAL LECTURE FREE WITH EACH SET.

A. J. CLAPHAM, *Manufacturer of Fine Art Slides*
130 WEST 37th ST.   NEW YORK
THE PLACE FOR FEATURES.

(24) Advertisement for A.J. Clapham Moving Picture World 4 May 1912

The A.J. Clapham company of 130 W. 37th Street, New York City, released *The Titanic Disaster*, which presented the news story in a choice of anything from 10 to 40 slides, in monochrome or colour, the different sets costing from $2.50 to $20. Supplied free were posters (1-sheet to 3-sheet or herald size), and a special lecture to be read to the pictures. These slides came from photographs of the National Press Association ('exclusively') and from the Central News Syndicate in London, and included pictures from before and after the disaster 'showing the ship, her commander, the notables among her passengers, the icefields, the arrival of the rescue ship, officers and survivors.'[12] Again Clapham stressed that these slides were from 'Genuine Photographs'. But he included one diagrammatic slide:

'Mr. Clapham obtained from a scientist an accurate drawing of an iceberg showing the proportion submerged, thereby giving the spectator an idea of the consistency of bergs.'[13]

The *Titanic* was not the only news story of disaster at this time, and the Novelty Slide Company of Chicago and New York City (20 East 14th Street, just a few doors away from Pryor and Claire) offered a choice of two disaster slide sets, each with 22 coloured slides: there was either the *Titanic* story, or the *Mississippi Flood*. These were taken from photographs, and were 'the only original, authentic and copyrighted' slides, so Novelty claimed, the emphasis in the advertising being on 'authentic'.[14] Lithographic posters were supplied too. The price of the *Titanic* story was $12, which was $2 more than the Mississippi set, though a couple of weeks later the price was reduced to parity at $10.[15] (Such a price

(25) Advertisement for the Novelty Slide Company
New York Dramatic Mirror
1 May 1912

The Only Original, Authentic and Copyrighted
TITANIC DISASTER
22 Colored Slides, $12.00
AND
MISSISSIPPI FLOOD
22 Colored Slides, $10.00
NOVELTY SLIDE COMPANY
20 East 14th Street, New York
1928 Milwaukee Ave., Chicago

reduction is typical as news images become out of date.) The *New York Clipper*'s writer considered the Novelty company's *Titanic* slides some of the best he had seen, partly because they included some exclusive images:

'Mr. Coufal, of the Novelty Co., has some photographs which his camera man got at the first hearing of the investigating committee, which, we understand, no one else has. These should prove of great interest to exhibitors.'[16]

Such photographs of a committee meeting (this was the committee set up by the American Senate to investigate the sinking) do not sound terribly exciting, but as we see repeatedly in visual news coverage, it is not the content of the image which defines its news value, but its significance to the story, its authenticity, and often its exclusivity too.

Also based in New York City, at 207 West 34th Street, was slide dealer, W. Lindsay Gordon. This dealer already offered 'feature lecture sets' on *Dante's Inferno*, *Paradise Lost* and *White Slave Traffic*, and when the *Titanic* disaster hit the headlines he rapidly put together a set on this theme. He offered 30 coloured slides of the *Titanic* disaster for $12, and later on also supplied a smaller set of 15 for $6, which were claimed to be 'The most realistic slides on the market'. Also supplied were a 'great lecture' and 10-colour posters 'cut for herald and newspapers', which referred to the size of publicity flyers or posters a showman could display. Interestingly this dealer was still advertising these slides as late as the beginning of June, when most of the others had given up.[17] The sets sold very well, as one trade journal reported:

'W. Lindsay Gordon's lecture set of slides illustrating the great sea disaster, the wreck of the *Titanic*, are in such demand that it has been found necessary to put on extra help in order to fill orders promptly. When the *Moving Picture News* man called on Mr. Gordon he saw a desk full of telegrams from managers and lecturers all over who wanted the slides.'[18]

(26) Advertisement for W. Lindsay Gordon New York Clipper 18 May 1912

TITANIC SLIDES

The most realistic slides on the market, showing the great sea disaster. Thirty Beautiful Colored Slides, great lecture, elegant special lithos, ten colors, and cut for herald and newspapers.

SPECIAL PRICE, $12. 15 Slides, Lecture and Lithos, $6.

Wire your orders quick. Other big feature lecture sets.
W. LINDSAY GORDON, Mfg. Sensational Lecture Slides 207 W. 34th St., N. Y. C.

It is not possible to know the exact content or style of many of these *Titanic* slide sets, as the sets appear not to have survived. With one exception. Some years ago James Card of George Eastman House discovered a set of *Titanic* news slides in Colorado, which had been distributed by Hinton-Fell-Elliott Inc of New York. Hinton was a subscription news service, and their slides were taken from, and credited to, photographs by the American Press Association and Underwood and Underwood. (Underwood was one of the world's top producers of stereoscopic slides at the turn of the century, concentrating on travel and news – they released many Boer War stereographs, for example, taken at the front). Some of the Hinton *Titanic* slides seem to be the same or similar images as those described above from other slide distributors, and it is not clear how much borrowing and rights-purchasing went on in the news slide business at this time. This sequence of photographic images, which included captions at the bottom, demonstrate just how effective slides could be in putting a news story over in visual form. Eight slides are reprinted in an article by Card.[19] The slides show:

1. Montage of the *Titanic* ship with an inset of the Captain, E.J. Smith.
2. Crowds of anxious relatives at White Star's offices in New York.
3. Survivors of the *Titanic* in a ward at St.Vincent's Hospital in New York, including crew members John Thompson, a fireman, and Thomas Whitely, a waiter.
4. Senate investigating committee, with Harold Bride, *Titanic*'s second wireless operator on the stand.
5. Montage of three images of: Captain Rostron of the *Carpathia*, survivors being taken aboard his ship, and the *Titanic*'s lifeboats in New York.
6. The *Carpathia* at dockside in New York, with survivors greeted by relatives and friends.
7. The deck of the *Mauritania* showing the extra life boats and rafts placed on board in the wake of the *Titanic* disaster.
8. Montage of the beneficiaries of the fortune of John Jacob Astor, who drowned on the *Titanic*.

It should be remembered that these *Titanic* slide sets were mainly intended for screening in movie theatres, as part of programmes which would also include dramatic, comic and scenic films. This practice of combining the media of lantern and film is made explicit in ads for the Feature Film Company of Columbus, Ohio. This company offered both moving pictures and slides of the *Titanic* disaster, which could be booked separately or together. 'Book it quick...The big money getter', it proclaimed.[20]

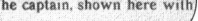

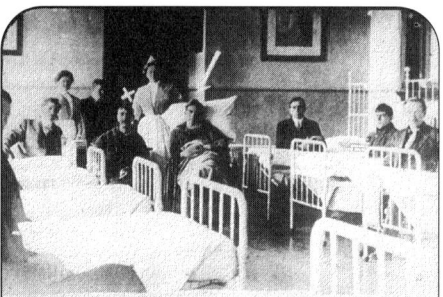

(27). Set of Titanic *news slides distributed by Hinton-Fell-Elliott Inc of New York* (James Card collection)

The hero of the rescue of part of the Titanic's voyagers is Captain Rostrom of the Carpathia, shown here with pictures of the taking aboard of the Titanic's people by the Carpathia and the lowering of the Titanic's boats by the Carpathia when the latter vessel reached New York.
Photographs by American Press Association

Thousands of people, many of them relatives and friends of those rescued from the wreck of the Titanic, greeted the Cunarder on her arrival with the horror stricken survivors.
Photograph Copyright, 1912, by American Press Association

These are busy days for boat builders, for every one of the big steamship lines has ordered more lifeboats and rafts, after the Titanic disaster. The picture shows extra boats and life rafts (the latter marked with an X) placed on the Mauretania.

Sharers in the Fortune of the Late John Jacob Astor

This Columbus firm brings to ten the number of American companies listed above which were offering slides of the *Titanic* disaster. This is an incredible figure by any standards, attesting to both the extraordinary public interest in this news story of maritime disaster, and to the continuing major presence of the slide format in the theatrical marketplace at a period when most film historians would probably suspect that the movies had 'won out' over the old slides. Such high numbers of suppliers surely indicates that slide shows must have been popular with audiences, though direct testimony about audience reactions is in short supply. In fact I have found only one contemporary comment on exhibiting such slides in America, but one which confirms their popularity: a show of Press Association slides of 'the wreck of the *Titanic* and scenes following the deep sea tragedy' at the Avenue film theatre in Kentucky, was said to be 'a head-line attraction during the past week'.[21]

So intense was the fascination with marine disaster generated by the *Titanic* events that almost any screen story about shipwrecks and the sea attracted interest. In early May 1912 Louise M. Marion, based in New York, advertised her 'refined and entertaining...new novelties', *The Shipwreck* and *The Lifeboat*. These were both series of slides, with accompanying recitations, each described as: 'A beautiful poem with 20 pictures and music, recited between films in picture theatres.' I have not discovered if these picture series had been available before May, nor if they referred to the *Titanic* per se, but clearly the timing of this

(28) Advertisement for the Feature Film Company of Ohio
Moving Picture World 4 May 1912

Book It Quick   **The Big Money Getter**

THE TITANIC

MOVING PICTURES and **SLIDES** of the Ill Fated Steamship, showing **CAPTAIN SMITH** Inspecting Ship, Loading of Baggage, Life-Boats, Promenade Decks, Boat Leaving, and Great Crowds at Pier, **SURVIVORS** and Many Other Scenes of this Great Disaster. **FILMS** and **SLIDES BOOKED** Separately or Together as Desired. Wire us your Order at Once.   Packing them everywhere.

A FEW OF OUR OTHER FEATURES

White Slave—Nero and the Burning of Rome—Trip Around Niagara Falls—Turkish & Italian Cavalry—Golden Wedding—Christian Martyrs —Dante's Inferno—Life in the West—War on the Plains—Passion Play—Cincinnati Auto Road Races, and 40 other Good Ones. Send for Prices and Complete List.

FEATURE FILM CO.
9½ WEST BROAD STREET.   COLUMBUS, OHIO.

advertising was designed to exploit the current disaster, and the free posters and banner Marion offered would have helped to attract audiences. The ads claimed that these 'illustrated poems...crowd the theatres in every state.'[22] (Slides of *Our Lifeboatmen* and the like were already a well known staple of lantern shows.)

British *Titanic* shows

In Britain, *Titanic* slide sets were apparently not quite so numerous nor so well promoted as in the USA, and seem to have included more non-photographic slides – to represent the sinking, in particular – than the US companies. It was not until early May that slides of the disaster were being advertised in the British trade press. The Kinematograph Exchange at 81 Aldersgate Street in London offered three designs of coloured slides based on the song 'Nearer My God to Thee'. Each showed the foundering of the liner, and with either the whole song overprinted on the slide or just the title, or just a single verse. Each option cost 1s. 6d.[23]

More ambitious was the Tyler Apparatus Company, which 'had a flood of orders' for a set of 16 coloured slides: these were supplied for five shillings per week, to include two posters and a copy of the song, 'Be British'. Multiple copies of this sheet music could be purchased by the exhibitor at 12s. per hundred, for retail to the audience for 3d.[24] Jury's Kine Supplies also marketed a set of *Titanic* slides (giving no details about how many were in the set), including ones showing 'Captain Smith on the Bridge' and depicting the sinking itself.[25] These news slides may have been like the American Hinton set described above, in which a caption was incorporated in the projected slide image. This was a technique regularly used by the Walter Tyler Company, the news photograph on which the slide was based sometimes coming from the Topical Press Agency in London.[26]

A couple of lantern slides of the *Titanic* are preserved in the private collections of David Francis and Lester Smith, the latter illustrated here. Furthermore, at least one private individual, Frederick S. Bowen, took photographs of the *Titanic* and *Olympic* during construction, which were turned into lantern slides, rediscovered by his grandson in the 1970s, and reproduced in an article that he wrote.[27]

In Britain most of the *Titanic* slides on offer were based on photographs from news agencies, though some sets included one or two artists' impressions of the disaster. The Bamforth company, based in Yorkshire, also followed the 'artistic' route in their images dedicated to the *Titanic* sinking. Bamforth was probably the leading producer of 'life model' lantern slides in Britain at the turn of the century and also one of the main manufacturers of picture postcards. In the case of the

Titanic we know that they produced a series of Bamforth Memorial postcards consisting of six cards. All six are basically photographic, but greatly retouched and montaged, as was the company's house style: they show the half-submerged ship, and five of them include a photograph of a young woman in a white gown, with her long hair matted together with the image of the sinking ship. Verses from Arthur Sullivan's hymn, 'Nearer, my God, to Thee!' appear on the cards.[28] The cards seem to have had quite a long life, and those in Richard Crangle's collection are postmarked in mid 1913, and, strangely, one as late as May 1915 to commemorate the *Lusitania* sinking.

But we also know from one of the former Bamforth child performers, Mrs Winifred Jackson, that the company produced a series of images entitled simply 'The *Titanic*' in which she appeared as a child actress. She was too young to have been the woman in the white gown, which implies that this production was different from Bamforth's postcard series.[29] As it seems unlikely that two postcard series would be produced, it is more probable that Winifred was appearing in an entirely separate lantern slide series devoted to the disaster.

(29) A British slide of the Titanic
(Lester Smith)

(30) Part of Bamforth's postcard series to commemorate the Titanic *disaster. Bamforth may also have made a* Titanic *lantern slide set* (Richard Crangle)

*(30) Bamforth's
postcard series
(Continued)
(Richard Crangle)*

Apart from the film dramas which I shall discuss in a later chapter, the most elaborate 'artist's impression' of the *Titanic* story on screen that I have yet come across was a so-called 'Myriorama'. The Poole family had been presenting diorama shows from the 1840s, specialising in topical and war-related subjects, and under the name of Poole's Myrioramas (meaning 'many views') they exhibited paintings on fine gauze screens, manipulated one in front of another.[30] One of their presentations in 1894 was of the collision of the British battleship *Pretoria* with the *Camperdown*, in which the former sank with the loss of 357 lives.[31] As the disaster took place the previous year, this was still a 'news' story, and to add the spice of authenticity a survivor of the *Pretoria* gave a descriptive account of the disaster as the pictures were shown (a practice which was repeated with films about the *Titanic*'s sinking).

The Poole's Myriorama entitled *The Loss of the Titanic* opened at the Synod Hall in Edinburgh prior to Christmas 1912, as the main feature of the Pooles' shows that season.[32] It was exhibited elsewhere in 1913 and 1914. This 'gigantic reproduction', as they called it was advertised for the week commencing 5th October 1914 at the Empire Palace, Ripley, Derbyshire, presented by Charles William and John R. Poole. Their advertising postcard stated:

'The spectacle staged in its entirety by John R. Poole, and every endeavour made to convey a true pictorial idea of the whole history of the disaster...Unique Mechanical and Electric Effects, special music and the story described in a thrilling manner.'[33]

The scenes, described on the postcard, were as follows:
LOSS of the "TITANIC": The Immortal Tale of Simple Heroism
In Eight Tableaux, comprising:-
1. A splendid marine effect of the Gigantic Vessel gliding from the Quayside at Southampton.
2. Cork Harbour, showing the return of the White Star Tender to Queenstown and the "Titanic" outward bound.
3. MID OCEAN. The "Titanic" brilliantly illuminated, speeding along at 21 knots.
4. The S.S. "Touraine" in the icefield, and carefully steering her way through the towering bergs.
5. The approach of the iceberg. The collision and grinding crash. Lowering out the lifeboats.
6. FOUNDERING. The great vessel sinking by the head. The extinction of the lights. The Sinking.
7. The arrival of the "Carpathia" and rescue of the survivors.
8. The Vision.[34]

We know what some of these images looked like because, remarkably, collector Peter Jewell has found a small scrapbook containing a set of photographs of five of the images. The most striking of these is a photograph showing John R. Poole, the 'guide' to the show, standing in front of the image of the *Titanic* going down. (Scene 6).

It seems clear from some of the scenes, especially numbers 6 and 8, that the presentation would have been a highly emotive performance by John R. Poole, in which the artificially created images would have helped spin a tale 'of simple heroism', as the subtitle puts it. Apparently the show 'often reduced audiences to tears'.[35] In the text of the narration which is reproduced in the Pooles' 'guide book', the language for this show is emotive, describing the awful fate of the people plunged into the icy waters, and concluding with a peon of praise to 'the simple courage which remains for ever a proud heritage of the Anglo-Saxon race.'

(31) Below and Right: Pooles' 1912 Myriorama show,
The Loss of the "Titanic": The Immortal Tale of Simple Heroism
(three of five photographs in an album, scenes 1, 5 and 6.)
(Bill Douglas and Peter Jewell Collection,
Bill Douglas Centre, University of Exeter)

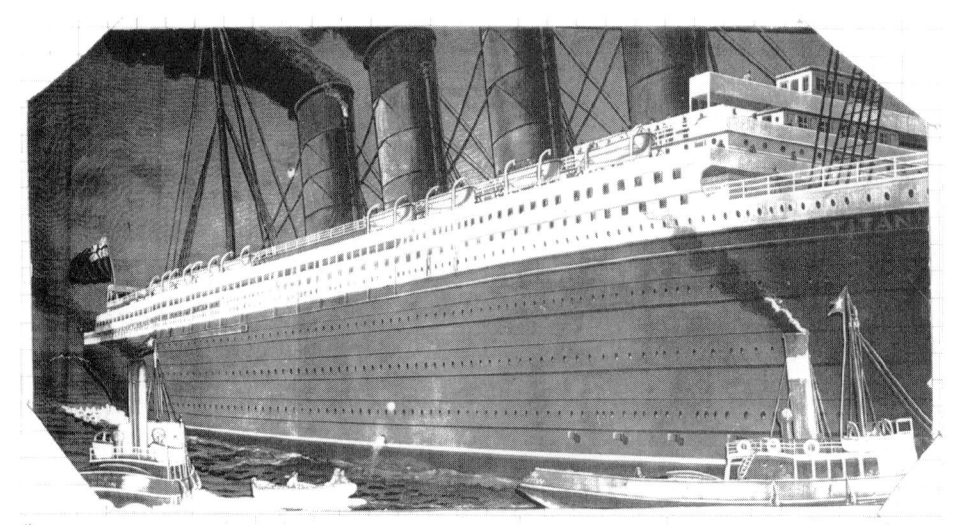

"Suddenly, there is a slight shock, followed by a curious shivering movement from stem to stern."

"It was as tho' some great hand were pushing her down"

It is indicative of the lasting fascination of the *Titanic* story that this spectacle could be mounted – and so presumably attract audiences – two and a half years after the actual event. The fact that it was put on during wartime might have imbued the show with an additional poignancy and audience appeal. Interestingly, a number of short films were exhibited during the Myriorama show as an interlude.

Conclusion
It is clear that the sinking of the *Titanic* produced a flurry of activity in the lantern trade on both sides of the Atlantic. In the United States there seems to have been more uniformity of product, with slides mainly based on news photographs, in sets of from 8 to 40 individual slides, with dealers also offering advertising posters and accompanying lectures. In Britain dealers were perhaps slightly slower off the mark, with fewer of them participating, and each offering fewer slides. On the other hand, there was a rather more varied product available from British dealers, including both artists' impressions and slides based on news photographs. In general, it is clear from this case study that the lantern slide industry, particularly in its news role was in rather robust health in the early teen years, and by no means as yet killed off by the cinema.[36]

Titanic News Films

News of disaster

In the autumn of 1998 the world heard the news of the loss of Swissair flight 111, in which all 229 people on board met their deaths as the aeroplane crashed into the North Atlantic. For those looking for such connections, the site of this tragedy in the North Atlantic brought echoes of the *Titanic* sinking in April 1912 when over 1500 lives were lost. While the *Titanic* was an even bigger news story, there were some interesting parallels in the media coverage of the two events.

Though the *Titanic* disaster took place at the dawn of the newsreel age, then as now in the news business, speed was of the essence, and the story was on screens within days of the event. Of course the television news of today is even faster in its coverage, and it is also different in another sense. The news today is, at least in dealing with disasters, more *honest* than the newsreels of 1912. Though one might well level accusations of general bias in the 'news agenda' of the modern media, there is less of the *crude* deceit that was so marked in the early part of the 20th century.[1] As we shall see, there were several instances of deception surrounding news film of the *Titanic* disaster in 1912 (and fakery was also an issue in other news films in this era). In this and the following chapter I will look at these and other issues surrounding news films of the *Titanic*, here concentrating on production, while in the following chapter turning more to exhibition.

Since mass media became a major industry in the late 19th century, whenever there was a major news event, there was an accompanying scramble by journalists for all and any information about it. When the *Titanic* went down the scramble became a positive melée, with reporters and photographers hunting out any information they could find related to the ship and its passengers. This frenzy certainly struck Bert Garai, later one of the great pressmen of the twentieth century, who was starting out at the Havas news agency in Paris when the *Titanic* story broke: 'It was most impressive and it gave me a glimpse of the speed, efficiency and enthusiasm such work entailed', he later recalled.[2] Indeed, in the immediate aftermath of the *Titanic* disaster, the press demonstrated just how quickly and imaginatively it could cover a news story pictorially. Within a day or two of the sinking, newspapers and periodicals published artists' impressions of the disaster, along with numerous photographs of the victims and other aspects of the story. A photographic periodical noting this 'ubiquity of photography', pointed out that such pictorial coverage was achieved despite considerable problems:

'The disaster took place under circumstances which, of course, precluded all question of a photographic record. If an event had been designed so as to cheat every possibility of being memorialised in the shape of a graphic record, it could hardly have been more successfully carried out. Yet the truly wonderful thing is that within a day or two of the calamity memorial numbers were on the streets containing upwards of a hundred photographs, all bearing more or less upon the event, and long before any pictures could reach them from New York our illustrated papers were in possession of a mass of pictorial material which filled interminable pages. It may truly be said that in the rare cases when photography is not on the spot it still seems to be only just round the corner.' [3]

But while the print media could successfully skate around the lack of primary visual material of the *Titanic* disaster, the problem was more acute for the nascent news film medium. There was no film of the sinking itself, nor any film taken during the maiden voyage (apart from what was filmed by the cameramen aboard, all of which had gone down with the ship), and there was not much film of the ship prior to its maiden voyage. Furthermore, the montaging of hand-drawn and photographic images available to the press journalist, was not so straightforward in films.

Yet the sinking took place at the dawn of the newsreel age, when the public was becoming accustomed to seeing a selection of filmed news at their local picture palaces, in newsreels including Pathé Gazette, the Animated Weekly and Topical Budget. So somehow, to satisfy expectations if nothing else, the *Titanic* story had to be covered on film, and finding or shooting appropriate news images became of urgent importance to these companies. They tackled this task with speed and energy.[4]

In Britain the Topical Budget newsreel may have been first on screen with the disaster, and included two items in its issue of 17th April:

'The *Titanic*: at Southampton, prior to her maiden voyage which has proved so disastrous.'[5]
'The White Star Line: Anxious crowds awaiting news outside the London Office.'[6]

*(32) The Topical Budget's issues of April 17th and 20th
included three items about the* Titanic *disaster
The Bioscope 25 April 1912 (British Film Institute)*

If this issue of Topical's newsreel was indeed available on the 17th April, it was a very rapid response indeed: the ship had sunk in the early hours of the 15th April, and some newspapers didn't cover the story till the 16th. The second of the items in Topical's issue was freshly shot, which makes their speed in releasing this issue doubly impressive. But the first item was existing or 'archive' film, and was one of the few moving images that had ever been taken of the *Titanic*. Interestingly, Topical may have been the only company with this footage of the *Titanic* at Southampton – but unfortunately the film has been lost. Topical's issue three days later also included a *Titanic* item, this one showing the memorial service which had taken place at St.Paul's Cathedral.

The Topical company's releases were certainly up-to-the-minute, and they were also genuine, a point they emphasised in their ads, to contrast their work with all other companies who they claimed were not so scrupulously truthful about their *Titanic* news films: 'we did not bluff you with flaring adverts', claimed Topical.[7] Genuine they may have been, but none of Topical's *Titanic* items was exactly startling footage. Other newsreels aimed to obtain something a little more original.

Animated Weekly/Gaumont's *Titanic* Wreck Special

Our focus now shifts to the United States and the Animated Weekly newsreel. Though the fact was not widely advertised, the apparently all-American Animated Weekly was produced by the Gaumont company, which originated in France.[8] Indeed it was so closely tied to Gaumont that its editor, Frank E. Holliday, was also editor of the Gaumont Weekly newsreel, which was also releasing in America at this time.[9] The Animated Weekly may even have been called The 'Gaumont Animated Weekly' in early 1912.[10] Gaumont had first released in America through the Patents Company, but left on 1st January 1912 for the open market, in other words joining the Independents.[11]

The Animated Weekly certainly had energy and brio, the qualities one would associate with the maverick Independents, which were in ongoing conflict with the Patents' Trust companies. It was issued by the Motion Picture Distributing and Sales Company (the Independents' umbrella organisation). The Animated Weekly, which called itself 'a visualized newspaper', had ambitious plans: it was pushing to become one of the world's major newsreels, and was already said to have a hundred cameramen around the globe.[12] They claimed in one ad: 'No matter where, how difficult to get at or the cost, if it happens, the Animated Weekly will have it.'[13]

THE MOST FAMOUS FILM IN THE ENTIRE WORLD

THE SALES COMPANY
ANIMATED WEEKLY

SCORES THE BIGGEST SCOOP OF THE YEAR IN THE MATTER OF THE

TITANIC
DISASTER

| WHEREVER THE SUN SHINES | | WHEREVER THERE'S HUMANITY |

OUR CAMERA MEN WERE THE FIRST TO REACH THE WRECK

THE ANIMATED'S SPECIAL BULLETIN WAS ISSUED IN NEW YORK AND MAILED TO 15,000 EXHIBITORS AT THE SAME TIME THE DAILY PAPERS PUT OUT THEIR EXTRAS—DID YOU GET YOUR BULLETIN?—IF NOT, WRITE QUICK, SO YOU WILL GET NEXT WEEK'S. IT'S WONDERFULLY ATTRACTIVE AND WILL DRAW THE CROWDS TO YOUR THEATRE. THE BEST ADVERTISING EVER DESIGNED FOR M. P. HOUSES—THE NEWS AND PHOTOGRAPHS OF CURRENT EVENTS AS THEY HAPPEN.

MOTION PICTURE DISTRIBUTING & SALES COMPANY
111 East 14th Street, NEW YORK

ANIMATED WEEKLY DEPARTMENT
31 East 27th Street, NEW YORK

(33) The Animated Weekly's newsreel about the disaster
Moving Picture News 27 April 1912

The newsreel was undoubtedly an aggressive news gatherer. For this *Titanic* mission, instead of waiting for the news to come to them, the Animated Weekly chartered tugs to get to the story.[14] Apparently they initially headed for the site of the wreck itself:

'Camera men were started in specially chartered tugs to the scene of the disaster, but were overtaken by wireless when news finally reached New York of the *Titanic*'s sinking – the boats were then turned southward and met the steamer *Carpathia* bound for New York. Many views of the rescue ship were taken. Another camera man at Halifax, Nova Scotia, took pictures of the funeral boat, *Mackay-Bennett*, as she started, coffins loaded, to pick up dead bodies.'[15]

It is not clear how many tugs were involved in this operation. The Animated's ads proclaimed: 'Our camera men from a dozen ports started immediately in specially chartered tugs, our entire staff working night and day.'[16] But Hearst newspapers also chartered tugs, and there may have been some co-operation between these and other news organisations.

On one of these tugs, the *Mary Scully*, was Jack Binns, the famous wireless operator and hero of the *Republic* shipwreck of 1909 (see Dramas out of a Crisis chapter). Binns had begun to work for a newspaper in New York just a day before the *Titanic* sank, so his interests were now as much journalistic as anyone's.[17] He may have been working for the *New York American* for it is said that the *Mary Scully* had been hired by this newspaper.[18] There is confirmation that he was actually on this tug, as one shot in the final newsreel is introduced by a title stating: 'the Mary Sculley with Jack Binns and camera men leaves from Providence, R.I.' and in the shot itself the boat bears a sign stating that it is a 'New York American press boat'. But Binns was not acting as a mere reporter: the idea was that he would take over as wireless operator on the *Carpathia* (which was carrying survivors from the *Titanic* to New York), as the *Carpathia*'s man Cottam was tiring after two days continuous work. Binns also brought a back up operator and a semaphore signalman. It is not clear how successful his mission was. One report says that fog made contact impossible, no one could see the semaphore, and rivals were already busy using the only wireless link on the *Carpathia*. Jack and the *Mary Scully* returned to port with nothing to show for their efforts.[19] On the other hand another report says Binns did indeed locate the *Carpathia* by wireless, and then the cameramen of the newsreel obtained the shots of the survivors.[20]

Certainly someone from the Animated Weekly managed to film the *Carpathia*, for their newsreel includes a shot of this rescue ship which bore the 703 survivors. A title states: 'The Animated Weekly draws close to her side. The survivors are plainly seen on deck.' As we discovered in our discussion of lantern slides one of the slide dealers, the enterprising Charles A. Pryor, chartered a tug which took him to the *Carpathia*, where he photographed the survivors and crew. With him on this trip was a Mr. M.M. Robinson, said to be a moving picture cameraman for Gaumont. The source for this story says that they were the first operators on board the *Carpathia*.[21]

(a)

(b)

(34) Titanic Disaster *(Gaumont) (NFTVA)*
(a) The Mary F. Scully, *chartered by the* New York American, *going out to meet the* Carpathia *at sea*
(b) Famous wireless operator Jack Binns (on the left), boarding the Mary F. Scully
(c) Reporters gather to interview survivors

(c)

Sending cameramen out to meet the *Carpathia* proved to be a smart move by the Animated Weekly, because the little Cunarder wouldn't arrive into New York until 18th April, and when she did come in she was met by a scrum of boats chartered by newspapers. Reporters shouted questions up to the passengers on the *Carpathia* through megaphones and the night was illuminated as they took dozens of flashlight photographs. When the ship stopped to pick up the pilot, several reporters tried to force their way on board: one offered $200 to be allowed on the ship, another had to be punched away by a crew member, and a third was cornered on the bridge.[22] At the pier there were even more reporters. All of this media frenzy would have made the cameramen's job very difficult.

This *Carpathia* footage was edited together with other appropriate *Titanic* footage to make up a special issue of the Animated Weekly newsreel. I have worked out the contents of this special issue mainly using an ad from the *New York Tribune* and an article in the *Moving Picture News*, neither of which description appears complete (or they may be describing slightly different versions).[23] The film went roughly in this order (incorrect spellings retained):

1. Laying the keel of the *Titanic*
2. Launching of the *Titanic*
3. The "hero skipper is shown in realistic poses" [ie. Captain E.J. Smith]
4. "A series of views showing icebergs..."
5. "The screen is darkened for a minute and the "C.Q.D." [the then equivalent of the S.O.S.] is flashed on in vivid reality"[24]
6. Funeral ship leaving Halifax, N.S., with coffins to pick up bodies at sea[25]
7. The tug, the *Mary Sculley* with Jack Binns and camera men leaves from Providence, R.I.
8. Scenes at the White Star offices on Broadway, where crowds await news of relatives and friends
9. Docks "where society ladies in private automobiles are bringing clothes and supplies to the relief of the rescued, when the *Carpathia* arrives."
10. The *Carpathia* bearing the 703 survivors. "The Animated Weekly draws close to her side. The survivors are plainly seen on deck."
11. Captain Rostron of the *Carpathia*
12. Robert Hitchens, quartermaster of the *Titanic*, who stood at the wheel when the vessel struck
13. Various views of the survivors
14. William Marconi, who invented the wireless
15. Lifeboats and life preservers
16. *Carpathia* at dock
17. The grave of the *Titanic*[26]

This was released as *The Titanic Wreck Special*. It was 900 ft in length, and premièred at Weber's Theatre on Broadway, New York on Sunday 21st April: that is, less than a week after the sinking, which had been in the early hours of Monday 15th April. It was released to other theatres the following day. (This was in addition to the Animated Weekly's regular newsreel release).[27] An ad from the

New York Tribune described the film as a 'gigantic scoop', and 'the most famous film in the whole world'. But even a relatively neutral source, the *Moving Picture News* declared: 'It is a truly wonderful film, and the Animated Weekly, with its staff, come in for credit for getting the biggest picture scoop the world has ever known.'[28] Another journal praised the film for its completeness:

'...especially when one realizes how little there was left to take and the energy and method required to obtain the exceptionally surprising amount of scenes and subjects, which are to be found in the film. It has been compiled with distinct care and order, creating by its sequence and interpolation of scenes an exceptionally vivid and impressive exposition of the subject.'[29]

One must agree with this assessment. Given how little footage of the actual *Titanic* had been available, this newsreel version of the disaster manages to marshal the footage that was available and the newly shot material to great effect, and builds up an extremely moving account of the tragedy. It is a fine example of how far the newsreel had already progressed by 1912.

The Animated Weekly's newsreel even attracted the great wireless pioneer Marconi, who was featured in the film. He attended a screening at Weber's Theatre, partly for the thrill of seeing himself on screen. He took some friends along the following night, arriving too late for a regular screening but when the theatre boss Bert Adler discovered that he had such a famous spectator in his building, a special showing was at once arranged.[30]

The Animated Weekly's film included material from a number of sources. The second scene was from existing footage of the launch of the *Titanic*, which had taken place almost a year earlier. The ship was launched in Belfast on 31st May 1911, the event having been filmed by Films Limited, a local firm conveniently located in the High Street, Belfast. A trade writer in June 1911 enthused about the film:

'Thousands who were unable to see the launch will avail themselves of this opportunity. Even those who saw the launch may in this film see some feature that they missed.'[31]

The Animated Weekly's footage was probably from this version shot by Films Limited. But Kinemacolor footage purporting to be of the *Titanic* launch was also re-released after the disaster – this incidentally being one of the first *Titanic* disaster-related screenings to be reported – it was premiered on 17th April 1912

(35) *The frontage of Weber's Theatre advertising the* Animated Weekly's Titanic *newsreel*
Moving Picture News 4 May 1912

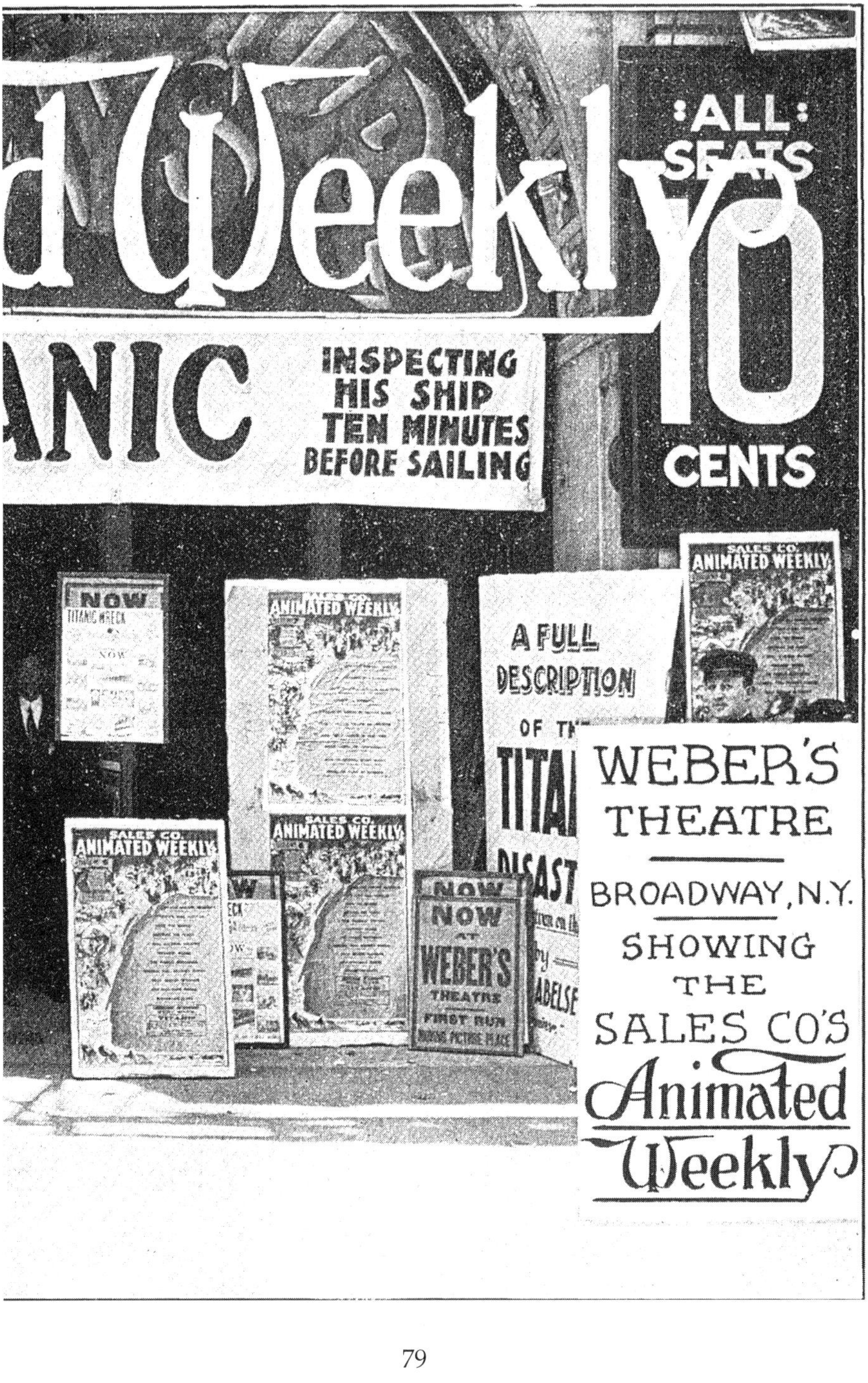
Weekly
ALL SEATS
10
CENTS
INSPECTING HIS SHIP TEN MINUTES BEFORE SAILING
NOW
TITANIC WRECK
SALES CO. ANIMATED WEEKLY
A FULL DESCRIPTION
SALES CO. ANIMATED WEEKLY
SALES CO. ANIMATED WEEKLY
NOW AT WEBER'S THEATRE FIRST RUN
WEBER'S THEATRE
BROADWAY, N.Y.
SHOWING THE SALES CO'S
Animated Weekly

at the Garden Theatre in New York, as an added feature to the existing programme.[32] The Kinemacolor screening also included film of Captain Smith, claimed to have been taken just before his last sailing from America.

'This most lifelike Kinemacolor portrait in color-motion-photography shows the hale and hearty septuagenarian surrounded by his chief officers, a remarkable specimen of vigorous old age crowned with honors. The compact figure and broad shoulders, even the good-humored twinkle in the alert gray eyes, so familiar to thousands of ocean voyagers, are reproduced with perfect fidelity.'[33]

Very possibly, the footage of the launch was actually of the *Olympic*, and the colour footage of Smith taken earlier on a different ship.

Despite all the praise heaped on the Animated Weekly's special *Titanic* newsreel, there was to be some criticism on the grounds of authenticity and misleading advertising. In one ad the Animated Weekly claimed 'Our cameramen were the first to reach the wreck', but this was plainly untrue, as the company's cameramen had not been at the wreck of the *Titanic*, which had long since disappeared under the waves by the time any press boat could have been alerted.[34] As a further instance of an inaccurate claim, in the *Tribune* ad the shots of the iceberg or icebergs (scene 4) are described simply as 'The iceberg that sank the *Titanic*'. The *Moving Picture News* article was more accurate, and made clear that it was not the iceberg, and explained what the scene really was:

'...a series of views showing icebergs taken three days before the *Titanic* struck by one of the Animated Weekly men who was returning from Europe. Several of the survivors who were present declare these icebergs to be identical with the one which foundered the *Titanic*'.[35]

However a critic in the *Moving Picture World* disagreed even with this explanation, declaring that, while several scenes in the film were genuine, the iceberg one was nothing like the real thing:

'The icebergs, represented as being near the spot where the *Titanic* went down, had in the background, clearly revealed, a rugged promontory, and one could easily see that the bergs were in a bay near some Northern shore. There are many films from which this scene could have been taken. So with the so-called grave of the *Titanic*. [the final shot in the film] That bit of northern sea, with the golden glint of sunset, and an iceberg in the offing, was taken many moons since, by whom I do not know.'[36]

Despite such quibbles about accuracy (which would be amplified in Europe) the *Titanic Wreck Special* was enormously successful. It was taken up by several regional distributors in the United States, who had obtained the rights for their own localities. These included the Central Film Service Company, Cincinatti; the American Feature Film Company, Pittsburgh; and the Syracuse New York Company.[37]

Animated Weekly/Gaumont's *Titanic* Film in Europe

Through the Animated Weekly's link with Gaumont, their *Titanic* newsreel was to become the most widely seen version of the disaster in Europe too. On April 24th, three days after its New York premiere, a copy of the film was dispatched on the *Mauritania*. It was in the care of a uniformed Western Union man, with instructions to disembark at Fishguard, first landfall on the British mainland, where he was to take a train direct for the Gaumont company's headquarters (presumably in London).[38]

The film was released in Britain in early May. I have no precise date for this British release, but it was projected in Paris on 2nd May (see following chapter) and so it would probably have been re-edited for British release about the same date. A detailed list of the contents of Gaumont's film was published in Britain at the time of release. There were 18 scenes in the British cut, and it was 710 feet long. (Versus 17 scenes in 900 feet in the USA). Gaumont rented it at the standard 4d. per foot, and could also supply a synopsis and posters in two sizes. The striking quad crown poster cost 6d and showed the liner sailing towards camera, with the text, 'The ill-fated *Titanic*: scenes before and after the Disaster.'[39]

Gaumont's ad in the trade journals proclaimed: 'Once again the Cinematograph has a solemn duty to perform, in recording incidents in connection with the greatest shipping disaster the world has ever known'. The ad, apparently telegraphed from New York, listed the scenes:[40]

1. Captain Smith on the bridge.
2. The graveyard of the sea. Icebergs and icefloes in the neighborhood of the disaster.
3. The yacht "Mary Sculley" [sic] leaving Providence to meet the "Carpathia" at sea.
4. Jack Binns the noted wireless operator, boarding the "Mary Sculley." [which bears a sign saying it's a press boat.]
5. Society women bringing clothing for the survivors to the Cunard docks, prior to the arrival of the "Carpathia."

THE "TITANI

Once again the Cinematograph has a solemn duty to
greatest shipping disaster
There can be no shadow of doubt that the remarkable
received, and now offer, will create a great sensation,
The films were secured at enormous expense, and the
cable from

1. Captain Smith on the bridge.
2. The graveyard of the sea. Icebergs and icefloes in the neighbourhood of the disaster.
3. The yacht "Mary Sculley" leaving Providence to meet the "Carpathia" at sea.
4. Jack Binns, the noted wireless operator, boarding the "Mary Sculley."
5. Society women bringing clothing for the survivors to the Cunard Docks, prior to the arrival of the "Carpathia."
6. The "Carpathia" nearing New York with survivors.
7. The "Carpathia" docked.
8. Captain Rostrum of the "Carpathia."
9. Some survivors of the "Titanic's" crew.

Quad Crown Coloured Poster 6d. each.

Length 710 ft.   Price 4d. per ft

GAUMONT'S,

(36) Gaumont's advertisement for the British release of their Titanic *newsreel*
The Bioscope 2 May 1912 (British Film Institute)

C" DISASTER.

perform, in recording incidents in connection with the
the world has ever known.
and quite exclusive series of films which we have
and will fill picture theatres for weeks to come.
following description was sent word for word by
New York.

10. Quartermaster Hitchens of the "Titanic" who went down with the ship, but was afterwards picked up.
11. Father Hogue, a passenger on the "Carpathia," who first sighted the "Titanic" lifeboats.
12. Some of the heroes of the "Titanic's" crew picked up at sea.
13. Reporters interviewing survivors.
14. The crowd at the White Star Offices, New York, awaiting news.
15. Scene at the Cunard Docks the morning after the "Carpathia's" arrival.
16. Marconi, whose marvellous discovery saved over 700 lives.
17. The "Mackey Bennett" leaving Halifax in search of the dead.
18. Their last resting place.

Double Crown Poster, Synopsis of Film, 2d. each.
(less 2½ per cent. cash 7 days).

CHRONO HOUSE,
PICCADILLY CIRCUS, LONDON, W.

6. The "Carpathia" nearing New York with survivors.
7. The "Carpathia" docked.
8. Captain Rostrum of the "Carpathia." [ie.Rostron]
9. Some survivors of the "Titanic's" crew.
10. Quartermaster Hitchens of the "Titanic" who went down with the ship, but was afterwards picked up. [Filmed in a New York street.]
11. Father Hogue, a passenger on the "Carpathia," who first sighted the "Titanic" lifeboats.
12. Some of the heroes of the "Titanic's" crew picked up at sea.
13. Reporters interviewing survivors.
14. The crowd at the White Star offices, New York, awaiting news.
15. Scene at the Cunard Docks the morning after the "Carpathia's" arrival.
16. Marconi, whose marvellous discovery saved over 700 lives.
17. The "Mackay Bennett" leaving Halifax in search of the dead.
18. Their last resting place.

Gaumont boasted that their film 'will create a great sensation and will fill picture theatres for weeks to come'. The *Kine Weekly* devoted an entire page to describing the film, and praised Gaumont 'for this excellent and most interesting subject'.[41] But there were issues of authenticity. The first scene showed Captain Smith on the bridge of a ship, and one would assume it was on the *Titanic*'s bridge. In fact it had been taken on the bridge of the sister ship, the *Olympic* the previous

(37) Titanic Disaster (Globe) (NFTVA)
(a) Title used to introduce the shot of Smith
(b) Captain Smith on the bridge of the Olympic, *probably filmed in the summer of 1911 in New York. The ship's name on the bulkhead has been inked out frame by frame to suggest that this was filmed on the* Titanic

summer. Initially Gaumont failed to make this clear. Embarassed by potential accusations of mendacity, a week after the film's release, a letter from Gaumont's Mr Welsh appeared in the *Kinematograph Weekly*, saying:

'...in my circulars and announcements on the subject I have never suggested that this portrait of Captain Smith was taken on the "*Titanic.*" As a matter of fact I believe it was taken on the '*Olympic*' and I should be glad if you would insert this letter in your next issue as I have no desire to lead anyone to believe that this section of the film was taken on the '*Titanic*'. It must be looked upon as a portrait of Capt. Smith and as such is surely of interest in the series we have produced.'[42]

So this was a mere 'portrait of Captain Smith'? And yet in Gaumont's ad a week earlier the Captain Smith shot was described as, 'Captain Smith on the bridge,' with no location given, whereas most of the other 17 shots do give some idea of the location where they were filmed. This would seem at the very least somewhat misleading, and Gaumont did not offer to augment the intertitle.

But others were even more deceitful in this matter. In a copy of a *Titanic* newsreel – of indeterminate source – held in the Library of Congress, the opening intertitle is cleverly worded to stop just short of an outright lie in introducing the shot of Captain Smith as:

'Captain E.J. Smith, Commander of the ill fated S.S. *Titanic* – a final inspection of his vessel ten minutes before sailing time'.[43]

'His vessel' meaning – the *Olympic* ! But it should be made clear that it was not only filmmakers who were guilty of confusion over the *Olympic* and *Titanic*. Some postcard publishers at this time brought out cards of the *Olympic* mislabelled as the *Titanic*.[44] (Similarly, an 'in memorium' postcard released after the *Lusitania* sinking was actually a picture of the *Titanic*!)[45] In more recent times one of the most authoritative books on the *Titanic* uses illustrations of the *Olympic* where no equivalent is available for the *Titanic*: 'in the belief that a picture quite representative of *Titanic*, though not actually of her, is preferable to no photograph at all.'[46] And indeed the ships were virtually identical apart from the forward half of their A decks, the pattern of windows on their B decks, and some internal fittings and partitions. One author has even speculated recently (unconvincingly) that perhaps the two ships had been switched prior to the voyage, in a plan to scuttle the already damaged *Olympic* in the icefields of the North Atlantic![47]

Warner Beats Them All

Greatest Feature Release of the Year. Positively the only negative in existence of the late

CAPTAIN E. J. SMITH, R. N. R.
Commander of the ill-fated
S. S. TITANIC THAT WENT DOWN IN MID-OCEAN

Captain Smith is seen on board the sister ship Olympic, ten minutes before sailing time, giving his boat a final inspection.

The Olympic, being a sister ship of the Titanic, was built by the same company and is exactly alike in construction. The very same life boats and rafts as well as other life saving devices are clearly shown, as well as the most interesting points of the boat, and the thousands of cheering passengers as the boat starts on her maiden voyage across the Atlantic.

An Absolute Perfect Production, and the
ONLY ONE IN EXISTENCE
Total Length 400 Feet

WIRE MONEY WITH ORDER   5-COLOR ONE-SHEETS, 10 CENTS EACH

Warner's Features
145 West 45th Street   -   -   -   New York City

(38) Advertisement for Warner's newsreel, which in fact showed the Olympic rather than the Titanic Moving Picture World 27 April 1912

Globe/Warner's *Titanic* Disaster

Gaumont/Animated Weekly were not the only newsreel companies to seek to mislead on the issue of Captain Smith and the *Titanic/Olympic*. By the beginning of May the Globe Film Company in London had acquired a 400 foot news film of the *Titanic* disaster, which it put on the market.[48] Their ad listed the scenes, and these included Captain Smith (the same shots used in the Animated Weekly/Gaumont version), and also views of different parts of the ship, including the emergency telephone, the engine room chart, the first, second, and third class cabins, and promenade decks including lifeboats. It also showed passengers' baggage being loaded, the crowds cheering as the ship departed, and Captain Smith as he 'makes his bow'.[49] But what Globe initially failed to mention in their handouts was that none of this was of the *Titanic*, but was in fact taken on the *Olympic*, *Titanic*'s almost identical sister ship, filmed a year earlier in the summer of 1911 on her maiden voyage to New York. A week after Globe's misleading release the company changed an intertitle in their film, adding a phrase to the effect that the film was taken on the sister ship rather than on the *Titanic*. One suspects this was possibly done following objections, or as the *Bioscope* put it: '...to avoid any possible misconstruction.'[50]

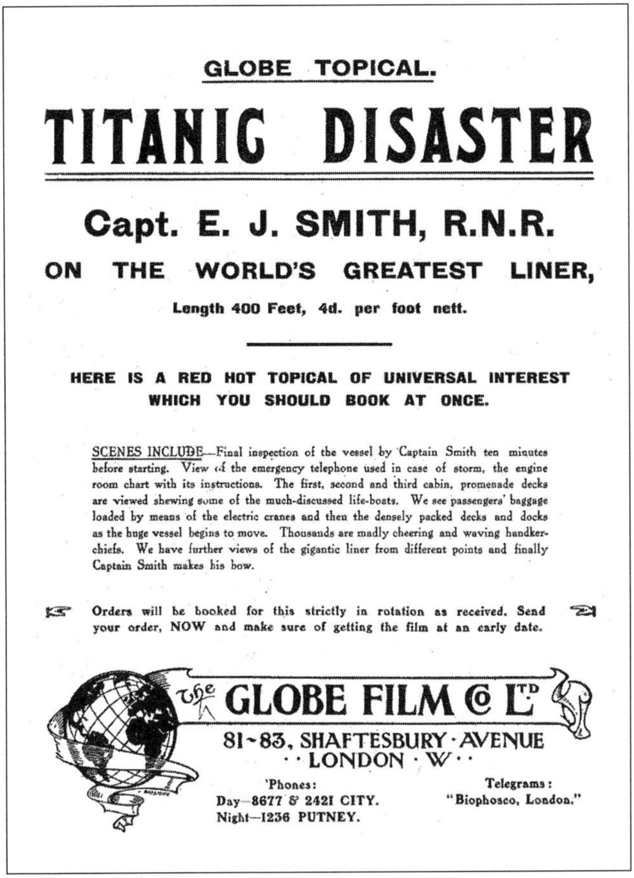

> **GLOBE TOPICAL.**
>
> # TITANIC DISASTER
>
> ## Capt. E. J. SMITH, R.N.R.
> ### ON THE WORLD'S GREATEST LINER,
> Length 400 Feet, 4d. per foot nett.
>
> **HERE IS A RED HOT TOPICAL OF UNIVERSAL INTEREST WHICH YOU SHOULD BOOK AT ONCE.**
>
> SCENES INCLUDE—Final inspection of the vessel by Captain Smith ten minutes before starting. View of the emergency telephone used in case of storm, the engine room chart with its instructions. The first, second and third cabin, promenade decks are viewed shewing some of the much-discussed life-boats. We see passengers' baggage loaded by means of the electric cranes and then the densely packed decks and docks as the huge vessel begins to move. Thousands are madly cheering and waving handkerchiefs. We have further views of the gigantic liner from different points and finally Captain Smith makes his bow.
>
> Orders will be booked for this strictly in rotation as received. Send your order, NOW and make sure of getting the film at an early date.
>
> ## GLOBE FILM C° L°
> ### 81-83, SHAFTESBURY AVENUE
> ### · · LONDON · W · ·
> 'Phones: Telegrams:
> Day—8677 & 2421 CITY. "Biophosco, London."
> Night—1236 PUTNEY.

(39) *Handout for the Globe (Warner) newsreel about the* Titanic
(British Library)

(40) *Titanic Disaster (Globe) Tugs nosing the* Olympic *out of the dock, probably filmed in the summer of 1911 in New York. The tug names have been inked out to suggest that the ship was the* Titanic *filmed in Britain*
(NFTVA)

This is much the same film as that released in the United States by the Warner Theatre Film Company, or Warner's Features, located at 145 W. 45th St., New York City – even the length of 400 feet was the same as Globe's. (Though some versions of the Warner film were shorter at 290 feet.)[51] It was being screened in various parts of the USA within a few hours of the *Carpathia* docking.[52] This film had been purchased by Warners from I. Bernstein of the Republic Company.[53] The difference from the British Globe version is that, instead of ending with Captain Smith, Warner's release ended with a black screen flashing 'S.O.S.'[54] (In contrast to the Animated Weekly version which flashed 'C.Q.D.') At the time of release Warners made it clear in a trade journal ad that the sequences mentioned above, including shots of Captain Smith, had not been filmed on the *Titanic*, but on the *Olympic*, which 'is exactly alike in construction'.[55] 'NOT A FAKE' they trumpeted.[56]

But the Captain Smith controversy would not lie down. The real nature of the Smith shots was not made clear in the title cards in the Globe film itself, and it would be easy for a viewer who had not seen the printed advertisement to assume that Smith had been filmed on the *Titanic*. This was partly because the title preceding Captain Smith's appearance was: 'The *Titanic* Disaster: Captain Smith, R.N.R. on the World's Greatest Liner.' And everyone knew that the *Titanic* had indeed been the world's greatest liner, so one would assume if one had not read their ad, that the shots in question were indeed on the *Titanic*. Even the *Moving Picture World*'s critic seemed to have come to this conclusion to judge from his review of the film.[57] One trade journal criticised this deception, but noted that it was easy to detect because all the people on deck wore summer costumes, while the *Titanic*'s voyage was in April. Apparently the Pathé news organisation had turned down the chance to acquire this *Olympic* footage, due to their concern about it being misleading: in a highminded statement the Pathé company claimed they had 'no use for fakes'.[58]

Someone tried to hide the deception. In a surviving print of the Globe film at the NFTVA (304 feet long) we can see that the New York pier number and the names and ports of registry on accompanying tugs have been inked out on each frame of the negative, and in the scene with Captain Smith the sign behind him, presumably saying *Olympic*, is inked out too.[59] It is not at all clear who did this, though it might have been an exhibitor rather than Globe/Warner's themselves. But clearly the intention was to efface any evidence that the ship was indeed the *Olympic*. Frank Thompson, author of *Lost Films*, notes that such footage still exists today as stock shots, and is still represented as being the *Titanic*.

The final tally: Genuine films of the *Titanic*
So where does this leave us regarding genuine films of the *Titanic*? When and where was the actual ship filmed? It seems probable that there were less than half a dozen sequences ever taken of the *Titanic*, which were:

* *Laying the keel of the Titanic*. (in Belfast, 31 March 1909). Included in the Animated Weekly version. It is not known which production company filmed this.

* *Transport of Titanic's Largest Anchor in the World*. (c1911?) This film of 400 feet was described as 'unique' when offered for hire by a Worcestershire cinema in May 1912.[60] Production company unknown.

* *Launching of the Titanic*. (in Belfast, 31 May 1911). Filmed by Films Limited of Belfast. Included in the Animated Weekly newsreel, and in some versions of the Gaumont newsreel. (Purportedly also filmed in Kinemacolor, but this was probably footage of the *Olympic*).

* *Titanic leaving Belfast Loch for Southampton* (2 April 1912) This was on sale by one cinema in early May 1912, in a print of 125 feet in length.[61] Production company unknown. This material survives in some prints of Gaumont's newsreel (see Appendix: Extant Films).

The Titanic: at Southampton, prior to her maiden voyage. (10 April 1912). Filmed by Topical Budget and released in their newsreel in April 1912.

In recent years, as the interest in the *Titanic* has reawakened, a number of commercial film libraries or collectors have continued to claim that they have a genuine film of the *Titanic*, when what they actually have is the infamous footage described above with the giveaway names of the *Olympic* and of the harbour tugs inked out. The stakes are high – such is the notoriety of this great disaster that any genuine film of the ship at the centre of it all would have an extraordinary value. In these circumstances the quest for, and arguments about, 'real' *Titanic* footage have taken on almost mythic proportions, and the issues of authenticity raised at the time will continue to haunt us.

Exhibiting *Titanic* News Films

As we have seen in the previous chapter, some of the newsreels released about the *Titanic* disaster included shots which were not entirely as their makers claimed in their intertitles and publicity. But it turns out that this was just one aspect of the false claims made about *Titanic* 'news' footage, and in several cases the mendacity was on the part of the showman rather than the producer. It was in the United States where controversy about false or misleading footage of the *Titanic*, and also general concern about exploiting the *Titanic* tragedy on screen, reached its height. In this chapter I will look at these issues, and will also examine the success of genuine and not so genuine films of the disaster in attracting audiences.

Titanic Fakes?
When it emerged that films would be released about the *Titanic* disaster some critics expressed themselves against any screening of such reels. In a May 1912 issue of *The Implet*, a house journal for the Imp film company, a writer suggested that all *Titanic* films should be banned. This was somewhat hypocritical, given that the same issue of the journal prominently featured their own Imp film, the marine drama *From the Bottom of the Sea*, which was surely a promotional decision based on the current interest in the *Titanic* sinking.[1] And other companies also promoted ship-related films at this time (see the following chapter).

It did seem that there was some resistance to showing *Titanic*-related films. But the real opposition was to come over fraudulent films about the tragedy, or false claims about the content of films. This really raised the hackles of spectators and critics alike. The *Moving Picture News* reported in May that a New York theatre was showing films purporting to be of the *Titanic* disaster:

'...and what was our astonishment to find the *Lusitania*, the *Olympic* and one or two scratch films of ancient days posing as pictures of the *Titanic*. We protested to the manager, who immediately ordered his operator to send them back to the exchange from which he had them and if possible to destroy them.'[2]

In the same issue of the journal an outraged letter from a reader in Los Angeles, dated 26th April, was published, complaining of the 'money mad' behaviour of the three most prominent independent exhibitors in the city:

'As soon as the news of the *Titanic* disaster was flashed to Los Angeles, these unscrupulous exhibitors immediately went to the film exchanges and rented several old reels which show the *Mauritania* and the *Olympic* steamers in action. After securing these old rainstorms [old, scratched prints] they papered their lobby with fake posters and lithographs which advertised the only genuine negatives of the disaster.'[3]

But the controversy about *Titanic* news films really took off in America in early May, when a rumour circulated that on hearing the first news of the sinking a cameraman had chartered a tug in Cape Breton and rushed to the scene while survivors were still in the water. Possibly this rumour originated in the Animated Weekly's claim that their cameramen 'were the first to reach the wreck' (see previous chapter), when the truth was that they were first to reach the survivors. In any case the trade writer who reported this bit of gossip expressed his horror at the thought that a cameraman might have been there, callously filming:

'...while the lives of brave men and devoted women went out under the faint glimmer of the stars, and that no hand was stretched out to save them. No; there can be no moving pictures of this fearful catastrophe. To have any, reputed as being such, would be gruesome, ghastly and ghoulish.'[4]

The writer admitted that this suggestion of an operator filming as passengers drowned was unfounded and indeed impossible. For one thing the *Titanic* sank within two hours of the collision with the iceberg, so there would not have been time for a cameraman to charter a boat and travel to the scene, and also the collision happened at night when it would have been too dark to film.

Nevertheless in early May some theatres in cities including New York were said to be exhibiting pictures representing the sinking. We do not know what film this was – perhaps an existing shot of a shipwreck, or perhaps a lantern slide. The *Moving Picture World*'s correspondent listened to some of the critical reactions of the audience as they came out of one such show, including this comment:

'I'll stand for almost anything if it is based upon and shows facts, but I certainly will not stand for "bunk." It hurts my feelings to be gulled into sitting down and looking at a lot of impossible stuff that is cooked up almost before a thing happens. It makes me sick to see either a newspaper or a picture show portray so-called actual occurrences when impossibility is stamped upon the pictures and illustrations. Take, for instance, this picture showing the *Titanic* with about a sixth of her forward length stuck into the iceberg which is supposed to have sent her to the bottom. Everybody knows that the collision did not occur in that manner. It was on the side that the vessel was damaged.'[5]

At this point the proprietor intervened to justify himself, saying that no-one could expect to see films of the actual events surrounding the *Titanic*'s fate, and that anyway this was not claimed, merely that the pictures were reproductions of actual scenes. In that case, argued another member of the audience:

'...put that on the banners in front of the houses, and don't hold back the truth until after the people pay their money. Some of the banners I have seen displayed at the cheaper houses on the East Side and other places were misrepresentations to the point of criminality.'

He added that the makers of films should intervene to stop this practice, for if not, like newspapers which deal in falsehoods, the public would stop buying the mendacious product. Another couple of bystanders who intervened were not so concerned with this possible faking, but the *World*'s critic was, and argued that the fact that movie theatres now showed news as well as entertainment films 'should not be taken as a license to distort or misrepresent.'

There were a number of other scams in connection with *Titanic* newsreels. As we have seen, moving picture footage of the *Titanic*'s launch had been around for almost a year, and after the disaster this footage was rapidly dusted off and shown (it made up the second scene of the Animated Weekly's version). But this footage was sometimes exhibited at American theatres with misleading advertisements outside. At the Savoy Moving Picture Theatre on 34th Street in Manhattan (presumably one of the cheaper houses on the East Side mentioned above) a sign went up advertising:

FIRST PICTURES OF THE TITANIC
sunk in
OCEAN DISASTER

The middle line was in very small type, and if one failed to read this it gave the impression that films of the disaster itself would be shown. But in fact the showman merely screened 'the most uninteresting views of the *Titanic*'s launching'. Needless to say, this was not what most spectators expected based on the main lettering.[6]

FOOLED PATRONS AT TITANIC SHOW

Audience at Savoy Sees Only Pictures Taken in Belfast and Lecturer Who Saw Ship There.

EXPECTED TRAGEDY SCENES

George Seybolt of the Lambs Gets Up in Theatre, Demanding His Money Back in Vain.

George Seybolt of the Lambs came to THE TIMES office yesterday afternoon with Mrs. Seybolt. He said:

"I was passing along Thirty-fourth Street near Broadway this afternoon, when I saw a sign outside the Savoy Moving Picture Theatre on the south side of the street, advertising pictures of the Titanic and a lecture by a survivor.

"We paid fifty cents and went in. After waiting for two hours, some views of the Titanic taken in Belfast were shown. A lecturer got off a long talk about 'the dangers of the briny deep,' 'the terrible tragedy' and the 'matchless heroism' of Col. Astor, Maj. Butt, Mr. and Mrs. Straus and others who had perished.

"When he finished, I got up and asked him:

"'Are you a survivor of the Titanic wreck?'

"He replied:

"'No, let me explain.'

"I cut him short with this:

"'Then this whole thing is a fraud and I want my money back.'

"Some one came up to me from the rear of the house and said:

"'Come out, you'll get your money, keep quiet, it's all right.' When I got on the street, I was told I could whistle for my money.

"I think it is an outrage that the public interest in the Titanic disaster should be capitalized and I consider it my duty to call public attention to it.

"This is the same theatre which had a riot when they advertised pictures of the Jeffries-Johnson prize fight at Reno July 4, 1910, and when they got a crowd in expecting moving pictures, showed them some snap shots which had appeared in an afternoon newspaper. The crowd to-day was a different sort of crowd and didn't make the kind of demonstration made by the disappointed sport followers on the occasion of the earlier fraud."

Mr. Seybolt referred to the wrecking of the kiosk and lobby of the theatre on July 7, 1910.

When a TIMES reporter reached the theatre he found employes hustling off with signs eight feet high and a yard wide advertising pictures of the Titanic and a discussion by "A Lecturer Who Was on Board."

Patrolman Cohen of the Old Tenderloin Station, who was on duty at Broadway and Thirty-fourth Street, said:

"I just ordered those signs taken inside, because I think they were misleading and there have been several complaints."

Julius Rosenberg, manager of the theatre, was found on the balcony floor. He said that the lecturer was Eugene West, who had been aboard the Titanic before she was launched at Belfast and other times in Belfast harbor. He admitted that West had not been a passenger on the disastrous trip of the liner. He said:

"Those signs don't say he was a survivor."

When asked why he had not given Mr. Seybolt his money back, Rosenberg explained:

"Of course, I didn't give him his money back. That sign didn't misrepresent anything. I spend hours thinking up my signs. It's a crime to get money by false pretenses. West was on the Titanic. The sign didn't say when he was."

"Was this place under your management when it had the riot over the Jeffries-Johnson pictures?" the reporter asked.

"Yes, and we didn't misrepresent anything then. We didn't say we had moving pictures. We said we had the first pictures. We showed slides taken at the ring side. If people were foolish enough to think we meant moving pictures, that was their fault, not ours."

(41) Article about one of the fraudulent screenings of Titanic *films*
New York Times
21 April 1912

> **MAKING DIRTY MONEY.**
> The versatile Herbert Corey writes from New York to the Cincinnati *Times-Star* as follows regarding a picture show manager of New York who made "dirty money" out of the *T̄itanic* disaster:
>
> He is the proprietor of a moving picture house on Thirty-fourth Street. The day that the *Carpathia* reached port he put up this sign:
>
> FIRST PICTURES
> OF THE TITANIC
> sunk in
> OCEAN DISASTER.
>
> The three lines capitalized were in immense letters. The two words, "sunk in," were in the smallest and least conspicuous type. The pictures themselves were the most uninteresting views of the *Titanic's* launching. About one man in three who had been stung demanded his money back. Each would be assured that if he stepped outside the gentlemanly attendant would hand it to him. Outside each was given the raucous hoot. That was not the way to make money, said the proprietor. "And there's nothing untruthful in that sign, either," said he. "I bet I worked three hours trying to get that to suit me. It isn't my fault if these boobs don't read it all."
> The first night, and each succeeding night thereafter, the proprietor was knocked down and other-

(42) Article about another Titanic film 'scam'
New York Dramatic Mirror
15 May 1912

This show practiced another misleading play on words, claiming to offer a talk 'by a lecturer who was on board'. But it turned out that this lecturer (one Eugene West) had merely visited the *Titanic* before her launch in Belfast. He was certainly not on the ship during her maiden voyage as the placard implied. (Though in a number of other American cities exhibitors secured the services of genuine *Titanic* survivors to give talks while *Titanic* news films were shown).[7]

Many spectators at this show were disappointed and aggrieved. The *New York Dramatic Mirror* noted that: 'About one man in three who had been stung demanded his money back. Each would be assured that if he stepped outside the gentlemanly attendant would hand it to him. Outside each was given the raucous boot.'[8] Another spectator was told quite simply: 'I could whistle for my money'. Then this ingenious immigrant showman devised yet another cleverly misleading sign to advertise his show:

ENTIRE RECEIPTS
from 9 a.m. to 12
GIVEN TO TITANIC SUFFERERS.
All seats ten cents.

Again the 2nd and 4th lines were in very small type, and the scam was that the show never opened before noon, and after that the tickets cost 25 to 50 cents. So the spectators would always have to pay at least 25 cents, and the *Titanic* sufferers would of course receive nothing. The *Dramatic Mirror* noted that the sheer cheek of the proprietor had enraged some members of the public who had fallen for the tricks, and that the proprietor bore the marks of this anger:

'His face has suffered considerably during his administration of this swindle. Both eyes are blacked and several teeth have been lost, and a blue-black bruise...now covers almost the entire southern aspect of his face. "But I'm getting the money," he whistles cheerfully through the gaps in his ivories. "Even after I pay the doctor and the dentist I'll clear five hundred dollars. And there isn't an untruthful word in those advertisements. There ain't nobody can say that I ain't a gent.'

The *New York Times* revealed that the theatre had a history of falsification: in 1910 their posters advertised 'pictures' of the Jeffries-Johnson fight, but the claimed 'pictures' turned out to be slides, not films.[9] However these several tales of the sheer effrontery of this man and his many con tricks suggest caution – should we believe these accounts? Can anyone really be that shameless (even in New York City?) Or might the tales be partly apocryphal?

In any case such anecdotes apparently had an effect, and, by the end of April the possibility of such blatant fakery helped convince an official in Memphis, Tennessee to ban *Titanic* films from his city entirely: Fire and Police Commissioner Uttley barred any 'moving picture reels portraying the *Titanic* disaster or any phase thereof'. Said the *Moving Picture World*:

'Commissioner Uttley avers that *Titanic* pictures can be nothing more than fakes and his opinion that the public has read and heard enough of the holocaust is backed by a majority of Memphians. The Tennessee city is one of the few yet discovered which has refused to allow the *Titanic* feature reels to be shown within its precincts.'[10]

Uttley was not alone in his firm action. Mayor Blackenburg of Philadelphia had already, it seems, banned *Titanic* films from his city entirely, with the same justification as Uttley (ie. to prevent the screening of fake films). He proclaimed:

'These pictures are all "fakes" in the first place... I think it is about the limit for the proprietors of moving picture houses to commercialize such a terrible disaster.'[11]

Apparently the mayors of Paterson, Boston, and other cities took similar action, all objecting to so-called *Titanic* 'fakes'. But 'Spectator' of The *New York Dramatic Mirror* ridiculed what he called these 'little mayors', and denied that any fake films of the *Titanic* as such had been produced at all. The only deception, he thought, had been in the 'misleading advertising' which had sometimes accompanied news films of the tragedy. (Though one could argue that this is exactly what a fake is: something represented to be what it is not, whether that false representation is on the part of the producer or the exhibitor). 'Spectator' laid into this mendacious advertising: 'No more absurd, shallow-brained exhibition of cheap, fake, swindling advertising methods was ever known in this country.'[12] Some exhibitors, he claimed (repeating the rumour we mentioned above) even advertised that they had films of the wreck of the *Titanic* itself on exhibition.

Honest exhibition
Ironically, though, it is quite likely that there was no solid financial reason for such mendacity and false claims. 'Spectator' himself pointed out the power of the genuine film to attract spectators: 'The truth was all that was needed in connection with an event so great. Not a penny more business could be attracted by lies.' And it is clear that the genuine *Titanic* footage, described accurately, could be shown with great success.

Films of the *Titanic* were certainly in tremendous demand. Warner's Features claimed that they sold over a hundred copies of their film in 48 hours, and over 150 prints within about a week of release.[13] It was, they said, 'packing houses

GREATEST FEATURE
OF THE YEAR
CAPTAIN SMITH of the
"TITANIC"
Over **100 COPIES SOLD** in 48 hours. Packing houses wherever shown. The biggest money maker in Filmdom.
WIRE, WRITE OR PHONE, QUICK
Will ship subject to examination to prove our rightful ownership to the only genuine negative of this Feature.
WARNER'S FEATURES, 145 W. 45th Street, New York City

(43) There was great demand for Warner's Titanic *newsreel*
Moving Picture World
4 May 1912

wherever shown. The biggest money maker in filmdom.'[14] This newsreel was shown at the Crystal Theater in Louisville exactly a week after the sinking, and: 'The Warner feature proved to be one of the biggest hits ever offered in a local playhouse.'[15] The film was accompanied by the orchestra playing 'Nearer, My God, to Thee', which the orchestra of the *Titanic* was supposed to have played as the ship sank. The Animated Weekly's *Titanic* newsreel seems to have enjoyed the same success. A telegram from a distributor, urgently ordering another print, is reproduced in the *Moving Picture News*.[16] This suggests that the film had a big audience appeal. Such was also the case at the Weber Theatre where the première of the Animated Weekly's film attracted immense crowds.[17]

An Illinois exhibitor noted that people were so eager to see pictures of the disaster, that when he screened his print of the Animated Weekly film it attracted no fewer than 3,700 people on one day alone (26 April), which 'Beat all previous records of the house.'[18] The Comique Theatre in Boston decided that such was the drawing power of the *Titanic* story that they would try a little profiteering, and in the week of the 22nd April they advertised: 'owing to the overwhelming public demand for these pictures, we find it necessary to limit our show to this magnificent, thrilling film. Admission, ten cents.' By showing a newsreel alone and cancelling all other films drastically shortened their usual programme, and allowed this theatre to pack in many more spectators per day. The *Moving Picture World* sniffed a scam, commenting sarcastically that 'It must be a quality show, because the quantity is so small!'[19]

(44) An order by a Chicago distributor for the Animated Weekly newsreel. (The Twentieth Century was the train from New York)
Moving Picture News
27 April 1912

At this time news films and other images related to the disaster were truly ubiquitous, and this did not pass unnoticed by one *Titanic* survivor, Ernst Ulrik Persson. While in New York on 20th April he wrote to his family in Sweden noting that the survivors had been much photographed, and that these images were to be seen in 'all newspapers, all motion-picture theaters all bookshops'.[20]

News films of the *Titanic* were shown successfully all over the world. Australia was quick off the mark, ads appearing in the trade press there by 27th April, promoting a news film which showed the *Titanic* survivors landing from their rescue ship, the *Carpathia*.[21] In Germany the Gaumont *Titanic* newsreel was distributed through the German affiliate Elge-Gaumont, and made the rounds 'through all of the first-class cinemas in the major cities'. The film was said to be, 'An event that must serve to fill the cinemas: dreadful, tremendous, awe inspiring'. By the middle of May in Germany the Martin Dentler company advertised 20 copies of their *Titanic* film for hire, a film which would 'guarantee a full house!'. From the description, this six scene film seems like a cut down of the Gaumont newsreel.[22] A more complete German-titled version has survived in the SDK in Berlin.[23]

As in America, in Germany some people objected to the commercial exploitation of the disaster, and one spectator in Kattowitz wrote to his local newspaper to complain about the Gaumont version. He was especially outraged, for some reason, by the accompaniment of the film with the singing of 'Nearer, my God, to Thee' ('Every patron will receive the text of the song free', promised the theatre).[24] Fred Berger, the owner of the cinema, responded to the criticism:

'We are still all under the influence of the terrible *Titanic* catastrophe, and however much lusty singing took place at this screening we may nonetheless be edified. We have read how heroically members of the ship's orchestra behaved as they approached their inevitable fate. It is deeply moving to imagine how hundreds came to their deaths on the great ocean as the ship sank further and further into the water, and yet in the face of certain death the strains of the ship's orchestra playing "Nearer, My God, to Thee!" wafted across the sea. For many people this noble melody has become a funereal song.'[25]

The hymn 'Nearer, my God, to Thee' was used to accompany other screenings of *Titanic* newsreels, (and also accompanied *Titanic* film dramas: see the chapter on *Titanic* dramas). In Britain during fairground showings of the Gaumont newsreel one showland family accompanied the film with a medley of sea-related tunes played on their Gavioli organ, including 'Afloat on the Ocean Blue', 'An Iceberg',

Page 40.   THE PHOTO-PLAY.   April 27, 1912.

Moving Pictures OF THE "TITANIC" DISASTER

Were not taken. The world will never know the real situation, when the stern of the great ship tilted into the air looming up against the sky, every porthole blazing with light, and the apalling cries for help from hundreds of people in the icy water.

Scenes on Board the "CARPATHIA"

showing the Survivors landing in New York and the battered "Titanic" life-boats, were secured by our Live-wire American purchasing office, and will be ready for our customers immediately upon arrival.

Next Week Another Double Header

We recently received an anonymous communication (presumably from a competitive film exchange), accusing us to a considerable length, that we were spoiling the Exhibitors by giving them several long Feature Exclusives a week, and that two a month, as they were formerly in the habit of receiving, was entirely sufficient. Here is our reply:

Special Feature Releases--Week to begin MONDAY, APRIL 29.

"ZIGOMAR VERSUS NICK CARTER" (Eclair), 3,600 ft.   A Duel of Wits between two Celebrated Characters
"THE MURDER OF A SOUL" (Pasquali), 1436 ft.   A guaranteed Exclusive Success Backed by our Co-

We have been, and will continue, giving the Exhibitors of Australasia as good film service as can be obtained by brother showmen the world over. We can see no good reason why the Picture Showmen of Australia and New Zealand should not get the pictures they deserve. We are not kicking about any lack of support. Our present and increasing volume of business is entirely satisfactory. We will continue to distribute films of such quantity and quality to warrant advertising our Motto.

INTERNATIONAL PICTURES--NO BETTER FILMS MADE

Remember, Mr. Exhibitor, that we don't advertise all the pictures we buy. We receive a number of exceptionally good films each week that are not announced in our regular advertisements. We want to call your attention to Bison's "Indian Massacre," which film has been announced by others to give the impression of being an exclusive subject. "The Indian Massacre," produced by the Bison Co., 2,190ft., is not held exclusively by any one company. Our copy was purchased on the open London Market, and no combine could possibly corner this excellent Moving Picture Star Feature. Our copies of "Indian Massacre" are available to independent Showmen, as well as all Gaumont Star Features, which are handled on the open London Market. Try us out on the above assertions. Let us demonstrate how quickly you can secure Bison, Gaumont, and all the best films from the house of INTERNATIONAL PICTURES.

Direction - - J. D. WILLIAMS.   Management - - WILLIAM H. BELL.

International Pictures

Controlled by the Greater J. D. Williams Amusement Co., Ltd.
CAPITAL, £200,000.   WRITE OR CALL TO NEAREST OFFICE.

SYDNEY: Colonial Theatre Buildings, 610 George-st.   BRISBANE: Courier Buildings, Queen-st.
MELBOURNE: Sutton's Buildings, Bourke-st.   PERTH: Trustee Chambers.
WELLINGTON (N.Z.): Fowld's Buildings.

(45) An advertisement for a forthcoming screening of a Titanic *news film by the Greater J.D. Williams Amusement Co. Ltd. in Australia*
The Photo-Play 27 April 1912 (Mitchell Library, Sydney)

'Lowering the Boats', and ending with 'Nearer, My God, to Thee' and Chopin's 'Funeral March'.[26] Elsewhere in British picture palaces the song, 'Be British', written in the wake of the *Titanic* disaster, was often sung as a tribute.[27] News films of the *Titanic* were widely screened in the British Isles. One of the first newsreels to be released was seen in Yorkshire the same day as it was first shown in London, and there were also reports of screenings of *Titanic* newsreels in Dublin and further afield.[28]

The *Titanic* films seem to have made a lasting impression on spectators. In the 1930s a man in Britain was asked to recall the early films which really struck him at the time. He mentioned one he saw at a fair in 1912: 'I think the film which stands out in my memory most of all... was the landing of the victims and survivors of the ill-fated "*Titanic*."'[29]

In the wake of such a major tragedy as the *Titanic* sinking, and especially as there was so little film of the liner available, any film with a similar theme suddenly became relevant (as we shall also see with film dramas about the *Titanic*). In several British picture palaces films of icebergs and icesheets were being screened by the end of April. For example, in Bradford and Oldham audiences saw the *Yermak*, the largest ice-breaker in Russia 'at work opening out a way for ships in the ice-bound waters of the frozen north.'[30] And a film of an iceberg, which the cameraman Mr Bool had happened to shoot while returning from filming seals in Newfoundland, was now rushed out and promoted as 'taken on the same route as that taken by the ill-fated *Titanic*', and a publicity frame-still of this berg appeared in the trade press.[31]

In this period one often finds that news films are priced by their topicality, so a really hot news story rushed to exhibitors would be charged at a premium. But as the days and weeks passed the very same film would cost progressively less and less to hire.[32] Furthermore, a second-hand sales market often opened up for such news films, offering even better deals, often direct from the cinema which had originally bought a print outright.[33] By early May 1912 a second-hand market had indeed arisen for *Titanic* news films in Britain, with used prints being offered by cinemas all over the land, from the Clapton Cine Theatre to the Wavertree Picturedrome, Liverpool. On 2nd May there were six such small ads in the *Kine Weekly* for *Titanic* films, either available immediately or within a few days after the seller's run had finished. A week later this had shot up to no fewer than fourteen ads. But the market waned as fast as it had waxed. By mid May the number of ads had reduced to six, a week later there were four, and by the end of the month none at all.[34] The only subsequent small ads that I have found are

GAUMONT'S
ALWAYS FIRST.

We were absolutely the only firm to show pictures of

The Last Stand of the Paris Motor Bandits

in London cn Monday night, when it was exhibited at twenty halls in the Metropolis.

We have only time and space to say that the film teems with interest, shows every incident, and is about 400 ft. in length.

THE GAUMONT COMPANY, Ltd.,
Chrono House, Sherwood St., Piccadilly Circus, W.

(46) The capture of the Paris motor bandits was big news even in Britain
The Bioscope 2 May 1912 (British Film Institute)

want-ads, rather than from sellers: in June two cinemas in Ireland – Gazette Pictures in Ventry, and Kerry and Toft's Cinematograph in Roscommon – wanted to buy either Gaumont's *Titanic* newsreel or film of the *Titanic* leaving Southampton or Belfast.[35]

Titanic newsreels in France

In Britain there was also quite a market for another newsreel item sometimes known as the *Siege of the Paris Motor Bandits*, a subject that originated in France and was concerned with the violent arrest of the Bonnot gang at Ivry.[36] This was a big hit in Britain – 'amongst the most wonderful "topical" pictures ever secured', said one journal.[37] The Gaumont version of this subject, entitled *The Last Stand of the Paris Motor Bandits* (400 ft.), was shown in twenty halls in London on Monday, 29th April.[38] This Bonnot siege was a major news event in France, and both Pathé and Gaumont captured the siege as it happened.[39] (We should recall that the newsreel had started in France and was in a particularly advanced state in that country). Not surprisingly the Bonnot newsreels were an even bigger attraction in France than in Britain, and the Pathé version was shown in 50 theatres in Paris alone.[40]

The prominence of this Bonnot newsreel may be partly responsible for a lack of screenings of *Titanic* news film in France, for it seems that the one news event forced out the other. Such competition is an interesting phenomenon at this early date in the newsreel industry, and becomes clearer through a detailed examination of two French trade journals, *Ciné Journal* and *Courrier Cinématographique*.

Ciné Journal regularly listed the contents of the newsreel Gaumont Actualités, which was issued weekly in about half a reel, usually including somewhere between 10 and 15 news items from around the world. There was no item about the *Titanic* in their issue of 20th April,[41] nor in the issue the following week, though Gaumont did highlight a special film they were releasing about the raising of the *Maine* (the ship sunk in Havana harbour in 1898). In introducing this film in an article, significantly entitled **Les Grandes Catastrophes Maritimes**, the journal pointed out that the sunken *Maine* must inevitably remind readers of the *Titanic* tragedy.[42]

But in the week of 4th May, the story of the capture of the bandits Bonnot and Dubois broke, and the entire issue of Gaumont's newsreel was taken up with a special 12 scene film about this.[43] By Gaumont's issue of 11th May the *Titanic* sinking was old news, and we find only one small film item about the *Titanic* – a

British army parade in Southampton to benefit survivors of the ship, though significantly this was within a special issue of 10 items all about 'heros (sic) of the sea'.[44] At the end of June, among 13 items is one about Captain Rostron (misspelled Bostron) the captain of the rescue ship *Carpathia*, receiving his awards in New York.[45] I have come across no further listings of newreel items about the *Titanic* after this date in *Ciné Journal*.

This lack of items about the *Titanic* in the releases of Gaumont's newsreel in France is on the face of it still somewhat puzzling, in that there would seem to have been a window of opportunity for screenings at the end of April before the Bonnot story broke. And Gaumont in France would have been well placed to release a newsreel about the *Titanic*, as their American branch had produced the multi-scene special about the sinking described in the previous chapter. But this Gaumont *Titanic* newsreel including the *Carpathia* material wasn't projected in Paris until 2nd May, and this was just about the time when the Bonnot story broke.[46] In these circumstances the *Titanic* news films may just have missed a potential opening. Incidentally, it is not clear whether this 2nd May screening was for preview or in public, nor for how many days the film ran subsequently, nor whether it received distribution outside Paris. It did impress the *Courrier*'s correspondent, who described it as 'a highly arresting production, of the greatest dramatic interest.'

An examination of the small ads for second hand films in the French film journals indicates that even here there was a relatively small market for *Titanic* film items. I have found two such small ads: a print of *La dernière sortie du Titanic* (*The last Voyage of the Titanic*) was available from as early as 27th April.[47] And a *Titanic* film, presumably second hand, was on sale from a Swiss cinema at the end of May.[48] But many more Bonnot news films were advertised in the small ads than *Titanic* films – in *Ciné Journal* on 11th May no fewer than five exhibitors were offering second-hand Bonnot films, while none were offering *Titanic* items. The dearth of *Titanic* items is even more stark when compared with the British market, where, as we have seen, numerous second-hand *Titanic* news films were on sale by May. In addition to the competition from the Bonnot story, perhaps another explanation for this dearth of *Titanic* newsreels in France was the relative lack of French nationals involved in the disaster.

Newsfilm attractions
This survey of the exhibition of *Titanic* news films in several different countries shows how strongly national and regional conditions helped mould how, and indeed whether, the films were shown. In the United States, with its strong

traditions of showmanship and ballyhoo the films were blazoned and promoted in a more extravagant fashion than elsewhere, (sometimes to the point of dishonesty!) In Britain *Titanic* newsreels were promoted more straightforwardly, though the screening of 'related' films, of icefields and the like, might also be seen as stretching the limits of authenticity.

But behind the promotional strategies in both countries was a perception that there was an enormous public interest in this news story: and as the French case illustrates, where this interest was perceived to be lacking, another news story of greater appeal would be moved up the pecking order. It seems that even in the earliest days of the news film, the judgements of producers and exhibitors/showmen about which films to promote and how, were remarkably similar to the judgements that print journalists had been making for years. The overriding rationale was: whatever would sell more newspapers or fill more cinema seats.

Dramas out of a Crisis

> A thousand years since, Fate had planned
> To stage a playlet on the sea,
> And moved her pawns with patient hand
> To build a merry comedy.
>
> And when the scene and stage were set,
> And all things tuned in time and space,
> The puppet ship and iceberg met
> True in the long appointed place.
>
> (Thomas Doolan, 'Fates Comedy', 1912
> – a poem to commemorate the *Titanic* disaster)[1]

Titanic dramas to date

In late 1998 the NFTVA organised a screening of *Titanic*-related films dating from the silent period all the way up to the present day. It was a well researched and well presented show, including early actuality material as well as clips of various dramatised versions of the celebrated disaster, and it gave the audience a real insight into how one news event had been tackled so differently – in a variety of genres and styles – through this century. After the screening the organisers, Stacey Abbott and Simon Brown, voiced what seemed to be a general feeling in the audience: that of all the versions of the *Titanic* we had seen, it was perhaps those original actualities – despite their poor condition and paucity of real *Titanic* shots – rather than the glossy film dramas, which were the most moving and poignant screen testaments to the 90 year-old tragedy.

But perhaps one could never really succeed in turning this marine catastrophe into film drama. The organisers quoted the opinions of director Alfred Hitchcock who had concluded, after considering it as a project, that the *Titanic* disaster could not be filmed as a drama in a 'cinematic' way because of the inherent lack of suspense in the story (ie. we know what's going to happen). Against this, one might argue that even if a film of the disaster is not 'cinematic' in the Hitchcockian sense, it might still be 'effective'. But my other *Titanic*-related viewing of that week seemed to me to be neither. I saw for the first time the film which helped spark off the revival of interest in everything related to the famous sinking: James Cameron's mega-production, *Titanic*.

'Disappointing', was my first reaction to this film, with its well mounted effects masking a clichéd script. One feels that people of the time would have found the way in which it turns an extraordinary human disaster into a mawkish and improbable love story, tasteless if not offensive. Critical opinion has been divided on this film: some, such as the *Daily Telegraph*'s critic suggested that it is 'one of the great achievements in popular film-making',[2] while the *Los Angeles Times* critic took a very negative view (leading to a well-publicised feud with Cameron). While one cannot in a sense argue with success (and Cameron's *Titanic* has beguiled millions throughout the world), in my opinion a far better drama about the tragedy was the 1958 *A Night to Remember* (Rank Organisation, GB), a subtle and effective piece of film-making which had the added benefit of sticking fairly closely to the known facts (though I guess it wouldn't qualify as 'cinematic' in Hitchcock's sense of the term).

I raise these issues – apparently unrelated to silent film dramas – to show that controversies over dramatisations of this celebrated disaster are both as old and as new as the disaster itself. Just as the issue of faking of *Titanic* newsreels led to heated arguments outside American picture shows in 1912, so debates about authenticity and aesthetic worth have followed in the wake of film dramatisations of the *Titanic* from 1912 to 1998. Perhaps such controversy will arise again if and when the next film version is produced. With this in mind, let us return to the early years of this century, and further attempts to place this news story on the world's screens – as drama.

Saved from the *Titanic*
In 1912 the film business was yet to move entirely over to feature films, and most picture palaces in Britain and elsewhere typically offered a selection of short movies. A programme of six to eight films, each of ten to fifteen minutes in duration, would not be unusual, including such genres as news, travelogues, dramas and comedies. (Longer dramatised feature films of two or more reels were also coming onto the market at this time, and somewhat disrupting the exhibition policy of a multi-film programme.)

The news film within the programme would obviously take current events as subject matter, but other genres would sometimes do so also, though with a greater time lag. For example, several comedies were released on the suffragette issue, and dramas appeared on themes such as the White Slave trade, current wars, and various sports events such as horse races. Sometimes the connection with a specific current event was even more direct. Examples include Pathé's version of the *Assassination of the Grand Duke Sergius* (1905), and Lubin's 1907 reconstruction of the notorious Thaw-White affair, *The Unwritten Law* (which created a huge public controversy).[3]

One such film version of a real story was in a sense a direct precedent for dramatising the *Titanic* disaster. In January of 1909 a White Star liner, the *Republic* collided with another ship off the eastern United States. As the *Republic* began to sink, the wireless operator, Jack Binns, sent radio distress messages which happily resulted in all passengers and crew being rescued. Binns was fêted as a hero and the story was made into a film by the Vitagraph company, entitled *C.Q.D or Saved by Wireless*. But Binns objected to his portrayal in the film and took legal action against Vitagraph which dragged on for several years.[4] This was scarcely an encouraging precedent for filmmakers contemplating turning the *Titanic* disaster into film drama. Nevertheless dramatised film versions were in production within weeks of the shipwreck in 1912 and helped to keep this event in the public mind for the following year.

After the *Titanic* sank it soon became clear to film professionals that very little actuality film existed of the great ship (and certainly none of the maiden voyage itself). Thus it was almost inevitable that film dramas would be produced of such a major story. At the end of April one French film journal, *Le Cinema*, noting the lack of any film of the voyage itself, published a proposed 'scenario' for a film of the *Titanic*'s last days, in three parts: the departure, in mid ocean, and the catastrophe itself. The latter was to include touching scenes of loved ones torn asunder on the sinking ship ('scènes déchirantes se multiplieront').[5]

But even as this theoretical 'scenario' was being written, an actual film drama was being prepared. One of the most surprising aspects of the *Titanic* story is that the first dramatised film to be produced on the subject was released in the record time of a single month after the sinking, starring an actress who had actually been a passenger on the *Titanic*. Dorothy Gibson, aged 22, began her career as a model, posing for artists including Harrison Fisher.[6] The *Indianapolis News* of 18th April 1912 described her as '...one of the most beautiful models that have ever posed for American artists.'[7]

*(47) Dorothy Gibson,
Eclair film star,
and survivor of
the* Titanic
Moving Picture News
27 April 1912

Gibson certainly made her mark, and subsequently joined the Eclair Moving Picture Company on the opening of its American branch in the Autumn of 1911. She soon became a leading star of the company, and would appear in eight films over the next few months. She had considerable acting talent, if one is to believe a reviewer commenting on one of these Eclair films, a comedy entitled *Miss Masquerader*:

'Especially noticeable is the reposeful work of Miss Dorothy Gibson. She has acquired the knack of expressing herself without excessive gesture or facial contortion, a failing so common among photoplayers and so distressing to those who view them. Miss Gibson is to be congratulated upon her singular ability and the Eclair Company upon having secured her services...'[8]

On 17th March 1912, having completed the film *The Easter Bonnet*, Dorothy and her mother, Mrs Leonard Gibson, sailed for Europe and Egypt for a vacation.[9] But while in Genoa, Dorothy was summoned by Eclair to return to New York to appear in another production.[10] The actress and her mother booked their return passage on the *Titanic* in Paris, and boarded the vessel at Cherbourg on the evening of 10th April.

Gibson recalled that she 'spent a pleasant Sunday evening playing bridge with a couple of friendly New York bankers'.[11] These were William Thomson Sloper, member of a prominent New Britain family and Frederick K. Seward whom she knew from her Church. The trio carried on with their game until late. It was not until about 11.40 p.m. that Dorothy made her way to join her mother in their stateroom. Dorothy later recalled that on the night of the disaster she heard a 'long, drawn, sickening scrunch'.[12] She wasn't exactly alarmed, she stated to the *Dramatic Mirror*, but decided nevertheless to investigate. 'As I started to walk across the boat I noticed how lopsided the deck was.' She hurried to fetch her mother.

Lifeboat number 7 was virtually empty when Dorothy and her mother arrived on the boat deck. Women and children, naturally, had priority, but according to Sloper, he owed his life to Dorothy, who got into the life boat and insisted that he join her.[13] The French aviator Pierre Marechal was also saved in boat 7 (but proved, according to Dorothy, less of a hero than a nuisance). The boat was launched off the sinking liner, but shamefully carried only half its capacity of 65 passengers. For a while it looked as if the lifeboat would follow the *Titanic* to the bottom. Water gushed through a hole in the hull until, in the words of Gibson, 'this was remedied by volunteer contributions from the lingerie of the women and the garments of men.' Hundreds of people on the stricken liner could not find places in lifeboats, and Gibson told the *Moving Picture World*, 'I will never forget the terrible cry that rang out from people who were thrown into the sea and others who were afraid for their loved ones'. But Dorothy and her mother were safe, and when the rescue ship *Carpathia* tied up at pier 54 in New York on the evening of 18th April, both were on board.

A journalist for the *Moving Picture News* heard Dorothy's story of the wreck from the actress, and observed that she 'has the appearance of one whose nerves had been greatly shocked.'[14] But incredibly, within days of the sinking she appeared before the cameras to make a film based on the disaster, entitled *Saved from the Titanic*.[15] Dorothy played herself, even down to wearing the same dress that she was rescued in.[16] Filming took place on a derelict transport vessel in New York harbour. It is said that Gibson was still in shock during filming, and a journalist reported that at one point she burst into tears as a scene was being filmed.

Saved From The Titanic

ECLAIR'S EXCLUSIVE EXTRA

A *Startling Story of the Sea's Greatest Tragedy* By Miss **DOROTHY GIBSON**, A Survivor

SHE IS SUPPORTED BY A POWERFUL CAST

Six Color and Gold Posters, Herald's Photos

A FILM WITHOUT A PARALLEL

| TUESDAY MAY 14 | **Eclair Film Co.**
FORT LEE, N. J.
SALES COMPANY, Sole Agents | TUESDAY MAY 14 |

Opposite page:
(48) Eclair's film drama,
Saved from the Titanic,
was released within a
month of the disaster
Moving Picture World
11 May 1912

Right:
(49a) Scene from
Saved from the Titanic
Moving Picture News
4 May 1912

The plot was a romance, based on a story which had apparently been co-written by Dorothy herself.[17] Dorothy's parents and her fiancé, a naval ensign (or 'a liner's wireless operator' said the British review of this film), hear about the sinking of the *Titanic* and are sick with worry until Dorothy returns safely.[18] At home she tells them what happened: this was a flashback scene, apparently illustrated with genuine footage of the *Titanic*, and also included a mocked-up sequence of the collision. After her daughter's lucky escape, Dorothy's mother urges the girl's fiancé to leave the navy, as his is a job that will always worry Dorothy. The fiancé considers this for a while, but finally decides that his duty is to flag and country. The father accepts this decision, blessing the marriage.

The *Moving Picture World* praised the film, noting in particular that it had, 'a lot of the mechanical and vision pictures which have made fame for Eclair's American directors,' (the director was actually French, the talented Etienne Arnaud) and concluded, 'a surprising and artistically perfect reel has resulted.'[19] For its part the *Moving Picture News* praised the film for its:

'Wonderful mechanical and lighting effects, realistic scenes, perfect reproduction of the true history of the fateful trip, magnificently acted. A heart-stirring tale of the sea's greatest tragedy depicted by an eye-witness.'[20]

Dorothy worked on the film with her 'usual vim', but the experience of the shipwreck, and filming the re-enactment straight afterwards had been emotionally draining, and she went to stay in Atlantic City for a rest.[21] This was at the beginning of May, suggesting that shooting had finished by the end of April – a remarkably quick turnaround. Post production was equally fast, and the one-reel film was reviewed as early as 11th May, to be released on the US market on 14th May, exactly a month after the sinking.[22] Film prints were supplied along with photographs and a set of six colour and gold posters.

The film may well have attracted large audiences given the 'national demand' at this time for screen Titanica. The fame of Dorothy Gibson herself also rose a few notches, and one showman in Kansas took advantage of this, screening an earlier Gibson film, and noting on his handbills that she had been one of the *Titanic*'s survivors (a publicity practice that the *World* found distasteful).[23]

(49b) Moving Picture News 4 May 1912

(50a) Moving Picture World
11 May 1912

Scenes from Saved from the Titanic

(50b) Moving Picture World 11 May 1912

In addition to its American release, the film was also distributed in Europe, (and possibly further afield) but with considerable delay. It was submitted to the censors in Berlin on 6th July 1912 by the American Standard company, and released on the German market as *Was die Titanic sie lehrte*.[24] In France it was released on 19th July, with a one page advertisement in the leading trade journal, as *La Survivante du Titanic*, under the American Standard label.[25] The same company released it in Britain, but not until 25th July, with the title *A Survivor of the Titanic*.[26] The British version was only 660 ft, compared with what was apparently a whole reel, 1000 feet, for the American release.[27]

This apparent delay and shortened print both suggest that there was some nervousness among distributors about handling this film so soon after the tragedy: perhaps some footage was trimmed to remove any possible offence? This nervousness was not without foundation. I have already discussed the

(51) *The French release of* Saved from the Titanic
Ciné-Journal 29 June 1912

furore over the exhibition of 'fake' newsreel films of the *Titanic* tragedy and the bans on *Titanic* films instituted in some American cities. And sure enough protests also arose about this version. In a previous chapter I mentioned the diatribe of 'Spectator' in the *New York Dramatic Mirror* in early May against misleading advertising of *Titanic* newsreels – in the same article he extended his criticisms to the Gibson film, which was then in production, proclaiming:

'The bare idea of undertaking to reproduce in a studio, no matter how well equipped, or by re-enacted sea scenes an event of the appalling character of the *Titanic* disaster, with its 1,600 victims, is revolting, especially at this time when the horrors of the event are so fresh in mind. And that a young woman who came so lately, with her good mother, safely through the distressing scenes can now bring herself to commercialize her good fortune by the grace of God, is past understanding... [This] can occasion only apprehension of the gravest character by thoughtful people who have the best interests and good repute of the motion picture art and industry at heart...It is to be feared that the film...will be a melodramatic affair that will inevitably fall absurdly short of truth and hence can prove only a lamentable travesty.'[28]

After the film was released there was at least one further objection, in the form of a letter to the *New York Times* in early June:

'I am writing to you to protest against the moving pictures now being shown depicting the terrible *Titanic* disaster. I am sure many will agree with me that it will be many, many years before the calamity will be forgotten, and I should think it would have been far wiser for the censor to have condemned this film, which at its best can be only manufactured.'[29]

The film does not survive: it was apparently destroyed in a fire which devastated the Eclair studios in March 1914.[30] The only visual records remaining of it are the production stills in the *Moving Picture News* and *Moving Picture World* showing scenes of the family and Dorothy standing in front of a map of the north Atlantic. The fact that no copies of the film are known to survive today is a sad loss, as Frank Thompson rightly says:

'...to have an actual survivor of the *Titanic* playing herself in a film about the disaster would be interesting enough. That, for the filming, she costumed herself with the very clothes – a white evening dress, long sweater, gloves, and a pair of black pumps – in which she abandoned ship, is more intriguing still. And that all this was committed to film within days of the disaster is enough to make any

Titanic enthusiast sigh with frustration. No matter what melodramatic hocum found its way into the film – and the synopsis suggests that there was plenty – *Saved from the Titanic* is an irreplaceable piece of *Titanic* lore.'[31]

This was to be Dorothy Gibson's last year of film appearances: perhaps the emotional strain from her *Titanic* experiences had been too much, or perhaps she was quitting for romantic reasons, for Dorothy was having an affair with Eclair executive Jules A. Brulatour.[32] The affair was exposed when they were involved in a court case. Gibson had killed a man while driving around New York City in Brulatour's car. Brulatour eventually divorced his first wife and married Dorothy in 1917. The marriage was short-lived however, the couple separated in 1919, and Gibson was awarded $10,000 a year alimony. Dorothy never remarried. By the 1920s she was living alone at the Hamilton Apartments in Manhattan, next door to another former Eclair star, Muriel Ostriche.[33] Gibson eventually settled in Europe and died of heart failure in Paris, 17th February 1946.[34]

In Nacht und Eis

But Eclair's was not the only dramatised film produced in 1912 based on the *Titanic* story. As early as the 1st May, the Continental Kunstfilm company of Berlin announced that they would be releasing a film that month entitled, *Der Untergang der Titanic* (*The Sinking of the Titanic*), which would depict the entire story including a scene of the collision with the iceberg. Two weeks later they announced that the release had been delayed until the 22nd June.[35] Presumably it is also this film which was advertised in the Italian trade press as a major German production for release as an exclusive at the end of July. It was to be 1000 metres (3 reels) in length, under the title, *La Catastrofe del Titanic*.[36]

In the event production only began on the film in June 1912.[37] Due to the 'great technical difficulties in the artistic creation of the film,' release was also delayed.[38] It was eventually premiered, two months late, in August 1912 in Berlin, now entitled *In Nacht und Eis* (*Night and Ice*). The director was Mime Misu, and this was his first film for Continental. One of the cameramen was Willy Hameister, who went on to shoot the celebrated *The Cabinet of Dr.Caligari*, and another was Emil Schünemann. Schünemann later recalled dismissively that Misu had been a barber before becoming a film director, and that he had written the script of the *Titanic* film in a school exercise book.[39]

In Nacht und Eis was partly filmed at Cuxhaven and in Hamburg, and possibly some was shot on the HAPAG liner, *Kaiserin Auguste Victoria*. The company then

> **Continental Kunstfilm**
> Berlin SW.48. Friedrichstr. 235.
>
> Wir bringen für *Mai:*
>
> ## Der Untergang der Titanic
>
> Seedrama, umfassend die ganze Katastrophe, einschliesslich des Zusammenstosses mit dem Eisberge und schwer dramatischer Szenen an Bord. ::
>
> ## Le Miracle
> (Das Wunder)
> Legenden aus dem Mittelalter.

(52) An announcement for the film which would later be released as In Nacht und Eis Der Kinematograph 1 May 1912

returned to Berlin, and shooting continued at the Continental Film Studio at 123 Chausseestrasse, known as the Bioskop-Atelier.[40] But it seems that most of the shooting took place in what was little more than the backyard of an apartment block. The ship's boiler room set was erected here, and stokers shoveled real coal, while the fire brigade provided water to simulate the ship sinking into the sea, until the set was awash.[41] Several journalists were invited to be present for the filming, and one of them described the extraordinary scenes:

'In thoughtless naiveté a loafer wandered into the courtyard, and in the very same moment he sprang back terrified, for a powerful detonation shattered the air. "The boiler has exploded! Help! I'm dying!" echoed hollowly across the courtyard. Water, steam, fire, smoke and everything imaginable filled the air. One saw terrifying accidents across the disaster site, and while the heart skipped

(53) *Italian announcement for* In Nacht und Eis
La Ciné-Fono 6 July 1912
(Cineteca di Friuli)

> Alla fine di Luglio uscirà
> *il più sensazionale film fin qui edito:*
>
> **LA CATASTROFE**
> DEL
> **TITANIC**
>
> Dramma in 3 atti - di 1000 metri
> ricostruito con enorme dispendio di capitali
> e concorso d'artisti
>
> **Film** posto, come tutti i nostri, sotto la tutela della legge sui diritti d'Autore.
>
> **CEDESI IN ESCLUSIVITÀ PER ZONE**
> *Rivolgersi agli unici Concessionari:*
>
> **FLAM. RIGO & C.**ⁱ
> TRENTO

a beat and caused a paralytic terror, an apparently insane foreman called out: "More fire! The other boiler must also explode! Let the people drown! More water!" In the background, two cameramen worked implacably at their cranks, and since I recognized the capable and brilliant director Misu in the water under his stained makeup, and despite his missing clothes [sic!], I realised that this disaster was a planned one. One also saw that today's filmmaking demands exceptional realism.'[42]

The fact that Misu had 'stained makeup' suggests that he was performing in the film as well as directing. A Berlin newspaper also gave a description of the activities during production:

'There is a loud explosion and meter-high yellow flames beat upwards through the painted wall, the barrels of water spill out, a filthy flood submerges the coal, and the actors begin their play. They paddle over the wet floor, stagger in the coal, and fall in the flooded engine room. The captain screams and reaches out hopelessly to seize a stoker who is swimming in the water...'[43]

During all this the director was calling out such commands as: 'No more fire...only steam...more waves...' as the proceedings were watched by inhabitants of the neighboring buildings, staring out of their bedroom windows and applauding and cheering as the scenes were enacted.[44]

It was claimed by some later writers that neither notices nor photographs nor advertisements for the film were published in the contemporary press, but this is not true.[45] Multiple advertisements were placed in the trade journals in the weeks before the premiere, on full pages and sometimes double-pages, sometimes with production photographs.[46] There are no reviews of the premiere to be found, but the film was extensively discussed in the *Lichtbild-Bühne*, whose editors were it seems so impressed by the film that they themselves managed the official premiere on 17th August.

Between the lines of this discussion in the trade press one can detect a certain disapproval of previous films about the *Titanic* disaster that had been released. By contrast, the catastrophe as shown in Misu's film was praised in the *Lichtbild-Bühne*:

'...not a sensational piece created by a brutal director grabbing for cheap effects, but instead, in showing us the machinery of a ship, this may even be called a very educational picture.'[47]

Strangely, at the time of release no-one pointed out a factual inaccuracy – in the film the iceberg hits the port side of the ship, whereas in fact the ship collided with the berg on the starboard side. The full title of the film was *Titanic oder In Nacht und Eis: ein Seedrama*, but in deference to the finer feelings of some of the public the direct reference to the *Titanic* would be cut, shortening the title to *In Nacht und Eis: ein Seedrama*.[48]

The film was completed by early July, and on the 6th received a censor's certificate.[49] Its preview screening took place in the second week of July in Berlin. But this was the end of the season, so its release into cinemas had to be postponed until the beginning of the new season in August, and the public premiere was on the 17th August.[50] The problem was that by then interest in the *Titanic* issue had waned. Though *In Nacht und Eis* was said to be a 'grand success', circumstances suggest otherwise.[51] The film was distributed in the provinces less than two weeks after its original opening in Berlin, which suggests that it was not attracting large audiences.

(54) Image from the American copyright submission for In Nacht und Eis
(Library of Congress)

In Nacht und Eis was also distributed in several European countries. A print with Swedish titles used for the recent restoration of the film, proves that it was shown in Scandinavia. The film was a big hit in the Netherlands where it was screened from late September 1912 through to early 1913, under the title of *Titanic* or *The Disaster of the Titanic*. Based on advertisements in the fairground magazine *De Komeet*, there were at least six prints available in the country, one renter alone holding four prints.[52] It was distributed for a time by Desmet, whose first rental was to Albert Mullens, owner of the Grand Theatre in Amsterdam, for projection from 27th September to 3rd October. In November 1912 a film entitled *De Ramp Der Titanic*, which is almost certainly the Misu production was advertised in Harlingen (in the county of Friesland), probably rented from Desmet.[53]

The film was also shown at the Witte Bioscoop and the Cinema Parisien in Amsterdam. In the Witte Bioscoop the film probably ran for three weeks, with ten shows a day on the hour, for an entry fee of 25 cents.[54] An advertisement on 7th October reproduced a list of the main scenes in the film:

1. The departure of the "Titanic".
2. Life aboard.
3. In the open sea.
4. Soirée dansante.
5. The icebergs.
6. The collision.
7. The rescue.
8. Courage and sacrifice.
9. Nearer my God to Thee.
10. Wrecking of the ship.

Just as some of the screenings of the *Titanic* newsreels were accompanied by the hymn 'Nearer, my God, to Thee', so it was with Misu's film, though apparently only in the Witte Bioscoop. The anthem was sung by a Ladies' Quartet in the afternoon and by a Men's Quartet in the evening, accompanied by an organ, and with a lecture by Messrs G. de Jong and J. de Boer. One newspaper critic praised the film as a 'moving film-tragedy', and enormous crowds waited to see it outside the Witte Bioscoop, while hundreds were turned away. 'Everybody wants to see this', said a newspaper. Again the ethical issue reared its head, witness this defence by the exhibitors in a Dutch newspaper from 14th October:

'Some people consider it inappropriate to show such a film, but a large majority feels that the screening of this cinematic play should be praised rather than condemned. The moving scenes of this awesome world drama leave an unforgettable impression upon spectators, showing the serious side of life and

(55) Frames from In Nacht und Eis

convincingly proving the insignificance and uncertainty of human existence, demonstrating that in the face of death neither money nor standing count any more. This is the good and moral message of this film... We would advise everybody to go and see the film, and don't wait too long, as the show will only continue for a few more days. Don't be put off by criticism – there are differences of opinion in all things. But make your own judgement by visiting our cinema and seeing the drama.'

As this quotation suggests, the film did not meet universal praise in Holland. A review on 28th September said that the early scenes, showing the departure of the liner and life on board, were the best in the film, whereas, 'The wrecking of the ship, however, is like a melodramatic representation on the stage with stagelike fantasy.' The writer went on to suggest, bizarrely, that the disaster scenes might best have been avoided, the film re-titled 'A trip on a Atlantic steamer', and then 'the memory of that dreadful disaster could safely have been avoided.'

The film was not copyrighted in the United States until 29th October 1912 with the title *Shipwrecked in Icebergs* (for copyright purposes it was categorised, interestingly, as a non-fiction film).[55] It was apparently not actually released for screening in America though, or at least it was not reviewed by the *Moving Picture World*, the major trade journal. Nor it seems was it released in Britain: indeed the only mention of the film that I have found in the British trade press was for a showing in Paris in early October. The *Bioscope* article notes that the untitled film, attributed to the 'Continental Film Company', was 'screened and boomed' at the Terne Palace Cinema at a length of 4,500 ft. It adds a description which confirms this was indeed the Misu film:

'Part of it was photographed on a large steamship. Scenes include the embarkation of passengers, departure from port, life on board the boat, the Parisian café, the captain sighting the iceberg, launch of boats, down in the boiler rooms where the stokers are seen up to their ankles in water, and finally a view of Death with extended arm over the sinking boat.'[56]

This 'view of Death' scene is not mentioned in other sources. I have also found details of a further screening in France. As late as November 1913 a cinema in Lisieux, Normandy showed what was billed as a 'film d'art', *La Catastrophe du Titanic*, about the great maritime disaster, 1,500 metres in length and in '40 tableaux'.[57] Surely this can only be the Misu film. Also in 1913 a cinema in Ecaussines, Belgium opened with what was presumably this same film, entitled

Catastrophe du Titanic. The performance was accompanied by a lead singer, an orchestra, and twenty local children singing 'Plus près de toi mon Dieu' ('Nearer, my God, to Thee').[58]

Reassessing *In Nacht und Eis* and Mime Misu
When James Cameron's *Titanic* was released in Germany in early January 1998, one writer drew attention to Mime Misu's 'missing' film. But it soon emerged that it was not missing at all: two film collectors reported that they owned a black-and-white Super-8mm copy of the film.[59] Then the Stiftung Deutsche Kinemathek (SDK) added that they held in their archive a 35mm export copy of *In Nacht und Eis* with Swedish intertitles. They started work on a restoration of

(56) In Nacht und Eis was screened in Harlingen, Netherlands in November 1912 Welte Komt

the film, using material from their Swedish version, and from other versions including a German-titled print at the NFTVA; also censorship records were used to establish correct intertitle information. The premiere of this restored version, running about 40 minutes, took place on 23rd August 1998 in Bonn, and it has since been shown at other venues including the Pordenone film festival and in London at the Museum of the Moving Image.

The restored film is of great interest, not only for its connections with the *Titanic* disaster itself, but for its style, starting as it does almost like a newsreel. The film has some strong technical aspects, notably in the rocking sets used to simulate the effect of the ocean swell, but the model of the ship in the open ocean is quite unconvincing and some of the acting is melodramatic. As we have seen, the scene of the collision was even criticised at the time by one writer for its overly theatrical style, and this scene does indeed seem laboured and unconvincing to a modern audience, though it would be unfair to judge a film out of context of its time, when such acting styles persisted. Originally the film was to end with a shot of the Captain's hat in the water, but in the existing copy the story ends rather inconclusively as lifeboats full of people mill around the wreck-site. Given the controversy at the time over the shortage of life boats on the *Titanic*, it is notable that there is no mention in the film of this.

Historian Michael Wedel has made a special study of the film, and also knows his way around the other German productions of the era. In his opinion, far from being disappointing, in terms of filmic style, *In Nacht und Eis* is remarkable for its mixing of actuality with fully-fledged, feature length melodrama. He thinks it amongst the strongest surviving German films from that year:

'Especially remarkable is the regular use of closer framing, and both parallel and connecting cuts with which Misu ... nearly matched the American style, which had scarcely appeared in the German films of that year.'

But Wedel considers that the mixture of melodrama with realism did not help viewers relate to the film, and that this factor (along with the delayed release, discussed earlier) surely contributed to the film's poor showing on the German market. This style, mixing reality and melodrama, became something of a specialty of Misu, who for a brief while in 1912 was Germany's most prominent director. The film he produced immediately before *In Nacht und Eis*, was *Das Gespenst von Clyde* (*The Ghost of Clyde*), a two-reel version of a recent real event, a media sensation: about a certain Count Arthur Hamilton, who died in his castle in Clyde, in Britain in April of that year.[60]

After his *Titanic* production, the following year Misu was asked to direct and act in another film, *Eine alte Legende, das Marienwunder*, for the Union Film Company of Berlin. Descriptions of the stages indicate that the set design was very similar to that of his *Titanic* film.[61] Misu's last film in Germany seems to have been *Der Excentric-Club* (1913, *The Eccentric Club*), after which he returned to the USA to make *The Money God* for Metropolitan (1914), and then disappeared, only to turn up in Germany again with the Misugraph Film Company (Berlin), which seems to have made no films. There was some controversy in 1921 over claims that Misu had been a major figure at Famous Players Lasky; both Eugen Zukor and a Herr Nachmann, at Famous Players in Berlin, denied knowing him, although Nachmann remembered he had been a customer of the firm.[62]

Other early '*Titanic*' film dramas

Following the appearance of the two film dramas described above, in October 1912 another film was released which was almost certainly strongly influenced by the *Titanic* disaster. Nordisk's *Et Drama paa Havet* (*A Drama at Sea*) was a romance about a ship which catches fire at sea, and included a scene of passengers fighting for lifeboats as the ship sinks. The film, which was quite a success in terms of sales, was released in the USA as *The Great Ocean Disaster* or *Peril of Fire*.[63]

The following year in December Nordisk released another film which was also surely influenced by the grim events surrounding the *Titanic*. At eight reels *Atlantis* was the longest Danish film to date, though it lost 2 reels in its US version.[64] It was a spectacular production, with a budget of $60,000, shot on large sets and culminating in a major scene of the sinking of the liner. The film was initially written by Gerhart Hauptmann (1862-1946), based on his novel, *Atlantis*, which had come out shortly before the *Titanic* disaster.[65] Hauptmann had a formidable reputation and won the Nobel prize for literature that year, but Nordisk claimed that his adaptation was 'totally unusable'. Nevertheless, the subsequent writers on the project stuck closely to the novel.[66]

Atlantis was directed by the great August Blom with the assistance of Mihaly Kertész (later Michael Curtiz). It is best described as a melodramatic love story, and stars Olaf Fönss, Nordisk's leading actor at the time, and also has a strong appearance by Charles Unthan, the 'armless wonder'.[67] The *Titanic* disaster undoubtedly influenced the shipwreck scenes of *Atlantis*. The maritime aspect of the plot in *Atlantis* appears around the middle of the film, when the main character, Kammacher, boards the *Roland* at Southampton. While travelling through a heavy fog the ship is holed and begins sinking. Kammacher and his lover manage to clamber aboard a lifeboat which is eventually picked up by a freighter bound for New York.

The scene of the ship sinking was filmed in the North Sea using the 12,000 ton Scandinavian-American liner, C.F.*Tietgen*, which was chartered at a cost of $6,000, along with a complement of officers and crew and 500 passengers.[68] This scene was the heart of the film and its main sales attraction, and is shown in both photographs used in a big advertisement in the *Moving Picture World*. The *World*'s ad also claimed that the film was 'the last word in film realism', describing the shipwreck scene as 'one of the most remarkable and realistic ever produced in films'.[69] The film survives and these scenes of the disaster still have considerable visual power.

This was not the last film from the early era which necessitated the sinking of a ship during production. In Britain in 1913 there were plans to build a replica liner and have a mock shipwreck in the North Sea, and the following year in order to

(57) Scene from Nordisk's 1913 film, Atlantis
(Det Danske Filminstitut/Filmmuseet)

film scenes of a ship sinking in a dramatised film, *Lost in Mid-Ocean* (Vitagraph, 1914), a large vessel was really scuppered.[70] Other productions from this era also took the sinking of a liner as their theme, almost certainly influenced by the *Titanic* disaster. This even extended to the amateur market: an animated filmloop for a toy projector, surviving in the collection of Hans-Danklev Hansen, was probably made just before the Great War and shows a multi-funnel ship approaching and colliding with an iceberg, and then proceeding to sink.[71] The theme of the *Titanic* shipwreck had resonances all over the world, not least in Bulgaria, for at least 50 Bulgarians had been on board the liner, most of whom died. Historian Kostadin Kostov informs me that sometime in 1913 a Bulgarian showman, Jurden Engov, took scenes from *Atlantis* and sections from a newsreel about the *Titanic*, and showed them in country areas of Bulgaria, while presumably delivering a spiel on the maritime disaster.[72]

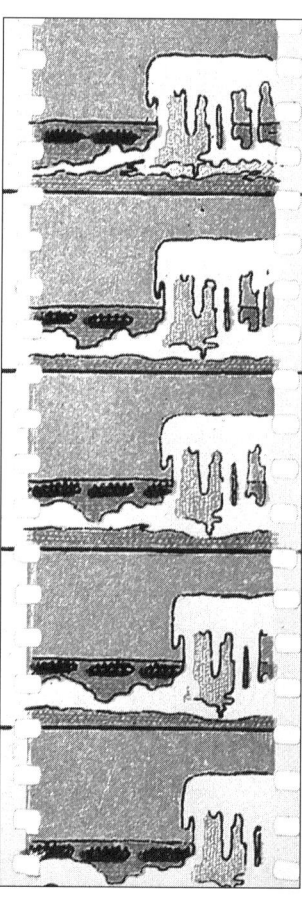

(58) Frames from a toy filmloop about a sinking ship. c.1912?
(Hans Danklev-Hansen)

The only other fiction film referring directly to the *Titanic* that I have found dating from the teens was a feature in five reels entitled *Bought* (Shubert Film Corp, dir. Barry O'Neill, USA, 1915), which includes a reference to a character who has died on the *Titanic*.[73] In the classic film of 1914 *A Fool There Was*, Theda Bara travels on board the *Gigantic* – perhaps a veiled reference to the late, great White Star liner.[74] In a scene on this ship, Bara confronts a former victim with her most memorable line, 'Kiss me, my fool'. The next film drama to be made which was exclusively concerned with the *Titanic* story comes just outside our time frame, E.A. Dupont's *Atlantic* being made in the early days of sound.[75] On the other hand a recent student film, *Titanic* (1998, directed by Rasmus Hirthe) was indeed silent, and was produced rather in the manner of early films. It tells the story of an Egyptian mummy carried on the *Titanic*, whose malign influence leads to the sinking of the vessel.[76]

Conclusion

For modern cinema and television audiences, dramas based on real life events and disasters are a commonplace. For producers they are a mainstay of the industry. A drama based on events that really happened may sometimes have the disadvantage (in Hitchcock's terms) of lacking suspense, but on the other hand it has the advantage of exploiting a celebrated news event that has already gained the public's interest through exposure in other media.

Furthermore there is a certain added fascination in watching a drama that one knows is more than the mere product of a writer's imagination. As a spectator one often feels a strong sense of identification for characters who were once real human beings with real problems and feelings. But there are also difficulties in reality-based dramas: issues may often arise over exploiting or seeming to exploit the lives and misfortunes of others, and in some cases, as we saw in the case of *C.Q.D.*, these issues may on occasion have legal implications.

The problems faced by modern filmmakers in adapting real-life stories are much the same as they were at the time of the *Titanic* disaster. At that time the knotty question of taking advantage and making money out of this greatest of maritime disasters was discussed by a number of commentators. But it is uncertain how much this issue affected ordinary filmgoers, and I suspect that feelings of guilt about raking over the embers of a disaster are unlikely to have deterred many spectators who were attracted by posters for *Saved from the Titanic* and *In Nacht und Eis*. For them the appeal was probably fairly simple: they had read the newspapers, seen the photographs – now, full of interest in the *Titanic*, they could go to see the film (and if tee-shirts had been available in 1912 they would no doubt have bought one of those too).

While critics like 'Spectator' railed against the 'lamentable travesty' of turning human misfortune into entertainment, ordinary filmgoers no doubt realised that such portrayals were in a sense simply one step on from the portrayal of news events in other media, such as newspapers and lantern slides. In a logical sense there is nothing inherently more offensive in having actors recreate events, with some embroidery, than in publishing detailed accounts of those same events and reproducing photographs of the real people involved. In fact one might argue that the former technique is somewhat less intrusive, in that public curiosity may be sated with the dramatic portrayal, thus saving the real persons further bothersome meddling from the press!

In any case, as so often in early cinema studies, such apparently 'modern' issues emerge with peculiar starkness in this pioneering age of the moving image, and may help us, perhaps, to understand the equivalent issues which crop up in the modern media. I will conclude by repeating the hope that a print of *Saved from the Titanic* might some day be rediscovered: it is unlikely to be a masterpiece, but to see a real survivor of the *Titanic* going through the disaster again for the cameras would be strangely compelling.

Credits

Saved from the Titanic (Eclair Moving Picture Company, 1912). Length one reel (c.1000ft) for US release, and 660 ft for British release. Director Etienne Arnaud. Producer: Harry Raver. Cast: Dorothy Gibson (Miss Dorothy), Jack Adolfi (Ensign Jack), Alex Budd Francis (Dorothy's father), Julia Stuart (Dorothy's mother), William H. Dunn, Guy Oliver (Jack's pals). [77]

In Nacht und Eis (Continental-Kunstfilm GmbH, Berlin, 1912), 946 meters. Director Mime Misu. Photography: Willy Hameister, Emil Schünemann, Viktor Zimmerman. Art director: Siegfried Wroblewsky. Cast: Anton Ernst Rückert, Otto Rippert, Waldemar Hecker.

Dorothy Gibson – filmography
(all were productions for Eclair)

The Musician's Daughter (1911) Dorothy plays the Prima Donna
Miss Masquerader (1911) plays the Heiress
Hands Across the Sea in '76 (1911) plays Molly Pitcher
Saved From the Titanic (1912) plays Miss Dorothy
Revenge of the Silk Masks (1912)
The Easter Bonnet (1912)
A Lucky Holdup (1912) plays The Daughter
Brooms and Dustpans (1912) plays The Girl
A Living Memory (1912) plays Her Memory
It Pays to Be Kind (1912) plays The Girl
The Kodak Contest (1912) plays The Wife
The Awakening (1912) plays The Girl
Love Finds a Way (1912) plays The Girl

Helping the Victims

Some 1500 people lost their lives in the *Titanic* disaster, and many of these were the sole breadwinners in a family. Of the nearly nine hundred members of the crew, three quarters died. In an age before universal social benefits this was likely to result in crippling poverty for the families affected, and within days of the tragedy a number of funds were set up in Britain and there were widespread calls for donations. The biggest of these charitable efforts was the Mansion House or Lord Mayor's Fund to which hundreds of people contributed – *The Times* published 2½ pages of donor names, with donations listed from £1 to £30,000. The eventual total collected stood at £412,000.[1]

Imaginative advertising strategies were employed to stimulate public generosity for the funds: for example, taking advantage of the British love of animals, a dog called 'Joe' was fitted out with a box strapped to his back into which donations could be dropped; and Joe's image was printed as an advertising card.[2] The entertainment professions and particularly the cinema trade were not slow to take up this charitable cause, especially in Britain, where benefit performances were put on in scores of picture palaces.

By 1912 British picture palaces already had some experience of fundraising drives, and on the occasion of the *Titanic* disaster, there was a massive effort to this end.[3] One pundit suggested that every picture palace could collect at least £5.[4] The *Bioscope* in late April predicted that 'there is not a single theatre in the whole of Great Britain which will fail to help, in one way or another.'[5] A bold claim, but it seems the response was indeed truly generous. Scores of picture palaces answered the call, either by organising a collection or offering a benefit performance. Sometimes this would include a *Titanic* newsreel, in among the eight or so films which made up a typical cinema programme in this era. The proceeds of these benefit shows went to one of the funds for the relief of families of those who had lost their lives on the *Titanic*.

One of the first of the benefit shows may have been in the Clevedon Picture House, for its inaugural performances on 20th April. The cinema advertised 'a special charity showing of newsreels of the RMS *Titanic* disaster', the proceeds to go to the Lord Mayor's Fund.[6] From early May news was coming into the trade press about the generosity of individual theatres all over the United Kingdom. In

(59) *A London newspaper highlights the suffering of relatives of those who died on the* Titanic.
Daily Sketch 22 April 1912

Opening of the
Picture House,
OLD CHURCH ROAD,
At 3 o'clock,
Saturday Afternoon, April 20

The whole of the proceeds will
be handed to the - -

LORD MAYOR'S FUND
FOR THE
RELIEF OF THE FAMILIES
of those who lost their lives in the
TITANIC.
Prices for this Matinee, 2/- and 1/- each.

The ordinary Entertainments will be from 7 to 10 each evening,
at Popular Prices, 3d., 6d., and 1/-

CLEVEDON PRINTING CO., LTD

(60) The inaugural performance at the Clevedon Picture House was a special Titanic *charity programme (Curzon Community Cinema, Clevedon)*

Hull, Liverpool, Dublin, Wolverhampton, Glasgow, Bolton, Falmouth, London, and many other places the call for donations was heeded. A typical amount collected from such a benefit performance was about £5 or £10, but figures ranged from £1 upwards.[7] At the top of the range, the Palais de Luxe cinema in Liverpool raised over £56, while the Empire in West Hartlepool raised over £40.[8]

In Lewisham the local cinema, the Rink (presumably a former skating rink), organised a collection, and the Mayor of Lewisham and councillors headed by a mace-bearer, walked in procession to the cinema to collect the donations of £5 10s (which was made up to £10 by someone).[9] On a recent visit to one of Britain's few surviving picture palaces of this era, the Phoenix in north London, I noticed a cutting displayed from the period, confirming that here too a *Titanic* benefit had taken place.[10]

Several exhibitors showed considerable imagination in their fundraising efforts, demonstrating again what a dynamic sector of the British film industry the exhibition side really was. The manager of the Clapham Junction Biograph Theatre, Mr. A.G. Cullingford, assiduously went to work on one of the large posters of the *Titanic* that he had received:

'This had its every porthole, mast and stateroom light, and wave crest laboriously punched out, backed with tissue papers and electrically illuminated. It drew more business than any amount of vociferating or bill distributing at the doors could possibly have done.'[11]

Meanwhile one of the few women to manage a British cinema at this time proved just as adept. Miss Fuller, manageress of Parkhurst Theatre in London was already known to the trade journals as a thoroughly efficient and go-ahead professional, seizing promotional opportunities and always concerned for her patrons' comfort. As soon as news was received of the *Titanic* disaster she reacted promptly:

'At once she showed a picture of the huge vessel leaving the dock at Southampton on its ill-fated voyage. For the Sunday night following she had a special slide made having on it the third verse of 'Nearer my God to Thee,' and a request that the audience should stand and sing the hymn to organ accompaniment. Every male hat was doffed and the heartfelt chorus resembled a church service.'[12]

(61) *The film trade organised collections for the victims of the* Titanic *disaster* Kinematograph and Lantern Weekly 25 April 1912

What the Trade is doing for the "Titanic" Sufferers.

"THE GREATEST OF THESE IS CHARITY."

Once again the outside world will have reason to recognise that our kinematograph industry possesses not only men with clever brains and commercial acumen but also sympathetic hearts—hearts to beat quickly in response to the call of the widows and orphans left by the dire calamity which befell the " Titanic." Prompt and generous giving has been the reply to our suggestion that we who have had the advantage of brave seamanship and speedy vessels to convey our traders and their wares to and fro between America and England should collectively assist the bereaved left by the brave departed.

We deeply mourn the loss to our own profession of Mr. Daniel Marvin, son of the President of the Patents Company of America, who was returning from a happy

Andrews' Pictures Ltd.	2 2 0
Bamforth & Co., Ltd.	2 2 0
R. Collier, Esq. (personal contribution)	2 2 0
Nordisk Films Co. (Mr. A. S. Paulson)	2 2 0
Robt. Rigby and Employees	1 13 11
J. Wrench and Sons	1 1 0
F. H. Heath, Ltd.	1 1 0
Royal Film Agency (Mr. G. B. Samuelson)	1 1 0
Gordon P. Firmin	1 1 0
Debenham and Co.	1 1 0
Mr. George Vickers (wholesale newsagent)	1 1 0
Barway Press	0 10 6
Baer and Co.	0 10 6
Lazarus and Son, Ltd.	0 10 6
Jury's Kine Supplies, Ltd. (Mr. Will Day)	0 10 6
Standard Feature Film Co.	0 10 0
Francis Kinematograph Co.	0 10 0
Total to Date	**£109 8 8**

This hymn had become a kind a theme song to the disaster, and was sung in several places, including cinemas in Tottenham, in Southend and in south London, while elsewhere there were other kinds of vocal accompaniment or interludes.[13] At the Central Palace in North Shields, the man who 'lectured' to the films (a common practice in the early cinema) wrote a poem which was sold on behalf of the *Daily Mail Titanic* fund.[14]

There were larger scale efforts too. The Pyke Cinematograph Theatres circuit placed collecting boxes in all its theatres, while the Albany Ward circuit pooled its collecting efforts and was able to send over £366 to the funds.[15] One of the major British film trade journals, *The Kinematograph and Lantern Weekly*, set up its own fund to which several of the major British film production and film services companies contributed.[16] The Gaumont Company headed the list, contributing over £35, followed by the Hepworth Manufacturing Company which gave £25. Ten Guineas apiece came from Vitagraph, Essanay, the Provincial Cinematograph Theatres and the *Kine Weekly* itself. Many other companies – Barker, Tyler, Hubsch, etc – contributed smaller amounts. Eventually over £200 was raised and sent to the Lord Mayor's Fund.[17]

Southampton suffered more than any other part of Britain in the disaster, as 535 of the 673 deceased crew had come from here.[18] Flags flew at half mast in the city, and in the districts of Northam and Shirley where nearly every man made his living from the sea, there were many stricken homes. Every one of the modest brick cottages in Russel Street contained a sorrowing family.[19] Perhaps because of this great loss, the city's film venues made a particularly energetic effort in their collecting. The Empire Theatre even went to the trouble of stationing two dogs with collecting receptacles beside the poster announcing the benefit screening.[20] At a benefit in another Southampton picture palace, the above-mentioned hymn 'Nearer, my God, to Thee' was sung as the films were shown. In a Hoxton picture palace there were benefit performances and speeches including an appearance by a representative of the British and Colonial Kinematograph Company, which often filmed naval stories in the region.[21]

The music halls were also collecting, and a common effort with the cinemas was organised, in which a joint cheque would be handed over to the Lord Mayor of London from 'the music-hall profession, the picture theatres, and their patrons.'[22] Eventually contributions to this central fund came in from over 150 picture palaces and amounted to over £256.[23]

(62) Two dogs were stationed with collecting boxes outside the Empire Theatre, Southampton
The Bioscope
2 May 1912
(British Film Institute)

There was also a specifically Irish dimension to the screening of Titanic news films. While most of the crew were from the Southampton area, the Titanic had, of course, been constructed in the Belfast shipyards of Harland and Wolff. There must then have been an extra note of sadness when the Titanic newsreels were screened in Belfast, and the number of Titanic films shown in the city attests to this special interest and concern among Ulstermen.

By the time the Titanic went down, cinema exhibition was well established in Belfast, and there were some ten picture palaces open in the city.[24] By the beginning of May the Picture House was advertising screenings of what it called The Fate of the Titanic ('taken immediately after the disaster'), which was presumably one of the commercial newsreels, eg. from Gaumont or Globe.[25] On Friday 3rd May the cinema management offered the total receipts of the day to the Titanic charitable funds. This sum, which turned out to be nearly £63, was I believe a United Kingdom record for an individual cinema's donation to these funds.[26]

A few days later, on 6th May, no fewer than four of Belfast's film venues were advertising *Titanic* films. As well as the aforementioned Picture House, the Alhambra was showing *Incidents Connected with the Titanic Disaster*; at St Georges Hall it was *Titanic Disaster Heroes, Etc* ('a special series of films from America'); while the Panopticon was screening 'the great prize picture', *Titanic's Fate*.[27] The latter three venues showed these films during the entire week, and on Thursday 9th the Alhambra promised 'the entire proceeds in aid of the *Titanic* survivors' to go to the Lord Mayor's Fund.[28] The screenings at the Alhambra attracted 'extraordinary interest':

'...and a great number of people who wished to witness some of the thrilling scenes were unable to gain admission to either performances on Monday evening, so great was the demand for seats'.[29]

(63) Four of Belfast's film venues were simultaneously showing Titanic disaster films
Belfast Evening Telegraph
6 May 1912

136

The *Irish News* also reported that these shows in the spacious Alhambra were 'packed to overflowing at both performances last evening' when this 'vivid and truly thrilling' film was shown. The newspaper highlighted, as if local audiences needed to know, that the great liner which was the subject of the film was 'a proud example of the magnificent workmanship of the artisans of Belfast...lost in the icy waters of the North Atlantic.'[30]

Incidentally, the screenings of *Titanic* films in Belfast was not the only intriguing connection between early cinema and Ulster. An even more momentous story was emerging at this time from the country which gave birth to the *Titanic* and to her sister ships. The Irish Home Rule struggle was entering its decisive phase in early 1912, and as the *Titanic* sailed there were big demonstrations in Ulster against Asquith's Home Rule Bill which was then going through Parliament.[31] The bill was wrecked largely through the strong sense of Unionist nationality among, for example, the Protestant workers at Harland and Wolff. The cinema newsreels were reporting on this political struggle in some detail, and the leader of the opponents of home rule was Sir Edward Carson who made regular appearances in the screen news. By 1914 the Union Defence League was even using film as propaganda, touring the United Kingdom with three large motor-vans equipped with projectors. They showed films of Ulster and the Ulster Volunteers drilling with weapons, while during the screenings lecturers commented on and explained the films.[32]

I have found much less evidence of equivalent benefit shows in other countries, presumably because so many of the victims came from Britain. Throughout the British Empire money was collected: patrons of two theatres in Rhodesia were particularly generous, benefit performances raising almost £100 between them.[33] In France the only benefit performances I have found were due to an expatriate British film star: William Sanders, aged about 6 years, was the child star of the French Eclair company, and had appeared in a long series of short films as 'Little Willie' (or Willy). He came from Liverpool, a port city like Southampton, and perhaps his parents would have prompted him to join the fundraising effort because of this maritime connection. Willie appeared in person in some Paris cinemas:

'Armed with a toy revolver in one hand and a silver plate in the other, he makes a sensational entry into the kinema halls and threatens to shoot those who do not "weigh out".'[34]

La première victoire. ∅ Willy tombe son adversaire.

(64) Popular child film star, 'Little Willy' collected in France for the Titanic *funds Courrier cinématographique 8 June 1912*

Captivated (or terrified) spectators gave generously, and Willie also appeared for fundraising in some of the big Paris hotels and restaurants, collecting £32 in this way.[35] The fruits of his labours were donated to the *Daily Mail* fund, which in turn gratefully presented Little Willie with a watch.[36]

I have come across only a couple of anecdotes about benefit performances in cinemas in America. One of these is the case of the showman mentioned in my earlier chapter on audiences, who falsely claimed all his takings from morning shows would go to the *Titanic* fund (the scam was that he didn't run any shows in the morning). But the other case is a far more positive story: in Champaign, Illinois, the Lyric film theatre gave a performance from which the proceeds would go to benefit *Titanic* victims. A competing theatre, the Crystal, helped out by closing its doors for its own shows at this time and 'directed its patrons down the street to its competitor,' a generous action which pleasantly surprised local residents.[37] It is possible, even probable, that there were many more benefit shows in the US and elsewhere, although I am not aware of any other reports.

The story which I have put together here – about benefit shows to help *Titanic* victims – not only demonstrates the great generosity of the public in this hour of suffering, but also indicates the importance and relative independence of regional and local cinemas in this period. We have seen examples of how individual cinema managers instigated imaginative publicity campaigns to benefit survivors, and also how specific regions of the United Kingdom exhibited particular responses to films of the *Titanic* disaster.[38] Readers may be wondering, in the wake of all these many figures for monies raised by the British film industry and cinema patrons for the *Titanic* funds, what was the final total. Sadly, it is impossible to say, as there were several separate funds, and also many independent efforts by picture palaces. It would be safe to say, however, that the amount would certainly figure in the thousands of pounds.

The Titanic and Silent Cinema: Conclusion

The *Titanic* disaster created a seismic shock in the society of its time. Given the awfulness of the event and the huge public interest in this disaster, it was perhaps inevitable that the cinema would become involved. That it did so in so many and varied ways demonstrates the sheer energy of this new mass medium.

Even well after the event the film business could not let the disaster lie. One particular hero who had emerged from the events of April 1912 was Captain A.H. Rostron of the *Carpathia*, the ship which rescued so many *Titanic* survivors from lifeboats after the sinking. The following year the captain was still being lionised, and when he visited his native town of Bolton a special performance, including a film of the *Rescue Ship Carpathia*, was put on by the proprietor of the Gem Picturedrome. It proved a big draw, and:

'...so great were the crowds seeking admission to his theatre, he was positively compelled to engage a posse of police to help keep the people out!'[1]

Even two years later in 1914 a trade journalist found it worthwhile mentioning that a violinist at a picture palace in Seacombe was none other than George Orrell, late bandmaster on the *Carpathia*, '...the vessel which went to the aid of the *Titanic*.'[2] Meanwhile inside an American cinema, the New Gem Theater in Baltimore, a more permanent memorial to the great news story was created: alongside murals of Swiss mountain scenes, there was 'a thrilling painting of the *Titanic* disaster.'[3]

In later years, there were, of course, to be many more conjunctions of the *Titanic* and the cinema, through several feature films based on the story. These include *Atlantic* (1929), *Titanic* (1943), *Titanic* (1953), *A Night to Remember* (1958), *Raise the Titanic* (1980), and of course the recent *Titanic* (USA, James Cameron, 1997).[4]

But in the early period, the connections between this great maritime disaster and the movies are particularly rich in significance and irony, not least in what they suggest about the representation of reality on film. Some writers on film and television have discussed the issues that arise in transposing the real world onto moving images as if these are of relatively recent origin: I recall earnest newspaper articles and television discussions in the 1980s about the 'new' phenomenon of drama-documentaries and the ethical issues this genre had introduced. But of course these issues are not at all novel, as early cinema historians are revealing. In fact, films in most of the genres of fiction, non-fiction and combinations thereof had been produced by the time of the Great War, and many of the theoretical and ethical issues about representation in the moving image were being discussed within this period.

In watching films from early in the 20th century it is all too easy to be hoodwinked by their apparent simplicity and 'primitiveness', and therefore to underestimate the achievements of early filmmakers. This is a failure of imagination. A more considered view of this subject might well lead to an abiding admiration for these filmmakers: admiration for how quickly these pioneers mastered a new medium and started to play with a profusion of techniques and styles, experimenting with form and function, and pioneering many of the genres and formats that are in use by the moving image media today.

The case of the *Titanic* and the cinema gives us an opportunity to study the film industry in 1912 in microcosm, and allows us to focus in on a number of issues. We can see how quickly newsreel producers reacted to the event; how news images were 'created' where none existed, by sending crews to film the aftermath of the disaster; how exhibitors exploited what images already existed through clever publicity campaigns; and slide producers put together sets of lantern images to supply this still-flourishing part of the screen industry.

We can also see that drama producers were almost as quick on their feet as the newsreels: re-releasing whatever existing sea-related films were already on their shelves; and in the case of Eclair, rushing into production a film drama that was on screens within a month of the disaster (a speed of turnaround that would surely be unimaginable today), and having the audacity to cast a real survivor of the shipwreck as the star. And, lest we think that the early industry was only concerned with maximising profit, we have the evidence of the many benefit performances and large donations to the *Titanic* funds, which suggest that both audiences and film professionals were as sympathetic to the victims of the *Titanic* as they were keen to see images of the disaster on their screens.

As we know, the film industry today is (and has been since the First World War) dominated by American production. But in 1912 there was far more of a balance in production between the old world and the new, and proportionately more international exchange and distribution of film than has been the case since. In these circumstances the considerable number of individuals on the *Titanic* who were connected with the film trade is further evidence of the robust state of the trans-Atlantic film industry at this time. And one of these filmmakers, William Harbeck, must surely be considered one of the more important figures in early filmmaking: the fact that he is so unrecognised in standard film history books is more a reflection of the neglect of early documentary production than evidence of his real significance.

These are some of the themes that I would draw out from this study of the *Titanic* and early film, but for me perhaps the most important theme is to do with the nature and practice of non-fiction filmmaking. While I have also discussed dramas in this book, my own particular interest (and professional life) is concerned with documentary filmmaking. Film historians are only now starting to realise that the subject of early documentary has been unjustly neglected. I would hope that this book might contribute to reestablishing interest in this field; and for my own part I will continue to pursue research into its many aspects.

Appendix 1: Extant contemporary films of or about the *Titanic*

Fiction
Titanic (*In Nacht und Eis*) (Continental Kunstfilm, 1912) reconstructed version held by SDK in Germany, 946 metres.

Non Fiction
Gaumont's newsreel (*Titanic Disaster*)
Several versions of the British release Gaumont film survive. In an NFTVA version of the film, scenes 11, 15 and 18 are missing, and the print is only 612 ft long. This is the catalogue description:

TITANIC DISASTER (Gaumont)
ACTUALITY. Events following the *Titanic*'s loss. Captain Edward J. Smith on the bridge. The graveyard of the sea, ice-floes and bergs. The yacht *Mary Sculley* going out to meet the *Carpathia* at sea. Jack Binns (wireless operator of the *Republic*) boarding the *Mary Scully*. Society women bringing clothing for the survivors to the Cunard docks. *Carpathia* entering New York with survivors. *Carpathia* docked. Captain Rostron of the *Carpathia*. Some survivors of the *Titanic* crew. Quartermaster Hutchins of the *Titanic* in New York street. *Titanic* crew members wearing life-jackets (?). Reporters interviewing survivors. Crowd at White Star offices, New York, awaiting news. Shots of Marconi, inventor of the wireless. The *Mackay Bennett* leaving Halifax to search for the dead (612ft).

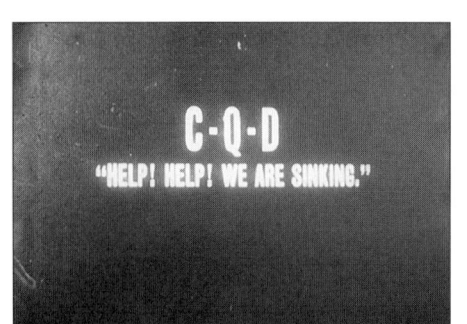

(65) Intertitle from some versions of the Animated Weekly/Gaumont newsreel with the distress call, C.Q.D.
(NFTVA)

There is no genuine film of the *Titanic* included in this version, but the NFTVA has now acquired a further version of the Gaumont film, which does include film of the *Titanic*. While it matches the published title list in other respects, it starts off with a shot of the *Titanic* (its name is on the bow) in Belfast dockyards. It also has the striking device of a flashing effect on a title card of the letters C.Q.D., the distress signal.[1]

A copy of the Gaumont film held at British Pathé includes even more footage of the *Titanic* in Belfast. And a version held at British Movietone opens with no less than 1 minute 25 seconds (at sound speed) of shots of the *Titanic* in Belfast, including an opening Gaumont title reading: 'The "Titanic" leaving Belfast lough for Southampton, April 2nd 1912.' There are seven different shots of the ship, taken from approximately three positions on the dockside, showing the ship floating a few feet off from the dock, with mooring ropes suspended from either side. There is activity on the dock, and smoke is seen coming from the *Titanic*'s third funnel, though she is not actually departing. (All but two of these dockside shots are included in a version of the Gaumont newsreel available on video from Kingfisher Productions, as *The Lost Film of the Titanic*.[2] My impression is that this video version may also include more footage of people on the *Carpathia* than appears in other versions.) Two films with footage from the Gaumont newsreel also survive at the Gaumont company's film library (headquarters in Neuilly-sur-Seine, France).[3]

SDK in Berlin also holds a version of the Gaumont newsreel, with Gaumont trademarks on the titles.[4] Total length is 119.3 meters – considerably shorter than the original NFTVA version. Here are the 13 German titles:

1. T: Zur entsetzlichen Katastrophe der "Titanic" der 1600 Menschen zum Opfer fielen (The terrible disaster of the Titanic, resulting in 1600 victims)
2. T: Kapitan Smith auf der Kommandobrücke (title 1 in British release)
3. T: C. Q. D. Zur Hilfe! Wir werden zu Grunde gehen (C.Q.D. Help! We're sinking!)
4. T: Ansicht verschiedener Eisberge, die Urheber der entsetzlichen Katastrophe (title 2 in British release)
5. T: Jack Binns, der mutige Marcono-Telegraphist geht an Bord der "Mary Sculley" (title 4 in British release)
6. T: Damen der hüchsten Kreise stellen den Geretteten Kleidungsstücke zur Verfügung (title 5 in British release)
7. T: Der Quartiermeister Hitchens, der sich zur Zeit des Untergangs an Bord der "Titanic" befand, wurde im letzten Moment gerettet (title 10 in British release)

(66) A German film dealer advertises the Gaumont newsreel
Der Kinematograph 15 May 1912

20 Titanic-Exemplare

ab 18. Mai zu vermieten.
(Dritte Woche und so fortlaufend). Gaumont-Fabrikat. Länge 130 m.

Dieser Film garantiert ein volles Haus!

Szenenfolge: Kapitän Smith auf seiner Kommandobrücke — Die Eisberge, die Urheber der Katastrophe — Die kolossale Menschenmenge vor dem Bureau der White-Star-Linie in New York — Ankunft der „Carpathia" mit den Geretteten an Bord — Einige Ueberlebende der „Titanic" — Herr Marconi, durch dessen geniale Erfindung über 700 Menschen das Leben gerettet wurde.

Erste
Woche frei, da Kunde mit Konkurrenz ältere Woche spielen will

Dritte
Woche frei. Schlagerwieimmer im Programm

Vierte
Woche in nächster Zeit zu vergeben 15-1600 m

Sechste
Woche. Sehr gut geschonte Films :: Schlager

Schlager-Einkauf
die meisten in mehreren Exemplaren.
Einzeln zu verleihen!

6. April:
                      Meter
Exist. Prinzess Cartouche wirklich 300
So stand es geschrieben . . . 851
Der Unbekannte 1200
Die Schatten der Vergangenheit 770
Rosenmontag 950
Der Schrecken der Wüste . . 446

13. April:
Die Rampe 900
Um fremde Schuld 850
Das Todesexperiment 713
Eine Million 360
Die Löwen sind los 354
Liebe und Leidenschaft . . . 310
Racheakt eines Eifersüchtigen . 261

20. April:
Die Schlange am Busen . . . 930
Marineleutnant von Brinken und die marokkanischen Wirren 299
Die Flucht vor den Indianern . 319
In Scheidung 918
In den Krallen der Wucherer . 1040
Stimme der Schuld 260
Eine indianische Mutter . . . 591
Die Konfektioneuse 625

27. April:
                      Meter
Wenn Frauen lieben 850
Die rote Maske 310
Geopfert 1150
Mamsell Nitouche 1035
Die Andere 765
Geraubtes Glück 320
Nur eine Schauspielerin . . . 850
Die Braut des Todes 1125
Die vielbegehrte Witwe . . . 366
Liebe gegen List 324
Echt amerikanisch 318
Die junge Witwe 312

4. Mai:
Um 100 Mark 800

Der fliegende Zirkus 1275 m

Auf dem Scheiterhaufen . . . 312
Ein Funken unter Asche . . . 800
Zwischen zwei Herzen . . . 990
Die Schlacht auf der Pottbuser Brücke 310
Genau um 3 Uhr 326
Wenn Vater mal später nach Hause kommt 320
Ein Irrtum und seine Folgen . 200
Die Schlacht der Rothäute . . 593
Die unschuldige Sekretärin . . 215
Die Macht des Gewissens . . 305

11. Mai:
                      Meter
Das Geheimnis der Brücke von Notre Dame 846
Die Falle 636
Eine Pferdekur 247
Die Pferdediebe 305
Der edle Blinde 720
Der Untergang des Hauses Randolls 324

18. Mai:
Blinde Liebe 508
Das verirrte Kätzchen . . . 187
Schwarzes Blut 1100
Das Geheimnis des Erfinders . 690

In der Nacht des Urwaldes
Das beste bisher erschienene
355 m Tierdrama. 355 m

Der Erfolg des Gaukelspiels . 240
    Max Linder Film.
Auf dornigen Pfaden 900

25. Mai:

Der Eid des Stephan Huller
ca. 1060 m   ca. 1060 m

Flammen im Schatten 825
Für immer kuriert 105
Des Vaters Racheschwur . . 317
Der Deserteur 563

☞ **Fordern Sie meine ausführliche Schlagerliste sofort ein.** ☜

Martin Dentler, Braunschweig

Telephon 2491 und 3098.   Telegramm-Adresse: Centraltheater.

8. T: Einige Helden der "Titanic"-Besatzung, die stundenlang im Ocean herumtrieben (title 12 in British release)
9. T: Reverend Hoque, ein Passagier der "Carpatia", welcher als erster die Rettungsboote der "Titanic" signalisierte (title 11 in British release)
10. T: Die kolossale Menschenmenge vor dem Büro der White-Star-Line in New-York in Erwartung neuer Nachrichten (title 14 in British release)
11. T: Herr Marconi, durch dessen geniale Erfindung 700 Menschenleben gerettet wurden (title 16 in British release)
12. T: Herr Branly, Mitglied der französischen Wissenschaftsakademie, der Hervorrufer der Drahtlose-Telegraphie (sic!) (Mr. Branly, of the French Academy of Sciences, who developed wireless telegraphy)
13. T: Der S/S. "Mackey Bennett" verlüflt Halifax, um die Leichen aufzusuchen (title 17 in British release)
14. T: Oceano Nox   O Wellen! von welch traurigen Ereignissen künnt ihr erzühlen (title 18 in British release)

One scene from the British release, 'Reporters interviewing survivors' is also in the German version, but without the corresponding title. On the other hand, the French Monsieur Branly was omitted in the British version.

Other companies' newsreels
Titanic Disaster (Globe Film Co., 1912) held in the NFTVA. This is the catalogue description:

TITANIC DISASTER (Globe)
ACTUALITY. 'Captain Smith, R.N.R., of the world's greatest liner'. Close shots of Smith on the bridge of his ship. 'Emergency telephone to be used in case of storm'. Close-up of telephone (speaking tube with earpieces). 'Engine room signal chart'. Close-up of chart on the Captain's bridge. 'First cabin promenade deck with a view of the lifeboats'. Pan shot of the deck. 'Second cabin promenade deck'. Looking along the deck. 'Third cabin promenade deck'. Shot. 'Loading passengers' luggage by means of electrical crane'. Lowering luggage into the hold. '"Bon Voyage!" Thousands madly cheering as the giant vessel begins to move from her dock'. Tugs nosing the ship out of the dock. 'S.O.S.' (304ft).
[As we have seen the liner featured is the *Olympic*, and not the *Titanic*.]

Lobster Films, Paris, holds a film of *le Titanic avant le grand depart*. This is a 35mm print of 180 meters (which would run a little less than 10 minutes). As with other

Titanic newsreels this one has areas inked out: the ship's name in the opening scene showing Captain Smith, and the names on the bows of the tugs in some of the scenes in the departure sequence at 'Southampton'.[5]

The Titanic Disaster (Pathé's Animated Gazette, 1912) held in NFTVA, 25 ft.

Titanic Disaster (Pathé, 1912) held in EMI-Pathé library, 194 ft. This film includes shots of the captain on the bridge, the ship leaving Liverpool(?) with crowds waving from the decks, and survivors and relatives crowding around the Cunard offices. Evidently some of this is mis-identified.

Titanic Disaster (Pathé) held in the NFTVA. Starts with an inter-title (see il. 69), followed by a wide shot of the liner *Lapland* arriving in Plymouth harbour (with survivors of the *Titanic* on board) with tugs in attendance, and a medium shot of the same, filmed from a boat.

Titanic (producer unknown, 1912) held in Library of Congress (FLA1870), 313 or 339 ft. (207 ft. of 16mm.) (Warner Feature Co. release. Material from Marshall, Atkinson and Kleine collections). The print I viewed included roughly the following scenes, interspersed with titles. (Evidently much of this is the Globe version with the *Olympic* footage):
Shot of Captain Smith.
1st cabin promenade deck and lifeboats.
People walking on 2nd cabin promenade deck.
Goods being loaded on 3rd cabin promenade deck.
Loading passengers' baggage.
Forward end view.
Crowds on dockside cheering, tugs pulling, several shots of the ship heading off to sea.
On dockside: various shots of the *Titanic* crew rescued by *Carpathia*.
Captain A.H. Rostron (of the *Carpathia*).
'Rev. Stuart Collett of Syracuse N.Y. a survivor of the sea horror' – 2 shots of him signing something (an autograph or telegram?)

A compilation about the *Titanic* disaster was shown at the Gosfilmofond Festival of Archival Films, 'Belye Stolby', in 1999. Compiled by Natalia Yakovleva and Ivan Tverdovskii, presumably the compilation was based on materials held in Russia.[6]

(67) The only genuine footage of the Titanic *known to survive was filmed in Belfast, probably on 2 April 1912*
(Encyclopedia Titanica website)

Encyclopedia Titanica information
The Encyclopedia Titanica website details the shots taken in New York of the *Olympic* probably on the occasion of her first arrival in 1911. These show Captain Smith on the starboard bridge, and with shots of the decks, loading luggage, and the ship in New York harbour. Frames have been retouched to eliminate the ship's signs and signs on the other vessels in harbour so that, when reshown in April 1912, the pictures might represent *Titanic* in the UK.

The site also reproduces frames from three shots of the *Titanic* in Belfast (possibly misdated on the site) which is probably the only surviving moving film of the actual *Titanic*. This footage also survives, of course, in various versions of the Gaumont newsreel preserved in film archives.

(68) Titanic Disaster (Gaumont)
(a) At the White Star offices in New York where crowds await news of survivors.
(b) Guglielmo Marconi, the inventor of wireless.
(c) Funeral ship (presumably the Mackay Bennett*) leaving Halifax to search for the dead.*
(NFTVA)

(69) Titanic Disaster (Pathé)
(a) The liner Lapland *arriving in Plymouth harbour with survivors from the* Titanic.
(b) Inter-title from the same film.
(NFTVA)

148

Appendix 2: the *Lusitania* and Early Cinema

The most notorious shipping disaster to follow the *Titanic* was that of the Cunard liner, *Lusitania* in 1915, which sank after being hit by a German torpedo. This event helped bring the United States into the World War, and it also inspired several newsreel stories and film dramas. But the *Lusitania* had been the subject of filmmakers' interest since its launch in 1906.

Filming the Liner

From the late 19th century there had been keen competition among the world's shipping lines to build ever bigger and faster liners. For many years Britain had the record-holders, but in the early years of the new century German shipyards were building the fastest, if not largest, Atlantic liners, with such ships as the *Kronprinz Wilhelm* and *Kaiser Wilhelm II*. But the *Lusitania* brought the mantle back to Britain, as she was then the longest (the length of two football pitches), and fastest (24 knots) ship in the world. The Warwick Trading Company had their cameras on hand to record the launch of this great liner in mid 1906. Their film showed Lady Mary Inverclyde performing the naming ceremony, and the launch of the huge ship, and:

'An excellent view of the deck taken from the stem is also given, which helps one to a realisation of the size of this vessel, which brings back to England the distinction of possessing the largest vessel afloat.'[1]

The following year the *Lusitania* went into service and Warwick released a film showing the start of a voyage on the great ship. This showed passengers embarking at Euston station in London and then disembarking at Liverpool. Many views of the *Lusitania* in the port were included (and another ship, the *Lacania*, was also filmed). One trade journal called the film a 'distinct triumph' and especially praised the shots of the dimly lit interior of Euston, and added that 'the views of the huge vessel, taken apparently in the course of a voyage completely round it in a tug give a good idea of its enormous proportions'.[2] The ship was also filmed in 1907 for the Walturdaw company by J. McDowell.[3]

The *Lusitania* was captured on celluloid in 1909, again by the Warwick Trading Company, as the ship left New York. This was part of Warwick's film of the

Hudson Fulton celebrations. Interestingly, after the *Lusitania*'s departure had been shot, the film negative was taken onto the ship itself and carried to England, and then speedily delivered to London where it was screened at the Empire music hall that very day. This was a graphic demonstration of the speed of both the liner and the filmmakers, for the Hudson Fulton events were on a Wednesday and the film was screened in London the following Monday. Despite the haste the film was said to be of 'excellent quality'.[4] Two films of the *Lusitania* were being distributed in 1907 in America: *Across the Ocean on the Lusitania* and *Arrival of the Lusitania* (the latter distributed by Miles Brothers), which may or may not have been versions of one of the 1907 Warwick or Walturdaw productions.[5] In subsequent years the *Lusitania* appeared on film again: in a Pathé Frères item of 1911 as the ship entered New York harbour, and in a Gaumont Graphic item of 1914, 'Harry Lauder Leaves for America' (both preserved in the National Film and Television Archive).[6]

The Disaster on Film

The *Lusitania*'s final departure from New York was on 1st May 1915 - the ship's 202nd crossing of the Atlantic in its 8th year on the New York to Liverpool run. The ship was hit by a torpedo from German U-Boat U20 just a few miles off the south coast of Ireland, and swiftly sank on 7th May with the loss of 1,195 lives.

Several newsreel stories about the sinking were released: versions from Pathé Gazette and the Warwick Bioscope Chronicle both survive in the NFTVA. (See below). As we have seen, there was considerable controversy over the screening of *Titanic*-related films after the 1912 disaster, but as far as I can ascertain there was not the same fuss about the screening of these images of the *Lusitania* events. The only note of doubt that I've found about the ethics of filming this disaster was in a press cartoon in which a German in uniform is shown filming cynically from a U-Boat as the *Lusitania* sinks and passengers drown.[7]

Interestingly, fairly soon after the sinking, there was also a non-film treatment of this news story. At the Panama Pacific International Exposition in San Francisco a spectacle called the 'World Wars' featured the sinking of the *Lusitania*. The display was not particularly successful in attracting spectators, but it received much valuable publicity when the consul of a certain 'foreign government', presumably Germany, objected to the implications of German criminality which were being put on the sinking.[8] (German censors had similar objections to a dramatised treatment of the sinking: see below). There were also several memorial cards issued: one was entitled, 'Lest We Forget', showing the *Lusitania* with lifeboats rowing survivors to safety.[9]

*(70) Cartoonist
W.A. Rogers
depicts the
U-Boat captain
callously
filming the
Lusitania's
drowning
passengers*
New York Herald
23 November 1915

One of the most intriguing issues surrounding motion pictures and the *Lusitania* disaster concerns the neutral status of the ship. Ever since the sinking there has been controversy about whether or not the *Lusitania* was carrying war materials. A more specific allegation emerged at the time, and again in the 1970s, that the ship had been armed with six-inch guns. Such arming of a supposedly neutral passenger ship would have offered some justification for the German attack, and so both the British and American governments were keen to refute the claim. Nearly a month after the sinking a newspaper editor wrote to President Wilson that a cameraman had taken 1000 feet of film as the *Lusitania* departed from New York, and that this should settle the question of guns. The State Department responded, asking for the name of the company. The editor wrote again to say that he had recently viewed the film, which showed the superstructure and the passengers, but no guns whatever.[10]

151

This film of the final departure was apparently owned by one Morris Spiers, a film producer. Spiers reported to the British consul in Philadelphia that he had been approached by a visitor with a German or Austrian accent who asked to purchase the film, and wanted the negative, not merely the positive prints. Evidently he intended to destroy the film because it showed no mounted guns, and this was evidence that Germany would wish to suppress. Spiers had come to the British representatives to see if their government might wish to acquire this unique evidence in the form of the negative. But after consultation with the Admiralty and Board of Trade, the British government turned the offer down. After all, if the film showed what they already knew to be the case - that the ship was unarmed - why go to the expense of buying it?[11]

The film in question still survives (at least one assumes that it is this film - though it is possible there were other versions). It shows the liner in New York Harbour, about to depart for its final voyage, with people boarding, and luggage being loaded by conveyor belt, and the ship itself leaving the dock. Images from this poignant film have been screened in documentaries about the *Lusitania*.[12]

(71) Emotive poster for a Lusitania *newsreel, displayed outside the Grand Cinema, Liverpool The Cinema 20 May 1915 (The Cinema Museum)*

152

Gaumont also released a newsfilm of the survivors reaching safety after the sinking. This was shown to great effect in the days after the disaster. For example, one trade journal reported on 20th May that the film had 'created a very deep impression throughout Scotland' in the previous week.[13] Meanwhile a Liverpool cinema owner attracted crowds to the film with a poster in purple and black ink ('to represent mourning') which proclaimed the victims from the *Lusitania* were sunk 'by the baby-killers.'[14]

Anger at the action of the German U-Boat was all too real, and on one occasion, at the Broadway Cinema in Hammersmith, it erupted into violence. As the newsreel of the *Lusitania*'s dead being taken ashore was screened, two well dressed men, said to be Germans, called out in loud voices: 'They only got what they deserved.' The rest of the audience responded with cries of 'throw them out', and then set about the Germans. The manager recalled: 'I thought they were going to be lynched. One of the Germans was struck in the jaw by a tall, massive Englishman.' Another man even pulled out a large knife. The manager and the excited crowd escorted the Germans outside, but they took to their heels before he could call the police.[15]

Rita Jolivet

One of the more extraordinary stories from the *Titanic* shipwreck was that of Dorothy Gibson, who had been on the sinking liner and soon afterwards appeared in a film about the disaster. But with the sinking of the *Lusitania* we can go one better: an actress who cheated death on the ship later appeared in not just one, but in two films about the event. Rita Jolivet was the actress in question, and I owe the following account to film historian Vittorio Martinelli.[16]

Born in Paris, Jolivet's family had a base in England and she started out as a theatre actress in London.[17] She reached her theatrical zenith with her performance in the 1911 show of *Kismet* at the Garrick Theatre, which ran for two years. American film producer George Kleine 'discovered' her on one of his European trips and suggested she should work in the Italian cinema industry. After a few films for the Ambrosio company, she went to Hollywood to appear in a film by Cecil B. de Mille, *The Unafraid* (1915). After more work in Hollywood, Arturo Ambrosio reminded her of her obligations in Italy. She was eager to return as she had fallen in love with Count Giuseppe de Cippico (whom she later married) during her Italian stay, and also had theatrical engagements in Britain. At the beginning of May she embarked on the *Lusitania*.

(72) Rita Jolivet (George Eastman House)

When the ship was hit by a torpedo on the 7th May and began to sink Jolivet was with a group including her brother-in-law, George Vernon; Alfred Gwynne Vanderbilt - 38 year-old head of the plutocrat Vanderbilt family; and Charles Frohman, the celebrated American impresario and executive of the Famous Players Film Company. They all joined hands for, as Jolivet said: 'We had made up our minds to die together.'[18] Frohman had apparently received a warning telegram that the ship would be sunk, and while Jolivet put on a lifejacket, he remained unperturbed, saying: 'To die would be an awfully big adventure!' (he recalled these words from his production of *Peter Pan*). Some time later 'a great wave of water swept along A deck', separating the group. Frohman was lost, but Jolivet was later rescued in a passing steamer, the *Katrina*. (Another actress and member of Frohman's group, Josephine Brandell, also survived).[19]

After witnessing the sinking of the ship, the exhausted survivors landed at Kinsvale, where Jolivet was reunited with Cippico. After a couple of months touring with theatrical productions in Britain, in September she arrived in Turin where she appeared in two films for Ambrosio, *La mano di Fatma* and *Zvani*. It is in the first film that she reenacts her experiences in the shipwreck. Jolivet plays Azyode, a Javanese dancer who has to seduce a young count in order to purloin a vital document from him, but the two fall in love and thus the diabolical plan of the gang of *La mano di Fatma* fails. As the tragedy of the *Lusitania* was still fresh in the public's memory, and it had been widely reported that Jolivet was aboard the ship, Ambrosio decided to exploit this by including in the film a sequence about the sinking, later highlighting this in the publicity campaign.

It is not clear how this maritime episode fitted into the story, but interestingly it was precisely this aspect which raised the hackles of one critic: 'The subject is not among the best,' wrote Antonio Rosso in a review in *Apollon* in April 1916, 'and it is made even worse by some scenes which come over as quite unreal or even grotesque, especially that of the *Lusitania*. Ambrosio has tried to show the shipwreck of a large transatlantic liner, the *Lusitania* on the cheap, using ... a tugboat, and ... this really doesn't work.'[20] According to the AFI catalogue *La mano di Fatma* was released in the United States by the Author's Film Company in four reels in March 1916, entitled *Her Redemption*.[21]

After appearing in a couple more films in Italy Jolivet returned to the United States with Cippico, now her husband, and made several Hollywood films. Most notable for our purposes was *Lest We Forget* of 1918, which again dramatised the *Lusitania* disaster. It was co-produced by Cippico for the Rita Jolivet Film Corporation and Metro, and directed by Léonce Perret.[22] In the film Jolivet plays a French singer, also called Rita, who at the outbreak of war decides to work for the resistance in occupied France. She is arrested and condemned to death by the Germans, but manages to escape and to reach New York. Meanwhile her American fiancé, thinking Rita has been shot to death, joins the French army in order to take his revenge. Rita then embarks on the *Lusitania* and is among the few survivors when it sinks. She reaches France, and manages to find and kill Baron Von Bergen, who knew in advance of the attack on the ship. In the end she is reunited with her lover who rests wounded in a hospital.

The film was a superproduction, costing 250,000 dollars, with 3000 extras, and required the construction of a French village in Westchester County. But the box-office results didn't reward the effort, despite the actress personally presenting it during a major tour around the United States accompanied by displays and passionate speeches. The audience was simply tired of the war. Even worse was the reception in Europe. The film arrived a year later, and in Italy it only appeared in 1923 entitled, *Quello che videro i miei Occhi* (*What my eyes saw*), later changed to *La rediviva* (*The revived one*). The reviews stigmatized the cruelty of some episodes, and the poorly worked out plot and the blind 'germanophobia' of the whole work.

Jolivet however made a full comeback with the mega-epic *Teodora* produced by Ambrosio and directed by Leopoldo Carluccio. The film was released in the United States first, where it attracted quite positive reviews and was a box-office hit. Ironically the film was released in Italy in January 1922, after the final closure of the Ambrosio studios: it was one of the last Italian megaproductions, as the Italian film industry had virtually collapsed by then. After that Jolivet's film career went downhill: she made a few more films in France, then her marriage with Cippico fell apart, and she retired from the cinema.

It is worth adding that Jolivet was not the only film star during the First World War who was on a ship attacked by a U-Boat. In mid 1917 a ship sailing off the west coast of Sweden with a company of Danish films actors and actresses on board was fired at by a German submarine, on two separate occasions. The company abandoned plans for filming and made for Gothenburg.[23]

Further cinematic links
In addition to Rita Jolivet, two film executives were also on board the *Lusitania*. Edgar Hounsell was a Birmingham film renter of the Midland Exclusive Film Company. He was travelling with Edward Barry, a New York film man who was linking up with Hounsell to start a new company, the Anglo-American Film Distributing Company, with headquarters in London. Both survived and Hounsell later cooly recounted his experiences to *The Cinema*. He was eating lunch at the time the torpedo hit, and, rather than joining the rush for the upper decks, he went to his cabin to don his life-preserver.

'The lights went out suddenly at this point, and it was only with great difficulty I gained the upper deck, where I found that most of the available boats were well away. There was such a slope on the deck - we had to hang onto ropes, etc, to retain a foothold - and all the time she was slowly sinking. I made a jump for it just as she finally settled, and as I felt the waters surging over my head the last thing I heard was the poor devils on the sinking liner singing "Tipperary" as they slowly sank to their doom.'

At this point he almost drowned in the down suction as the liner sank, but was picked up by a lifeboat and finally reached safety on a trawler. He was apparently not overly affected by the experience, and told the reporter that he was going straight back to work in his film business, which indeed he did.[24] His

(73) A reel of
The Carpet from Baghdad
(Selig, dir Colin Campbell, 1915),
salvaged from the wreck of the
Lusitania *in 1982*
(NFTVA)

colleague Barry was equally sanguine, and the following week appeared at a recruiting meeting at the Rookery Road Picture House in Birmingham, 'and stirred the audience very effectively with the recital of his exciting experiences on the *Lusitania*.'[25]

While in America Hounsell had secured the UK agency for the Alliance Corporation, and was bringing back 'show copies' of five recent films: *The Key to Yesterday, The Last Chapter, Jack Chanty, The Truth Wagon* and *Beulah*. All of these sank with the *Lusitania*.[26] They were never recovered, but, amazingly, during salvage work on the liner in 1982 a reel of another film was found.[27] Small sections of this reel were restored at the National Film Archive, which salvaged a few image-bearing feet, and also revealed the film's title, *The Carpet from Baghdad*, a Selig 5-reeler from 1915. The film was not copyrighted in the USA until a week after the voyage, and wasn't released in Britain until the end of the year, so the most likely explanation of what the film was doing on the ship is that, like the films Hounsell was bringing, it was being sent over to London for preview purposes.[28] (In principle the film could even have been projected during the voyage, for the *Lusitania* unlike the *Titanic*, did have a theatre on-board which could have been used for cinema shows.) *The Carpet from Baghdad* is unlikely to have been a lost masterpiece, says Clyde Jeavons, who supervised the restoration work on the reel. The review in the *Bioscope* called the film:

'...a difficult production to submit to the ordinary process of criticism, for it is less of a film drama than a series of gorgeous tableaux, fascinating, almost bewildering, in their vivid orientalism, their crowded animated scenes of native life and customs'.[29]

(74)*Winsor McCay's The Sinking of the Lusitania*. The Cinema 27 March 1919
(The Cinema Museum)

MARCH 27, 1919.   THE CINEMA.   5

The biggest box-office attraction ever put in an open-market programme.

Released on Thursday, May 22, in the Trans-Atlantic Open-Market Programme

A wonderful picture built up of 25,000 separate drawings taking 22 months of intensive work, by the famous artist WINSOR McCAY.

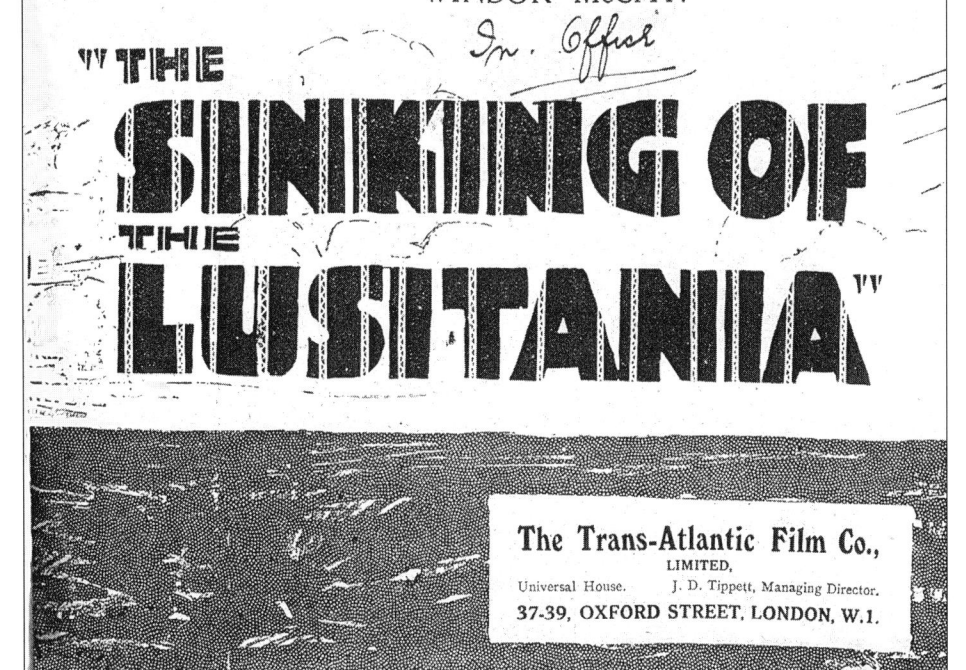

"THE SINKING OF THE LUSITANIA"

The Trans-Atlantic Film Co.,
LIMITED,
Universal House.   J. D. Tippett, Managing Director.
37-39, OXFORD STREET, LONDON, W.1.

But a far more significant film than this oriental hokum may also have been lost on the *Lusitania*. A print of *Ireland a Nation* (USA, 1914) was said to have been on board, destined for Ireland. This 5-reel film, partly shot in Ireland, depicted the life of Irish nationalist Robert Emmett, who plotted with Napoleon against England in the early 19th century. The film was written by Walter MacNamara (who had also written the celebrated *Traffic in Souls* of 1913) and was produced by his own company. In the event a replacement print did not arrive in Ireland until late 1916. It was due to be shown in January 1917, but the Easter Week Rising had taken place earlier in 1916, and the film was banned by the British authorities as likely to cause disaffection.[30]

As we have seen, the *Titanic* had at least two film cameramen on board, and it seems that the *Lusitania* also had one: Patrick L. Jones from the London office of the Hearst-Selig News Pictorial newsreel. During the sinking he was observed by another passenger (survivor C.T. Jeffrey) alone on the deck:

'He had a camera and was standing at the rail, balancing himself with one foot on the top rail - for the boat had a frightful list - and was taking picture after picture of the lifeboats that were being lowered and of those already in the water.'[31]

It seems somewhat unlikely that he was indeed filming the last minutes of the *Lusitania*, given the bulk of film cameras of the time, and the need to crank them - perhaps he was taking stills rather than moving pictures? I have not found Jones listed among the survivors, so I assume that he drowned. The same fate undoubtedly befell another passenger with a link to the movies. Elbert Hubbard (1856-1915) was not a film professional in the sense that Hounsell or Jolivet were but was a famous author, whose 1899 essay, **A Message to Garcia**, was the source for the celebrated Edison film of the same title, released in 1916. Novelist and author of several motion pictures (according to Kevin Brownlow) Justus Miles Forman (b.1875) was also drowned.

Apart from Jolivet's two films, there were to be several other films based or partly based on the *Lusitania* disaster. One of the Hepworth Cinema Interviews of 1916 is concerned with the *Lusitania*. The next film drama referring to the notorious shipwreck was an Italian film produced at the end of 1917 by Ambrosio. Directed by Augusto Genina, the film was entitled *Il Siluramento dell'Oceania* (*The Torpedoed Oceania*), and was a maritime adventure. Though the ship in the film was called the *Oceania*, the reference to the *Lusitania* and German responsibility for the sinking was clear, and was even made explicit in a title and an insert telegram. But the Italian censors demanded that all references to Germany and the sinking of the *Lusitania* be removed. The film was critically quite well received in Italy according to Vittorio Martinelli's researches.[32]

In 1918 there was a rash of films produced in America touching on the celebrated shipwreck. *The Kaiser, the Beast of Berlin* (Renowned Pictures Corporation/Jewel Productions, 1918) featured a character Captain Von Neigle, who is responsible for sinking the *Lusitania* and is then driven mad from remorse. In *The Price of Applause* (Triangle Film Corporation, 1918) a pacifist is finally goaded to fight by outrage he feels over the sinking of the *Lusitania*. A similar plot idea was used in *Over the Top* (Vitagraph, 1918, dir Wilfred North) in which hero James Owen joins the British Army after the sinking of the *Lusitania*. In the serial, *The Eagle's Eye*, Germans were portrayed plotting to blow up the *Lusitania* and preparing to spread infantile paralysis germs through the civilian population.[33] A documentary entitled *Crashing Through to Berlin* (Universal, 1918) used animation to depict the sinkings of the *Aztec* and the *Lusitania*. And Syd Chaplin reflected the disaster in surprisingly poor taste in *A Submarine Pirate* (1915).

The most significant cinematic version of the disaster however, was Winsor McCay's *The Sinking of the Lusitania*, (Universal-Jewel Productions) an animated film running 900 feet long. Released in Britain in May 1919 this was a highly skilful piece of work, in which the animation was achieved using cells, which later became the standard method for making animated cartoons. McCay was aided by several assistants, who helped turn out 25,000 drawings. The animation work is tremendously fluid and the tone and detail highly impressive. *The Cinema* praised the film highly, noting that: 'The best scene shows the explosion of the first torpedo. It is more real than reality...'[34] Advertisements for the film echoed this theme of realism, claiming that the film was, 'The world's only record of the crime that shocked humanity.' This impression of reality was achieved partly by setting the main animated part of the film within a live action framing story in which we see how the animation was achieved in McCay's studio. For an animated film McCay's production is surprisingly dark in mood, and depicts some of the gruesome details of the aftermath of the sinking - showing drowning children, for example. The tone of the narrative is powerfully propagandist.[35]

One further item of *Lusitania* lore is worth adding. In Fanny Hurst's story, **Heads**, written sometime before 1919, the plot deals with a family who decide on the toss of a coin whether or not to enter the movies in 1898. They succeed in the film business only to end up on the *Lusitania*.[36]

Extant films about the *Lusitania* disaster in the NFTVA

Lusitania Tragedy (Warwick Bioscope Chronicle, May 1915) 43 feet. Only scenes 6 and 7 survive: survivors waiting to board a train home at Queenstown station; shots of victim Alfred Vanderbilt and of his coaching business.

Anti-German Riots in Liverpool Following the Loss of "Lusitania" (Pathé's Animated Gazette, May 1915) 100 feet. Shots of broken shop windows and crowds looking on.

The Tragedy of the Lusitania: Germany's Foulest Crime (Pathé's Animated Gazette, May 1915) 231 feet. Shows the Lusitania leaving Liverpool. Anxious crowds waiting outside Cunard's offices in Liverpool, and weeping women walking away from the offices. Survivors arriving at a station and being met by relatives. Funeral of *Lusitania* victims at Queenstown, showing soldiers digging the communal grave, the coffins in it, and the funeral ceremony.

Lusitania Survivor's Appeal (Topical Budget, Sep 1915). 52 feet. Mrs Pye who lost her baby on the *Lusitania* makes a successful appeal for recruits, and George Robey watches swearing in at Trafalgar Square.

Strong Man of U.S.A. (Topical Budget, Nov 1915). 51 feet. Theodore Roosevelt quoted in a title that if he'd been President at the time of the *Lusitania* tragedy he'd have acted.

Lusitania Day (Topical Budget, May 1916). 103 feet. London-based Czech people march behind banners, followed by a large model of the *Lusitania* in a glass case carried on a cart.

(75) The Tragedy of the Lusitania
(Pathés Animated Gazette, May 1915)
(NFTVA)
(a) The Lusitania *leaving Liverpool.*
(b) Weeping women walking away from Cunard's offices in Liverpool.
(c) A survivor of the Lusitania.
(d) Funeral of Lusitania *victims at Queenstown*

Abbreviations of Periodicals

Bios	The Bioscope	MPW	Moving Picture World
FI	Film Index	NYDM	New York Dramatic Mirror
KLW	Kinematograph and Lantern Weekly	NYT	New York Times
LBB	Licht-Bild-Bühne	OLCJ	Optical Lantern and Cinematograph Journal
MPN	Moving Picture News		

Notes and references: Introduction

1. Quoted in John Wilson Foster, *Titanic* (Harmondsworth: Penguin Books, 1999). For fine selections of contemporary writings about the *Titanic* disaster see the same author's *The Titanic Complex: a Cultural Manifest* (Belcouver Press, 1997).
2. Quoted in Michael Davie, *Titanic: the Death and Life of a Legend* (New York: Henry Holt, 1986), p.183. See also Stephen Kern, *The Culture of Time and Space, 1880-1918* (London: Weidenfeld and Nicolson, 1983) for more on the symbolic impact of the disaster on the pre-WW1 world.
3. For a general introduction to liners in this period see Ernest Protheroe, *All About Steamers* (London: Collins, c1929) and McAuley below.
4. The *Olympic* had a darkroom, and therefore presumably the *Titanic* had one too. See Michael Moss, John R. Hume, *Shipbuilders to the World: 125 years of Harland and Wolff, Belfast 1861-1986* (Belfast: Blackstaff Press, 1986) p.146.
5. There was no cinema theatre on the *Titanic*, and as far as I can find out no film show was ever given or planned. A film show would scarcely have been a novelty on a major liner in April 1912. There had been film shows on ships almost from the beginnings of the cinema. Carl Hertz probably gave the first screening of films during an ocean voyage on his journey out to South Africa on the S.S. *Norman* in 1896, using his newly purchased Paul Theatrograph. Over the next few years – from 1904 onwards – films were shown on board ships from time to time, and by 1911 the *Oceana* offered '...up-to-date moving pictures and illustrated songs' on its voyages to Bermuda. (*MPW* 13 May 1911, p.1070.) By 1912 plans were announced for cinematograph theatres to be included on some of the big Atlantic liners. (*Bios* 21 Mar 1912, p.805.) And in April 1914 the new liner *Patria* left on her maiden Atlantic voyage from Marseille to New York with 'a completely equipped cinematograph theatre, wherein the passengers may while away the evenings when afloat'. (*Bios* 16 Apr 1914, p.246.)
6. Science Museum, Urban Collection, Urb 1, p.226. The signature of the Harland and Wolff representative is hard to read, but it may be Mr Carlisle.
7. *Bios* 27 Oct 1910, p.94. *The Times Engineering Supplement* 12 Oct 1910, p.14, cl. c: reported the launch was to be filmed. Interestingly, historian Tom McCluskey notes that White Star arranged little formality for launching either of the two ships: when completed 'they were pushed into the water with very little ceremony at all.' Quoted in Robb McAuley, *The Liners* (London: Boxtree, 1997) p.49.
8. *The Times* 23 Sep 1911, p.8, column b.
9. *Bios* 20 Oct 1910, p.39; *Bios* 27 Oct 1910, p.27.
10. British Pathé number ON186H. Topical Budget 274-2, released 25/11/16 – title: 'Hospital Ship Britannic The largest British liner, sunk by Germans'. Thanks to Simon Brown for this information.
11. *Titanic*-related books and other publications have included everything from discussions of the causes of the sinking to detailed biographies of the victims, from descriptions of the design and construction of the great liner, to highly specialist articles on the reception of the disaster among various different racial or social groups. Just to give a sense of the specialised nature of some publications I might cite, for example: Robert G. Weisbord, **Black American Perceptions of the Titanic Disaster**, *Journal of Popular Culture* vol. 28,3 (1994):245-250; Ann E. Larabee, **The**

American hero and his mechanical bride: gender myths of the Titanic disaster, *American Studies* vol. 31,1 (1990):5-23.
12. I have also tried to generalise from the particular in my other publications on non-fiction film. For example, see my article: **"An amazing quarter mile of moving gold, gems and genealogy":** filming India's 1902/03 Delhi Durbar, *Historical Journal of Film, Radio and Television* vol. 15,4 (Oct 1995).

Notes and References: Film People
1. *Motography* May 1912, p.233; *KLW* 25 April 1912, p.6.
2. The honeymoon may have been restricted to England rather than Europe as a whole: sources differ. The wedding date is given in *NYDM* 24 April 1912, p.26. The *Daily Sketch* of 16 April 1912 noted that Mr and Mrs Daniel Marvin were returning from honeymoon, and included photographs of them, but falsely stated, 'Young Marvin, who was associated with T.A. Edison in business...'(Courtesy of Mo Heard). Their address in London had been 58, Acre Lane, Brixton. See log of Marriages, Births, Deaths and Injuries, White Star Line 1912, Board of Trade 1912 (Public Record Office, London, BT 100/260).
3. *Daily Mail*, 17 April 1912.
4. *The Pictures* 15 June 1912, p.22.
5. Having one's wedding filmed was said to be a society fashion in this period: the previous year a Captain Brassey and his bride were filmed at St. Paul's, Knightsbridge. See **A kinematographed wedding**, *KLW* 2 Feb 1911, p.843.
6. For more on this studio see Richard Brown and Barry Anthony, **A Victorian Film Enterprise: the History of the British Mutoscope and Biograph Company, 1897-1915** (Trowbridge: Flicks Books, 1999) p.236.
7. *NYDM* 24 April 1912, p.26 op cit.
8. *The Times* 20 April 1912. See also *Daily Mail* 17 April 1912 and *Daily Sketch* 17 April and 20 April,1912.
9. *Bios* 25 April 1912, p.239.
10. Mary Marvin lived out her life in Herkimer County, New York where she owned a home at 12 Birch Road in the town of Thendara. She died on 17 October 1975 in New Hartford, New York at the age of 81. In her will she divided her estate between her children and grandchildren, specifically disinheriting her grandson, Wheaton Kitteredge, Jr., the only son of her daughter Peggy (who was the child of Daniel Warner Marvin). Thanks for this information to Phillip Gowan, David Huffaker and Peter Engberg-Klarström at Encyclopedia Titanica.
11. Stephen Herbert, **Animated Portrait Photography**, *History of Photography* vol.13,1, Jan-Mar 1989, pp.69-71 and pictures pp.70-74. Thanks also to Stephen Herbert for additional information on Biofix. Being 'Biofixed' was much cheaper than having a Kinora portrait taken, or buying an amateur film camera for oneself. Kinora portraits cost up to 3 guineas, and a Kinora camera was £19.
12. The flick books came in at least three formats. In addition to the London studio, there were several Biofix companies in other cities, including in Blackpool, Leeds, Portsmouth, Sheffield, and Southend, and there was also one on the Continent, in Bruxelles. See BT31 companies index in the Public Record Office.
13. *Daily Sketch*, 23 April 1912, pp.8-9.
14. **A Pocket Picture Palace**, *Royal Magazine* vol.28, May 1912, p.48. The picture also shows a cyclorama backdrop, with three artificial lights above.
15. **The mission of the Magic Lantern**, *Review of Reviews*, Dec 1890, pp.561-567. *Help* was published from the *Review of Reviews* office in London. Only four runs of this periodical are known to survive: in the British Library, vols 1-2, 1891-1892; in Hammersmith Reference library, for 1891-1892; in the Bodleian, vol 1, nos 1-4, 1891; and in Columbia University Library.

16. **The mission of the cinematograph** appeared in the annual of *Review of Reviews*, entitled *The Americanisation of the World, or the Trend of the 20th Century* (London: Review of Reviews,1902; reprint NY: Garland, 1972).
17. The American *Monthly Review of Reviews* ran articles about moving pictures in 1908, 1910, 1912, and 1914.
18. W.B. Northrop, *With Pen and Camera: Interviews with Celebrities* (London: R.A.Everett and Co., 1904) pp.157-161.
19. **At the toll of death – the world mourns**, *MPN* 20 Apr 1912, p.6.
20. The Cripple-Creek web-site claims that Margaret Brown ('the unsinkable Molly Brown') was a journalist, but Pat Behe has never heard that claim made anywhere else and has never seen any examples of Mrs Brown's 'professional' writing. Brown has become possibly the most famous passenger on the ship for her bravery during the disaster and she is commemorated in the Molly Brown Museum in Denver.
21. See information on Futrelle in Logan Marshall, ed., *Sinking of the Titanic and Great Sea Disasters...* (Philadelphia, The John C. Winston company, c1912).
22. *Daily Sketch*, 17 April 1912; article on Futrelle in *Eclair Bulletin* (NY) no.60, Feb 1914; Dennis Gifford, *Books and Plays in Films, 1896-1915* (London and New York: Mansell, 1991) p.60; Paul C. Spehr, *American Film Personnel and Company Credits, 1908-1920* (Jefferson: McFarland and Company, Inc., 1996). For a recent 'take' on Futrelle see the novel, Max Allan Collins, *The Titanic Murders* (Harmondsworth: Penguin, 1999).
23. Dave Bryceson, *The Titanic Disaster as Reported in the National Press, April-July 1912* (Sparkford: PSL, 1997), pp.82-83. See Futrelle's wife's account of their parting in Marshall Everett, *Wreck and Sinking of the Titanic* (Chicago: Homeward Press, 1912). There is a less dramatic account of the parting, along with a photograph of the Futrelles in their car, in Judith B.Geller, *Titanic: Women and Children First* (Sparkford: Patrick Stephens Ltd., 1998) pp.46-49.
24. *Le Courrier Cinématographique* 20 April 1912, p.16.
25. A brief death notice appeared in **Parisian Notes**, *Bios* 25 Apr 1912, p.273. Malachard is not listed in Henri Bousquet's invaluable catalogues of early Pathé films. My thanks to Jean-Jacques Meusy for checking French sources on Pathé. Thanks to Germain Lacasse, André Gaudreault and Bill O'Farrell for checking Canadian sources.
26. This information, credited to Hermann Söldner in Germany, and others, comes from the invaluable web-site Encyclopedia Titanica. Sources are given as: Contract Ticket List, White Star Line 1912 (National Archives, New York;NRAN-21-SDNYCIVCAS-55[279]); log of Marriages, Births, Deaths and Injuries, White Star Line 1912, Board of Trade 1912 (Public Record Office, London, BT 100/260). See also Günter Bäbler (with Linda von Arx-Mooser), *Reise auf der Titanic: das Schicksal der Schweizer* (Zürich: Chronos-Verlag, 1998) and Alan Hustak, *Titanic: The Canadian Story* [foreword by John P. Eaton] (Montréal/Québec: Véhicule Press, c1998).
27. *NYDM* 24 April 1912, p.26. *Le Cinema* 19 April 1912, pp.1 and 3 also speculates that perhaps Malachard was filming as the vessel sank, but if so his film went down with the ship. Frank Thompson also claims Malachard was assigned to film the maiden voyage.
28. Many thanks to Victoria Duckett for this reference. **A bord du 'Titanic' – Cruelle Angoisse**, *Cine Journal* 20 April 1912, p.15: 'La mère éplorée et les amis de Monsieur Malachart, un des vaillants opérateurs de la maison Pathé frères, traversent en ce moment de cruelles minutes. Malachart était, en effet, parmi les passagers du *Titanic*. Notre ami, qui se rendait au Canada pour y diriger une succursale, est-il parmi les rescapés? Nous le souhaitons ardemment mais, hélas, nous n'avons pas d'espoir bien ferme. Malachart a vingt six ans. D'origine lyonnaise, il s'était de bonne heure passionné pour la Cinématographie et son nom demeure attaché a maints films de voyage d'une execution supérieure. Puisse-t-il n'avoir pas été victime de sa glorieuse profession?' (My translation).
29. *l'Echo du Cinema*, 19 April 1912, p.1.
30. *NYT* 20 April 1912, p.9, column 3.

31. Wollstein op cit.
32. This information on Fahlström comes from the internet site Encyclopedia Titanica, and from Per Kristian Sebak, *Titanic: 31 Norwegain Destinies* (Oslo: Genesis Forlag, 1998), pp.19-20, 170.
33. These pieces of information come from *KLW* 9 May 1912, p.150.
34. Another person with a vague film connection who perished on the *Titanic* was Walter Miller Clark, whose grave and memorial is in Hollywood Cemetery, California. His son married actress Barbara Fritchie, and his family were friends of Cecil B. DeMille's family. See, Brian J. Ticehurst, *Titanic Memorials World-Wide: where they are located* (Swathling: B&J Printers, 1995); Bryceson op cit p.45. Thanks to Don Lynch, via George Behe, for this information on the family.
35. *Bios* 23 May 1912, p.569.
36. John P. Eaton, Charles A. Haas, *Titanic: Triumph and Tragedy* (Wellingborough: Patrick Stephens Ltd., 1986) pp.314-316; Marc Shapiro, *Total Titanic* (NY: Pocket Books, 1998) pp.167-168.
37. Advertisement in *Amateur Photographer and Photographic News* Supplement 29 April 1912, p.12.
38. *Daily Sketch*, 19 April 1912, quoted in Bryceson op cit, p.63.
39. Herbert Birett reports the 1000 meter figure, presumably based on trade journal sources of the time.
40. *MPW* 1 June 1912, p.869 published an ad stating that A.H. Woods was the exclusive rights holder of *The Miracle*, which was copyrighted in the USA on 12 January 1912. The theatrical production had played at the Olympia, London.
41. See *Bios* 9 May 1912, p.388; *KLW* 30 May 1912, p.385; *KLW* 27 June 1912, p.xviii; *Bios* 6 Feb 1913, p.397. I have not been able to consult a work which might shed light on the date conflict regarding *The Miracle*. This is Margit Zahradnik, **Max Reinhardt und der Film** (Diplomarbeit, Univ. Wien, 1989).
42. Walter Lord, **A Night to Remember** (Harmondsworth: Penguin Books, 1976)p.106.
43. *Daily Sketch* 19 Apr 1912; *Bios* 9 May 1912, p.397.
44. Logan Marshall, op cit. For more on Harris see the THS web site and Don Lynch, *Titanic* (London: Hodder, 1992). Also see Harris' article: **My relation to the American stage**, *The Green Book Album* vol.4, Oct 1910, pp.831-834, which notes that his most ambitious theatrical production was *The Christian Pilgrim*. His obituary appears in *NYDM* 24 April 1912, p.13.
45. *Daily Mail* 17 April 1912.

Notes and References: William H. Harbeck

1. The date of 1863 comes from 'recent contacts from family members' reported on the Cripple Creek website.
2. His father, John Samuel Harbeck Jr., was born 19 May 1836 in New York, and died 11 Sep 1921 in Long Beach, California. His mother, Ida was born in 1 Sep 1859 and died 15 Feb 1950. (Courtesy Don Lynch).
3. From undated *Toledo Blade* article: Mark Reiter, **Man finds a distant relative among victims of the Titanic**. This was sent me by Don Lynch (in turn from Mark Gable), and it concerns the researches of Karl Harbeck of Blissfield, Ohio, who has discovered more about his forbear than anyone else.
4. *MPN* 15 Jan 1910, p.10.
5. The details here are taken from Harbeck's answers to census questions, cited on the Cripple-Creek internet site, from which source the other information in this section also comes.
6. This is confirmed by Mark Reiter, op cit.
7. *MPN* 11 May 1912 says that Harbeck worked for Miles Brothers in San Francisco five years ago, then for Selig and Hales' Tours.
8. Letter from J. Frank Pickering, a lecturer, of Payson, Utah to Selig Polyscope Co., Chicago, dated 12 May 1908 recalls meeting Harbeck in 1906. A note from Selig says to send Pickering their list of Yellowstone films, which he says is on page 134 of their catalogue. From Charles G. Clarke Scrapbook no.2, p.19 – held in Academy of Motion Picture Arts and Sciences.

9. Selig Polyscope Co., *Everything Pertaining to Animated Photography and Projection* (Chicago, 1907) including *Catalogue of Original Selig Films, Animated Pictures...* pp.107-8, 134-5. (Selig had also referred to page 134 – see my previous note – supporting the attribution of these films to Harbeck). On reel two of microfilm: Charles Musser, *Motion Picture Catalogs by American Producers and Distributors, 1884-1908.*
10. The Hales carriages were rocked realistically during the screenings, which were accompanied by sound effects and a narration.
11. *Views and Films Index*, 23 Feb 1907 p.6..
12. *Selig Polyscope Co., Supplement* no. 44, Aug 1906, **Hale's Tours Films**. On Musser microfilm, op cit. Cameraman H.H. Buckwalter shot many western scenes for Selig, especially in Colorado.
13. *VFI* 23 Feb 1907, p.6. Harbeck filmed local scenes such as Seattle's regrading project on Denny Hill. See Seattle's information site at: www.historylink.org. The same site claims that Harbeck was based in Seattle from 1905. A 1912 article notes Harbeck had his own 'miniature manufactury' in Seattle where he could develop and print his own films. See **Interesting interview with Mr. W.H. Harbeck of Seattle**, *MPN* 17 Feb 1912, p.20.
14. *VFI* 23 Feb op cit.
15. From *Victoria Daily Colonist* article cited in the following note.
16. **Views of Victoria in realistic form: many pictures of City and Surroundings taken by Cinematograph Expert**, *Victoria Daily Colonist* 5 May 1907, p.3, cited in Colin Browne, *Motion Picture Production in British Columbia, 1898-1940: a Brief Historical Background and Catalogue* (Victoria: British Columbia Provincial Museum, 1979). A copy of the article and a summary by Browne was kindly sent to me by the National Archives of Canada. Harbeck's work for Hales is also mentioned in Hans J. Wollstein, **Dorothy Gibson: 'Saved from the Titanic'**, *Classic Images*, no.268, (Oct 1997): 35-36.
17. This had been opened in 1905 by J.D. Williams (who went on to form First National, which was by 1920 the second largest exhibition circuit in North America).
18. The Seattle city directories apparently still show him living in the city in 1910, as working in 'moving pictures' the following year, and as living in Seattle with his wife Katie L. Harbeck in 1912. Directories for Seattle are not yet included on the US City Directories microfilm so I am unable to confirm this information. Behe suggests that at the time of the Titanic sinking Harbeck had been a resident of Seattle for the past eight years.
19. **Canadian Pacific Railway's Matchless Film**, *MPN* 11 Dec 1909, p.12.
20. The exposition had been organised to highlight America's North West and its economic potential. See Ann Fienup-Riordan, *Freeze Frame: Alaska Eskimos in the Movies* (Seattle: University of Washington Press, 1995), which notes that there was an 'Eskimo village' at the expo (illus, p.28) and 100 real eskimos.
21. **Canadian Pacific Railway's Matchless Film**, op cit. Another source stated that the film was 7,000 ft. in length. See **The latest visitor to London**, *Bios* 27 Jan 1910, p.58.
22. At about this time there were plans to tour a Harbeck film through the United States, which may have been this CPR one, or another film of the Seattle Exposition. See **Mr. W.H. Harbeck, of the Canadian Pacific Railroad Company**, *MPN* 15 Jan 1910, p.4.
23. The photograph also bears a P.O. Box address in Seattle, and possibly a date (which cannot be made out from my copy). This photograph is held in the Historic Photographs department of the Provincial Archives of BC, Parliament Buildings, Victoria, and was sent to me from Colin Browne's collection. The photograph is also reproduced in **Canadian Pacific Railway's Matchless Film**, *MPN* op cit.
24. **Former Toledan gives friends picture treat**, *MPN* 15 Jan 1910, p.10. Also cited in *Bios* 27 Jan 1910, p.43 and *KLW* 27 Jan 1910, p.643. The screening was in the Crown Theatre, Summit Street on 7th January 1910.
25. **Mr. W.H. Harbeck, of the Canadian Pacific Railroad Company**, *MPN* 15 Jan 1910, p.4, op cit.

Also sailing on the ship was film executive Jules Brulatour, whom we shall meet again in connection with Dorothy Gibson.
26. **Messrs. Brulatour and Harbeck,** *MPN* 22 Jan 1910, p.4.
27. *KLW* 3 Feb 1910, p.687.
28. *MPN* 25 June 1910, p.11. According to the Encyclopedia Titanica website Harbeck made a light comedy, *The Ship's Husband*, about a matrimonial mix-up on board a ferry that ran between Vancouver, Seattle and Victoria. The American Film Index lists an Edison film of this title released in November 1910.
29. See my article: **Will Day: the story of rediscovery,** *Film Studies*, no.1, Spring 1999, pp.81-91.
30. **Weekly Notes,** *KLW* 23 Feb 1911, p.1063; see also **Latest news from America,** *KLW* 23 Feb 1911, p.1083.
31. **Motion Pictures Cure Seasickness,** *Motography* May 1911, p.103.
32. Courtesy George Behe; and *Bios* 27 Jan 1910, p.58.
33. **Moving pictures of valley scenes,** *MPN* 20 May 1911, p.22. Incidentally, Seattle seems to have had an imaginative policy on self promotion: the publicity director of the Seattle Chamber of Commerce was Charles Philip Norton, who was put in charge of American propaganda in Russia during the First World War. See James D. Scott, **American film propaganda in revolutionary Russia,** *Prologue*, vol. 30, Fall 1998, p.175.
34. Though Wills wrongly remembers Harbeck's initials as 'J.W.' *Times Colonist*, 23-24 August 1981, p.33. Courtesy National Archives of Canada.
35. Copyrighted by Harbeck, who gave his address as c/o Cadillac Hotel, New York.
36. **The Moving Picture educator,** *MPW* 17 Feb 1912, p.561. An article on Harbeck from this period which I have not managed to see may also have useful information: *Tacoma Daily News* 2 May 1912, p.7.
37. **William H. Harbeck's widow asks for injunction,** *MPN* 25 May 1912, p.23.
38. Pinchot took an active role in founding the new Progressive Party, commonly known as the Bull Moose Party. The forester represented the more radical wing of the party's politics and made strong statements on the need for stricter antitrust laws and innovative social reforms.
39. **Moving pictures of southern Alaska,** *MPN* 10 Feb 1912, p.36.
40. **Interesting interview with Mr. W.H. Harbeck of Seattle,** op cit.
41. Letter from Brownie Harbeck, Seattle, 31 Aug 1912, cited below.
42. These film subjects are noted in the article: **Harbeck lost on the Titanic,** *MPW*, 11 May 1912, p.506. The round-up takes place at Pendleton in N.E. Oregon each year in September, so Harbeck probably filmed it in September of 1911.
43. *MPN* 28 Jan 1911, p.5.
44. Information from the Historylink site, which adds that he exposed some 10,000 feet of negative.
45. *KLW* 18 Apr 1912, p.1385.
46. **Unexhibited films sink with Titanic,** *MPW* 29 June 1912, p.1231.
47. Raymond Fielding, *The American Newsreel, 1911-1967* (Norman: University of Oklahoma Press, 1972) pp.85,100. Contemporary sources state that the President of this concern was L.L. Burns, with H.K. Eakle as assistant manager and Eduard Gheller (formerly of Ambrosio, and later a cameraman for Goldwyn) running the European side. Fielding gives different names from these as the producers behind this newsreel.
48. Courtesy George Behe. Historylink claims the communication to his wife was a postcard.
49. Eaton and Haas, *Titanic: Triumph and Tragedy* (1986) op cit.
50. **Notes of the week,** *MPN* 25 May 1912, p.40.
51. Mark Reiter, op cit.
52. Possibly based on a *Seattle Times* article of 21 April, according to Behe and Historylink.
53. **Weekly Notes** by columnist 'Stroller', *KLW* 18 April 1912, p.1385. See also **Harbeck lost on the Titanic,** *MPW*, op cit. Day suggested that it was likely Harbeck had 'procured some vastly

interesting pictures"' See **The wreck of the 'Titanic'**, *KLW* 18 April 1912, p.1387.
54. See **A letter from the 'Titanic'**, *Bios* 18 April 1912, p.169.
55. **Weekly Notes** by columnist 'Stroller', *KLW* 18 April 1912, p.1385.
56. *KLW* 14 Mar 1912, p.1114b.
57. **The wreck of the 'Titanic'**, *KLW* 18 April 1912, p.1387.
58. The ticket information comes via Alan Hustak and Hermann Söldner on the Encyclopedia Titanica web-site. The source is given as the Contract Ticket List, White Star Line 1912 (National Archives, New York; NRAN-21-SDNYCIVCAS-55[279]). Places of abode and addresses are from the Titanic's log, Marriages, Births, Deaths and Injuries, Board of Trade 1912 (PRO London, BT 100/260). The address of Miss Yvois (some suggest her name was Yrois, though Brownie Harbeck used Yvois) was 5 Rue des Pyramides, Paris.
59. This letter is preserved in the official records in Halifax, and a copy was kindly sent to me by Don Lynch, who has a microfilm of this material. The letter from Brownie Harbeck read in full (with mistakes):
    'Seattle Washington Aug 31 1912.
    Dear Sir,
    Your letter of Aug 23rd Receiv ,
    Pardon me I don't quite understand figures to the amount of money in gold. Kindly inform me if the amount in gold was fifteen hundred dollars. what was the amount in travellers checks Thanking you for grateful kindness
    Referring to lady's articles among W.H. Harbeck's effects, I knew the lady well. I understand she was also lost on the *Titanic*. Her name was Henriette Yvois. Do you know if such Person's body ever been picket(?) up and being brought to Halifax,
    Mrs Brownie Harbeck, 1311- E. Marion St'
    This letter was received at the Provincial Secretary's office 6 Sep 1912.
60. Lawrence Beesley, *The Loss of the S.S. Titanic: its story and its lessons* (New York: Houghton Mifflin, 1912) reproduced in Jack Winocour, *The Story of the Titanic as Told by its Survivors* (NY: Dover Publications, 1960) pp.16 and 23. (A scene of a cameraman cranking his camera during the voyage was recreated for the 1979 film, *S.O.S. Titanic*).
61. Ibid. Presumably Beesley deduced the wife's nationality from her accent.
62. The game of 'Patience' was highly fashionable in France from the late 19th century, supporting the idea that the woman whom Beesley saw playing cards was indeed French. See Jaqueline Karas, *Patience Games by Jacqueline Harrod* (Tadworth, 1992).
63. There is another possible sighting of Harbeck during the voyage: he may have chatted with Elizabeth and Thomas Brown, a South African family who were also Seattle-bound. One author claims such a contact. See Judith B. Geller, *Titanic: Women and Children First* (Sparkford: Patrick Stephens Ltd., 1998) p.125. But the only source she cites, the autobiography of the Brown's daughter, [Edith Eileen Haisman, *A Lifetime on the Titanic* (1987)] fails to mention any such meeting (though perhaps Geller's information comes from personal contacts).
64. Several other prominent men were passengers on the *Titanic*, including John Jacob Astor and Isidor Straus.
65. This version is given in Wollstein op cit. Walter Lord, *A Night to Remember* (Harmondsworth: Penguin Books, 1976) p.104 has only Benjamin Guggenheim and his secretary dressing in evening clothes: 'We've dressed in our best and are prepared to go down like gentlemen.'
66. The account of steward, James Etches, in *NYT* 20 April 1912, p.9.
67. John H. Davis, *The Guggenheims: an American Epic* (New York: William Morrow and Co., 1978) pp.238-242. The blonde companion of Benjamin Guggenheim was a certain 'Mme Aubart', according to Jeffrey Kern, 17 July 2000 on Encyclopedia Titanica website.
68. Press reports said that his body was identified as 'W.H. Hambeck'. *Daily Sketch* 24 April 1912 (the official body recovery records kept in Halifax identified the body as 'W.H. Herbeck'). The *Mackay-*

Bennett pulled 190 bodies from near the site of the sinking, and along with two sister ships they recovered a total of 328 bodies. See Michael Davie op cit, pp.224-9 on the recovery of bodies by the *Mackay-Bennett* and other ships. The *Mackay-Bennett* embarked Apr 17th and returned to Halifax Apr 30th.

69. A detailed list of the clothes and effects of victims was made by the authorities at Halifax (Harbeck's body was number 35). A copy of the relevant pages (the lists are on microfilm) was kindly supplied to me by Don Lynch. The list is also given on the *Titanic* Historical Society's web site, and in the Box here.
70. Letters from Catherine Harbeck, 733 Michigan Street, Toledo, 23 May and 28 May, 1912, to Provincial Secretary, Halifax. Courtesy Don Lynch, from microfilm. Catherine signed for the effects at the Custom House, Toledo, on 8th June. Among her husband's effects collected by Catherine was his diary – if still existing this would give some interesting details of Harbeck's life.
71. **Harbeck lost on the Titanic**, *MPW* 11 May 1912, p.506. This source says he was 45 at death, and the 1900 census lists his birth date as December, 1866, making him 45. But according to the *Titanic Hind* online database he was 44 when he died; and if, as family claim, he was born in Sep 1863, that would make him 48.
72. Harbeck's wife Catherine was born c.1863 and died 17 May 1940 in Toledo, Ohio. She was survived by her sisters, Emma Stetter and Mrs. John H. Kerbel. Catherine and William's sons were: John S. Harbeck, one time reporter on Toledo newspapers, born 27 April 1887 and died 21 May 1917; and Stanley, photographer and salesman, born Feb. 1892 and died 21 July 1947. Neither of the sons ever married.
73. See **A letter from the 'Titanic'**, *Bios* 18 April 1912, p.169. This confirms his popularity in London film circles.
74. *KLW* 25 April 1912, p.6.
75. *KLW* 9 May 1912, p.150.
76. Brownie Harbeck's address was given as Flat A, 1311 E. Marion Street, Seattle.
77. On Harbeck's Library of Congress copyright application for *Alaska (Panoramic Views of) in animated maps*, submitted in January 1912 his permanent address was given as 1311 E. Marion St., Seattle. Interestingly this is not the same address as given when his body was recovered, 114, 24th Avenue (no city given).
78. Letter from John S. Harbeck, 733 Michigan St, Toledo, 25 Sep 1912. There was also a letter from him of 12 Sep. In the meantime Brownie had been informed that there had only been £15 in gold found on Harbeck's body, and that Catherine was the administratrix of his estate. Letter of 7 Sep from Deputy Provincial Secretary.
79. *NYDM* 8 May 1912, p.26.
80. One of only two Harbeck films copyrighted in the Library of Congress – the other being the 'Alaskan maps' film. A British source later suggested that a film of the great Montana round-up, made by Harbeck, was lost on the *Titanic*, but this was probably a confusion with Harbeck's Pendleton film. See **Sunderland Sidelights**, *Bios* 30 Oct 1913, p.405. Another source puts Catherine Harbeck's claims at $50,000 for 100,000 feet of lost motion picture films. It was also claimed that 110,000 feet of his films shot in Europe had gone down on the *Titanic*. **Notes of the week**, *MPN* 25 May 1912, p.40.
81. **Harbeck lost on the Titanic** *MPW*, op cit.
82. **William H. Harbeck's widow asks for injunction**, *MPN* 25 May 1912, p.23; **Harbeck Pictures in Litigation**, *MPW* 1 June 1912, p.805. See also *MPW* 3 Aug 1912, p.455.
83. **Does not represent the Harbeck estate**, *MPW* 17 Aug 1912, p.659. This gave Mrs Harbeck's address as 733 Michigan Avenue, Toledo (not the Seattle address cited above). See also **The late W.H. Harbeck**, *MPN* 10 Aug 1912, p.18, in which Catherine claimed she and her son John S. Harbeck held all the exhibition rights to the Round-up and Alaska films except for rights to a

couple of New England states. Tom Moore held Washington state's rights for The Pendleton Round-Up which he considered one of Harbeck's finest films, and it was shown for a very successful week at the Majestic theatre. **Washington Notes,** *MPN* 29 June 1912, p.10.
84. Mark Reiter, op cit suggests that Catherine moved back to Toledo in 1915, but Polk's Toledo City Directories suggests that she may have been there from as early as 1912. The 1911 directory (p.735) lists only Stanley and John S. Harbeck at 733 Michigan Street, while the 1912 directory (p.755) lists the two boys, but adds their mother Catherine as the main occupant. Incidentally, on the 25th anniversary of her husband's death she told a reporter that William Harbeck had once gone on a business trip to Russia in connection with his film work (no other source confirms this trip).
85. *The Implet* 4 May 1912, p.2. Held in the Library of Congress Motion Picture Division.
86. **William H. Harbeck,** *MPN* 27 Apr 1912, p.6.
87. **Harbeck lost on the Titanic,** *MPW,* op cit.

Notes and References: The Titanic and the Lantern

1. Little has been published about the news lantern slide business, and relatively little about the lantern in the Americas. The latter gap will be partially filled when X. Theodore Barber's book on the magic lantern in America finally appears.
2. Boleslaw Matuszewski, author of the 1898 pamphlet *Une nouvelle source de l'Histoire* and the 1899 book, *La Photographie Animée,* argued that the faking of films was much more difficult than the faking of still photographs – indeed he thought it would be virtually impossible – as so many more pictures/frames would need to be doctored.
3. *Der Kinematograph* 24 April 1912.
4. Slides of the S.S. 'Titanic' and the S.S. 'Titanic' in Belfast are listed in the 'Ships & Shipbuilding' section of the catalogue of W H Rau Corporation (of 238 South Camac Street, Philadelphia), volume 12, page 17, slides number 29454 and 29519. They were available as lantern slides or photographs. The catalogue is in the collection of David Francis who kindly sent me this information.
5. *MPW* 27 April 1912, p.354.
6. Ibid and *MPW* 4 May 1912, p.442 and *MPW* 11 May 1912, p.547.
7. **Pictures of the Titanic Survivors,** *New York Clipper* (Clipper) 27 April 1912, p.7.
8. Ad in the *Clipper* 27 April 1912, p.8; repeated 4 May 1912, p.5. Pryor's office address was given as c/o the De Commerce Slide Co., 46 East 14th St, NYC, or his branch office was with W.I. Neagle in Iowa.
9. *Clipper* 4 May 1912, p.6.
10. Ad for J. De Commerce in *MPN* 27 April 1912, p.42, and at the back of *Photoplay,* June and July 1912, n.p. I have also found him listed at 13th Street.
11. *MPW* 4 May 1912, p.471.
12. *NYDM* 1 May 1912, p.27 and ad on p.31; *MPW* 4 May 1912, p.397; 11 May 1912, p.579; 18 May 1912, p.646. The *NYDM* ad refers to the organisations as the National News Association of New York and the Central Press Syndicate of London.
13. *MPN* 11 May 1912, p.19. Clapham's ads for the *Titanic* slides continued appearing in this journal into June. He continued offering news slides – later in 1912 he offered a set about the Rosenthal murder from photographs of the National Press Syndicate of New York. See *MPN* 10 Aug 1912, p.10 and p.40.
14. *NYDM* 1 May 1912, p.27 and ad on p.34. See also *MPN* 27 Apr 1912, p.14 and p.38.
15. *Clipper* 4 May 1912, p.5, 18 May 1912, p.7.
16. *Clipper* 4 May 1912, p.6.
17. *Clipper* 4 May 1912, p.6; 18 May 1912, p.7; 1 June 1912, p.6
18. *Titanic* disaster slides popular', *MPN* 4 May 1912, p.21 and p.23.
19. James Card, **When Newsreels stood still,** *American Heritage,* vol. 36,2, Feb/March 1985, p.48-53.

Sadly, I have not been able to find the present whereabouts of these slides: Card once worked at George Eastman House, but a recent search at their Photo Collection has proved negative. Thanks to Joe Struble of GEH for this search. Hinton-Fell-Elliott also offered three posters with this slide set.
20. *MPW* 4 May 1912, p.457.
21. *MPW* 11 May 1912, p.550, column 1.
22. *MPW* 11 May 1912, p.540; 1 June 1912, p.869.
23. Small ad for the Kinematograph Exchange, *KLW* 2 May 1912, p.139.
24. **Items of Interest**, *Bios* 16 May 1912, p.467. See also *KLW* 16 May 1912, p.216; 23 May 1912, p.326.
25. **Items of Interest**, *Bios* 2 May 1912, p.317.
26. Steve Humphries, *Victorian Britain Through the Magic Lantern* (London: Sidgwick and Jackson, 1989) pp.152-157.
27. Malcolm Bowen Niedner, **Searching for a legend**, *Titanic Commutator*, vol.1,2, 1987, pp.3-36. Lester Smith informs me that *Titanic* slides were offered in a Newton catalogue of c.1913.
28. Richard Crangle tells me that Bamforth produced two versions of the set of six cards, one in black and one in sepia monochrome. The cards are reproduced in Mark Bown, *R.M.S. 'Titanic' – a Portrait in Old Picture Postcards* (Loggerheads: Brompton Publications, 1987) p.67.
29. Letter from Mrs Winifred Jackson in **50 years of films and listeners' recollections** (1946), File R19/363, BBC Written Archives Centre, Caversham. Her address was given as Butterley Lane, New Mill, near Huddersfield. She also appeared in the slide sets: 'Fireman save my child', 'Don't go down the mine Daddy', 'Lord Fauntleroy', 'Please Mr Conductor don't put me off the train', and 'A little child shall lead them'. She also featured in comic postcards with Alf Foy; and in films, including one with Queenie Thomas about 1912 and in another, 'watching the burning of an effigy of the Kaiser! probably 1914-15... I was about 8 or 9 at the time so naturally I only remember bits...'
30. Hudson John Powell, **H. and F. Poole's Myrioramas**, *New Magic Lantern Journal*, vol.8,1, Oct 1996, pp.13-15.
31. Recalled many years later by someone who had seen the original show. *Cambridge Daily News* 30 August 1938, p.3. The collision took place off Syria on 22 June 1893. The writer wrongly recalls the name of the *Pretoria* as the *Victoria*. The other part of this Poole's show was a reproduction of the Matabele attack on the Mashonas subdued by the British, ending with the capture of Bulawayo.
32. Reported in *The Scotsman* 24 Dec 1912, pp. 1 and 5.
33. An advertising postcard for this show, with many details, is reproduced in Mark Bown and Roger Simmons, *R.M.S. 'Titanic' – a Portrait in Old Picture Postcards*, op cit, pp.77-8. Copies of the same card exist which are overprinted with the names of other theatres in different parts of the country. The postcard was copyrighted. For more on Pooles' shows see John H. Bird, *Cinema Parade: 50 years of Film Shows* (Birmingham: Cornish Bros, nd.) pp.62-66. I have benefited much from discussing the Pooles with Peter Jewell, who in turn has received much information from Hudson John Powell.
34. The wording is almost the same as in the Pooles' *Guide Book* for their 1913 shows, (from Hudson John Powell collection). The guide book adds one detail for scene 5: the distress rockets were also depicted.
35. Hudson John Powell, op cit, p.14.
36. Other writers in recent years, notably Richard Crangle and Deac Rossell (at the Visual Delights conference, Sheffield, 1999) have made this point in more general terms about the continuing survival of the lantern industry, which they emphasise was not immediately 'killed' in 'giving birth' to the cinema (to use the terms parodied by Crangle).

Notes and References: News Films

1. See John Pilger, *Hidden Agendas* (London: Vintage, 1998), who argues that there are general distortions and lacunae in news coverage.
2. Bert Garai, *The Man From Keystone* (London: Frederick Muller Ltd, 1965) pp.11-12.
3. **Ubiquitous Photography**, *The Amateur Photographer and Photographic News*, 13 May 1912, p.479. Nicholas Hiley's paper **News of the Titanic**, presented at the conference Nights to Remember (University of Southampton, July 2000) discussed the circulation figures for British newspapers in the immediate wake of the disaster. Hiley suggested that illustrated papers seemed to show a different sales pattern compared with more 'serious' newspapers.
4. For more on early newsreel filming see Luke McKernan, *Topical Budget: the Great British News Film* (London: BFI, 1992) and my article, **'Have you seen the Gaekwar bob?: filming the 1911 Delhi Durbar**, *Historical Journal of Film, Radio and Television*, vol.17,3, 1997, pp. 309-345. The latter is the second of my three planned articles on how the Delhi Durbars were filmed and screened.
5. *The Titanic Leaving Southampton*, which may or may not be this Topical Budget film was shown at the Osborne Picture Hall, Oldham. See *The World's Fair* 27 April 1912, p.14
6. *Bios* 25 April 1912, p.236.
7. Ad: *Bios* 9 May 1912, p.394.
8. The Animated Weekly was produced by Gaumont from around February 1912 until July. After 24 July Gaumont ceased to release the AW, but continued to release their own Gaumont Weekly each Wednesday, which had appeared from 22 Feb. See **The Gaumont Weekly**, *MPN* 27 July 1912, p.19. (*Photoplay* June 1912, p.69 stated that the 'Animated Weekly' is 'published' by the Gaumont Company.)
9. A review of the Animated Weekly's *Titanic* newsreel credits a T.E. Holliday as 'the compiler and instigator of the film', or 'producer' as we would say today. (**Titanic Disaster**, *NYDM* 1 May 1912, p.27.) The initial of his name may be wrong, and another source notes that Frank E. Holliday was the editor of the 'Gaumont Weekly'. (*MPN* 8 June 1912, p.16).
10. Raymond Fielding, *The American Newsreel, 1911-1967* (Norman: University of Oklahoma Press, 1972) p.83.
11. From 31 March Gaumont appeared on the Sales Company's list and by June was lined up with the Film Supply Company of America. See *MPN* 8 June 1912, p.16
12. *MPW* 20 April 1912, pp.237, 251; *MPN* 13 April 1912, p.6.
13. *MPW* 4 May 1912, p.396.
14. They had just filmed another wreck, of the *Ontario*, on 8 April. Ad in *MPN* 20 Apr 1912, p.33. Thanks to Madeline Matz for this citation.
15. **United States Government recognizes worth of Titanic pictures**, *MPN* 11 May 1912, p.26. The Sales Company offered the film to be preserved in the Congressional Library, which was accepted.
16. Ad for the Animated Weekly, *MPN* 27 April 1912, p.44.
17. Karl Baarslag, *Radio Rescues at Sea* (London: Methuen, 1937) p.62.
18. See *Bios* 2 May 1912, p.312; and **Titanic Disaster**, *NYDM* 1 May 1912, p.27.
19. J.A. Fleming, *The Wonders of Wireless Telegraphy* (SPCK, 1913) p.238. Richard Garrett, *Atlantic Disaster – The Titanic and Other Victims of The North Atlantic* (London: Buchan and Enright, 1986) pp.167-9. Binns was accompanied by another operator, Elenschneider. See Baarslag pp.94-96, who also notes that the US Government sent two fast cruisers to assist the *Carpathia*.
20. *Bios* 9 May 1912, p.419. The report says the tug Binns travelled on was called the *Sea Witch*. Michael Davie, *Titanic: the Death and Life of a Legend* (NY: Henry Holt, 1986), pp.154-7 shows the desperation of the media for *Titanic* news – he notes, for example, the huge amounts of money offered by the *New York Times* to *Titanic*'s Marconi operators for their stories.
21. Ad in the *Clipper* 27 April 1912, p.8
22. Daniel Allen Butler, *Unsinkable* (Mechanicsburg: Stackpole Books, 1998) pp.170-172.

23. The *Tribune* ad is reproduced in John P. Eaton and Charles A. Haas, *Titanic: Triumph and Tragedy* (Wellingborough: Stephens, 1986) p.216, though my search in the *Tribune* from 16 April to 6 May has revealed no such ad. See also **Titanic wreck pictures amaze Broadway throngs**, *MPN* 27 April 1912, p.24.
24. The distress signal S.O.S. was generally adopted in 1908, but C.Q.D. lingered on for a few more years especially in the British service where it had originated. It was used by Binns in the *Republic-Florida* collision in 1909. The *Titanic* used both signals. See Baarslag, **Radio Rescues...** p.8; Peter B. Schroeder, **Contact at Sea: a History of Maritime Radio Communications** (Ridgewood: The Gregg Press, 1967) pp.12-13, 120.
25. This may have been filmed by cameraman, Charles K. Hall. See *MPW* 4 May 1912, p.412.
26. The latter shot is mentioned in **Chicago Letter**, *MPW* 11 May 1912, p.511.
27. This release contained just one *Titanic*-related item among twelve news items – about the charity baseball game between New York and Boston teams for the *Titanic* fund. See *NYDM* 1 May 1912, p.31. There were other newsreel items released showing the aftermath of the disaster. Late in May 1912 Andrews Pictures were offering *Funeral of Wallace-Hartley, the Late Bandmaster of the Titanic* in a print of 300 feet, for £2 10s. See ad in *KLW* 23 May 1912, p.326.
28. **Titanic wreck pictures amaze Broadway throngs**, op cit. A telegram from a distributor, the Anti-Trust Film Co., urgently ordering another print, is reproduced – emphasising the film's popularity.
29. **Titanic Disaster**, *NYDM* 1 May 1912, p.27
30. **Marconi interested in film**, *NYDM* 1 May 1912, p.27.
31. *KLW* 15 June 1911, p.261.
32. *NYT* 21 April 1912, part 7, p.10: ad for Garden Theatre, 27th Street and Madison Avenue, for **Durbar in Kinemacolor** and **Added feature, S.S.**Titanic, **launching and Officers, "Caught by Kinemacolor."** By 28 April 1912 (in *NYT*, part 8, p.7) the ad had been changed to offer films of **Durbar Maine** *Titanic* (the *Maine* in Havana harbour was salvaged at this time and the operation was filmed). The launch of the *Olympic* was also shown.
33. *Titanic's* **captain in Kinemacolor**, *MPN* 20 April 1912, p.9. And *Titanic* **in Kinemacolor**, *Clipper*, 4 May 1912, p.5.
34. **Alleged** *Titanic* **Views**, *NYDM* 24 April 1912, p.26.
35. **Titanic wreck pictures amaze Broadway throngs**, op cit.
36. **Chicago Letter**, *MPW* op cit.
37. *MPW* 11 May 1912, p.579; *MPW* 18 May 1912, p.658; *MPW* 25 May 1912, p.755. In these ads the title of the film and its length, 900 ft, confirm that it was indeed the Animated Weekly film. The film was attributed to the Motion Picture Distributing and Sales Company. (The Sales Company, for short).
38. *MPN* 11 May 1912, p.24. See also *KLW* 25 April 1912, pp.52-53. The ad lists the Gaumont company's six branches throughout the UK: in London, Manchester, Liverpool, Glasgow, Birmingham, and Cardiff.
39. The poster is illustrated in the ad in *KLW* 2 May 1912, pp.78-79. The synopsis was available for 2d.
40. *Bios* 2 May 1912, pp.312-313.
41. **The** *'Titanic'* **Disaster**, *KLW* 2 May 1912, p.67.
42. *KLW* 9 May 1912, p.149. Welsh's letter was prompted by the *Kine's* assumption that the shot was taken on the *Titanic*: See also *Bios* 2 May 1912, pp.312-313 and p.319.
43. Library of Congress print FLA 1870. Almost the same wording appeared on the frontage of the Animated Weekly's Weber Theatre during its *Titanic* screenings.
44. Three such *Olympic* postcards are reproduced in Bown, op cit pp.73-5.
45. About this *'Lusitania'* postcard, see Bown, op cit p.79.
46. Eaton and Haas, *Titanic: triumph and Tragedy*, op cit, p.8.
47. R. Gardiner and D. Van der Vat, *The Titanic Conspiracy* (New York: Birch Lane Press, 1996).
48. **Stop Press**, *Bios* 2 May 1912, p.377. It cost the usual 4d per foot.

49. *Globe Topical – Titanic Disaster*: one page handout held in the British Library at Cup.21.g.7.(5.).
50. **The Globe Special**, *Bios* 9 May 1912, p.391.
51. And a version 207 feet long of the Warner release is held in the Kleine Collection at the Library of Congress.
52. A.W. Thomas, **Just about the photo play business**, *Photoplay* June 1912, p.61.
53. *Bios* 9 May 1912, p.419; *MPW* 27 April 1912, p.359. Warners sold the film for $60: see *MPW* 27 April 1912, p.344. Lobby posters were available.
54. For more on Warner's version see Simon Mills, *The Titanic in Pictures* (Chesham: Wordsmith Publications, 1995) p. 17, which reproduces a shot-list for the Warner version on p.129.
55. *MPW* 27 April 1912, p.359.
56. In an ad for Warner's Features from the *New York Morning Telegraph*, 21 April 1912 (undated copy reproduced in Eaton and Haas op cit, p.216).
57. **The *Titanic***, *MPW* 4 May 1912, p.436.
58. **Alleged *Titanic* Views**, *NYDM* 24 April 1912, p.26 op cit.
59. In this print there is an additional penultimate shot of tugs nosing the *Titanic/Olympic* out of the dock. Another NFTVA print ends with shots of the *Carpathia* and Captain Arthur H. Rostron (here called 'Rostrum').
60. *KLW* 2 May 1912, p.139. – this source states that the anchor shown in the film weighed 17 tons.
61. From a small ad of sale by a Liverpool cinema: *KLW* 2 May 1912, p.139.

Notes and References: Exhibiting the News Films

1. Editorial in *The Implet* 18 May 1912, p.2 (and p.8). *The Implet* is held in the Library of Congress Motion Picture Division.
2. **Fake Pictures**, *MPN* 11 May 1912, p.6.
3. Ibid. Letter from Alex Feinstein. 'Rainstorms' meant films which had become scratched, dirty and spotted through repeated projection and handling. See ad in *MPW* 4 May 1912, p.476 for a company which made a coating compound, 'Cellukote' to protect films and prevent them from becoming 'rainstorms'.
4. **Chicago Letter**, *MPW* 4 May 1912, p.412.
5. 'Observations by our man about town', *MPW* 11 May 1912, p.518. Perhaps these images referred to were either lantern slides, or a dramatised film, *Tragedy of the Sea*. See my chapter on dramatised films of the *Titanic*.
6. **Fooled patrons at *Titanic* show**, *New York Times*, 21 April 1912, pt.2, p.11.
7. **Survivors as lecturers**, *NYDM* 8 May 1912, p.24.
8. **Making Dirty Money**, *NYDM* 15 May 1912, p.25. From Herbert Corey, New York correspondent of the *Cincinnati Star-Times*.
9. **Fooled patrons at *Titanic* show**, *New York Times*, op cit.
10. **Louisville**, *MPW* 25 May 1912, p.746.
11. **Bars *Titanic* pictures**, *NYT* 28 April 1912, pt.2, p.4.
12. **Spectator's Comments**, *NYDM* 8 May 1912, p.24. 'Spectator' was, of course, Frank E. Woods. He ridiculed the mayors by adding the name 'Squedunk' to the list of towns with bans.
13. **The *Titanic***, *MPW* 4 May 1912, p.436.
14. Warner's ad, *MPW* 4 May 1912, p.447.
15. *MPW* 11 May 1912, p.550.
16. Telegram from the Anti-Trust Film Co, reproduced in *MPN* 27 April 1912, p.24.
17. ***Titanic* wreck pictures amaze Broadway throngs**, *MPN* 27 April 1912, p.24.
18. **Chicago Letter**, *MPW* 4 May 1912, p.412.
19. **New England**, *MPW* 11 May 1912, p.552.
20. From the web-site Encyclopedia Titanica. Persson, aged 25, was emigrating to America with his sister and niece. They drowned, while he, evidently a tough, brave and calm soul, survived in the

water for 6 hours after the *Titanic* sank. Ernst's letter was sent to his parents, wife and children, and as well as mentioning the photographing, he noted that the survivors of the *Titanic* were being well treated and given clothes and money.
21. *The Photo-Play* (Sydney) 27 April 1912, p.40. (Held in Mitchell Library, Sydney Public Library).
22. It included what seem like, respectively, scenes 1, 2, 14, 6, 9, and 16 of the Gaumont film. See *Der Kinematograph* 15 May 1912. See also the small ad in *Licht Bild Bühne* (LBB) 4 May 1912, p.47.
23. This Gaumont newsreel, was among the restorations of the Bundesfilmarchiv in Berlin in 1992, entitled *Zur Entsetzlichen Katastrophe der Titanic, der 1600 Menschen zum Opfer Fielen* (121 Meters). Reported in *Kintop*, no.2 (Frankfurt: Stroemfeld/Roter Stern, 1993). See Appendix 1, **Extant Films** for more details.
24. *LBB* 8 June 1912, pp.20, 25.
25. Quoted in Wedel article cited in my dramatised films chapter.
26. Vanessa Toulmin, **Women bioscope proprietors: the Queens of Showland** in John Fullerton ed., *Celebrating 1895* (Sydney: John Libby Press, 1998).
27. *The World's Fair* (WF) 18 May 1912, p.14. This and other World's Fair references come courtesy of Vanessa Toulmin. This reference is to a Mr E. Evans singing 'Be British' in Brown's Picture Hall, Oldham as part of a general programme of entertainment films shown there. A recording of this song is held in the private collections of Ray Johnson of Stoke-on-Trent, and R. Brown.
28. Yorkshire: *Bios* 9 May 1912, p.395; Dublin: *Bios* 16 May 1912, p.524.
29. *Cambridge Daily News*, 5 Sep 1938, p.4. Thanks to Nick Hiley for this reference.
30. See *WF* 27 April 1912, p.14 (Oldham); *WF* 4 May 1912, p.14 (Bradford).
31. *KLW* 2 May 1912, p.109. Bool describes his filming expedition to Newfoundland.
32. See my discussion of this in my article '**Have you seen the Gaekwar bob?': filming the 1911 Delhi Durbar** in: *Historical Journal of Film, Radio and Television*, vol.17,3, 1997, pp.309-345.
33. It is unclear to me why some cinemas continued to buy prints when a system of rental existed.
34. *KLW* 2 May 1912, p.139; 9 May 1912, p.195; 16 May 1912, p.259; 23 May 1912, p.326; 30 May 1912, p.387.
35. *KLW* 13 June 1912, p.521, repeated 4 July p.710; *KLW* 20 June 1912, p.583.
36. *KLW* 2 May 1912, p.139; *WF* 11 May 1912, p.4.
37. **Items of interest**, *Bios* 2 May 1912, p.317.
38. See *Bios* 2 May 1912, p.314.
39. For more on the Bonnot newsreels see Jean-Jacques Meusy, *Paris-Palaces, ou le Temps des Cinémas (1894-1918)* (Paris: AFRHC/CNRS Editions, 1995) pp.260, 402-3. See the dramatic account of the battle of the outlaws with police in an advertisement for Pathé, in *Le Courrier Cinématographique* (CC) 4 May 1912, pp.16-17; and **Petites Annonces** in the issue of 25 May 1912; see also **Pour les victimes du** *Titanic*, *Ciné-Journal* (CJ) 27 April 1912. One cameraman, Trimbach, later recalled that the Bonnot gang arrest film was censored and 'never appeared in Pathé Journal', which seems clearly false given the extensive trade press advertising of this item. See Pierre Trimbach, *Quand on Tournait la Manivelle Il y a 60 Ans* (Paris: editions CEFAG, 1970) pp.46-49.
40. Pathé ad in *CC* 4 May 1912, pp.16-17. The Gaumont film survives in the Cinémateque Royale in Belgium, entitled *Toutes les Phases de la Capture tragique des bandits Bonnot et Dubois* (150 meters).
41. *CJ* 20 April 1912, p.73.
42. *CJ* 27 April 1912, p.59.
43. *CJ* 4 May 1912, pp.15-16.
44. *CJ* 11 May 1912, p.41. *Les héros de la mer* including 'Southampton. Parade des Territoriaux aux benefice des survivants du *Titanic*.'. Note that the issues of the Gaumont Actualités newsreel were numbered, that of 4 May being no.18, 11 May being no.19, etc.
45. *CJ* 29 June 1912, p.39. This was issue no. 26 of Gaumont Actualités, and was c.160 meters in length.
46. **La Tragedie de l'Océan**, *CC* 4 May 1912, p.32.

47. The *Titanic* item was available c/o the *Courrier Cinématographique*: see *CC* 27 April 1912, p.36; repeated 4 May 1912, p.36; 11 May, p.37; 18 May, p.38; 25 May, p.38.
48. *CC* 25 May 1912, p.38, and repeated on 1 June p.28, 8 June p.34, 15 June p.38.

Notes and References: Dramas out of a Crisis

1. The original poem of eight verses is reprinted in Steven Biel, *Titanica – the Disaster of the Century in Poetry, Song and Prose* (NY: W.W. Norton and Co., 1998) pp.17-18.
2. Quentin Curtis in *Daily Telegraph* 23 Jan 1998.
3. There was also a reconstruction of the Thaw-White murder for the mutoscope. This version was enormously popular when screened in Coney Island, and the enthusiastic crowds ('largely composed of women') 'fought in desperation for a chance to view the mimic scene'. See **Disposing of money by the bushel**, *Billboard* 4 Aug 1906, p.3.
4. For a humorous account of the filming see *FI* 27 Feb 1909, p.9. For the film's full credits see AFI catalogue op cit. **Binns' injunction refused**, *FI* 4 Sep 1909, p.10.
5. H. Rialc, **Le '*Titanic*' – vues cinématographiques**, *Le Cinema*, 26 April 1912, p. 1 (held at the Bibliotèque nationale, Jo-25161).
6. I have examined several of the published picture albums by Harrison Fisher, which reproduce his pictures of American beauties, eg. *Fair Americans* of 1911. They are mainly dark haired, dark-eyed girls, and while the models are unidentified, several could indeed by Dorothy Gibson. Several photos of Gibson taken from journal articles of the period are in an album in the Robinson Locke collection, Scrapbook series 3, vol 407, pp.99-102, New York Public Library Performing Arts Division. Dorothy Gibson (b.1890, d. 20 Feb 1946) and Pauline Boeson Gibson aged 45 (1867- ?): the dates are from Judith B. Geller, *Titanic: Women and Children First* (Sparkford: Patrick Stephens Ltd., 1998) pp.56-59.
7. Many girls – often from 'New York's best families' – became Fisher models. Gibson was not the sole film starlet to have started out by posing for Harrison Fisher: others included Kalem stars Marguerite Courtot and Alice Joyce. See *Photoplay* July 1914, pp.72-3, 85. Some contemporary articles about artists' models in America are cited in: Norman Taylor, **Re-presenting the field of restricted cultural production: the nude at the interface**, *Screen*, vol. 37, no. 1, Spring 1996, pp.21-22.
8. **A new star in the picture firmament**, *MPW*, 2 Dec 1911, p.720.
9. *MPW* 27 April 1912, p.344. And *Indianapolis News* 18th April 1912. Mrs. Gibson's maiden name was Pauline C. Boeson.
10. *Pittsburgh Leader*, 21 April 1912. From Robinson Locke collection, Scrapbook series 3, vol 407, op cit.
11. *NYDM* 1 May 1912, see following endnote.
12. Elsewhere she says there was 'a slight jar'. Her accounts of the misadventure appear in *New York Morning Telegraph* 21 April 1912, and *NYDM* 1 May 1912, p.13 which commented that her account was like 'a chapter from some book'.
13. **Titanic survivor dies suddenly at 71**, taken from an unidentified *New Britain*, Connecticut newspaper, May 2, 1955, which also revealed that Sloper was an author.
14. **Dorothy Gibson tells her story of the *Titanic* wreck...** *MPN* 27 Apr 1912, p.7.
15. The details surrounding *Saved from the Titanic* have been well covered in: Frank Thompson, *Lost Films: Important Movies that Disappeared* (NY: Citadel Press, 1996) chapter 2 **Saved from the Titanic**; reprinted with additions from: Frank Thompson, **Lost at Sea**, *Film Comment* vol. 30,3 (May-June 1994). See article, **Saved from the *Titanic*** in *Voyage* no.8 June, 1991, issue on '*Titanic* in Films'. See also Wollstein op cit; and Titanic Historical Society website listing on Gibson.
16. *MPN* 4 May 1912, p.27.
17. Simon Mills, *The Titanic in Pictures* (Chesham: Wordsmith Publications, 1995). The suggestion that she co-wrote the film is based on two quotations in the *MPW*: a review says she starred in the film 'which she constructed as well' (11 May p.539), and 'A startling story of the sea's greatest tragedy

by Miss Dorothy Gibson, a survivor' (11 May p.561). The plot is summarised in *MPW* 11 May 1912, p.566. I have not found an actual footage given for the American release, because in the *Moving Picture World* at this time exact lengths were only given for Trust films, not for Independent releases like this one. A 'standard' length of films, though, was one reel or 1000 feet.

18. **A survivor of the *Titanic*,** *KLW* 11 July 1912, p.i and p.ix.
19. *MPW* 11 May 1912, p.539. Wollstein suggests that in the film the father travels on the *Titanic* with Dorothy.
20. *MPN* 11 May, 1912, p.35.
21. *MPN* 4 May 1912, p.19.
22. The *Moving Picture News* (op cit) put the release date at 16th May.
23. *MPW* 25 May 1912, p.724.
24. Herbert Birett, *Verzeichnis in Deutschland gelaufener filme 1911- 1920* (Munich, 1980) p. 53. Information from Michael Wedel.
25. *Ciné-Journal* 6 June 1912, p.70; and *Ciné-Journal* 29 June 1912, p.32 with a picture of Gibson on the ad – courtesy Jean-Jacques Meusy.
26. **A survivor of the *Titanic*,** *KLW* 11 July 1912, p.i and p.ix.
27. *Bios* 18 July 1912, p.xxix.
28. *NYDM* 8 May 1912, p.24.
29. Letter from Strickland King, *New York Times* 9 June 1912, pt.2, p.14. Encyclopedia Titanica quotes the *Moving Picture World* which denounced certain opportunists, and the editor strongly suggested that 'the deplorable disaster should be given as little attention as possible as an exhibition feature.'
30. Geller pp.58-9.
31. Thompson, *Lost Films...* op cit, pp.17-18. Release date: see *Bios* 16 May 1912, p.507.
32. Jules Brulatour was one of the organisers of the Universal Film Company and later was associated with Eastman Kodak. His first wife was Clara Isabelle and they had two daughters (later Mrs Harry C. Mills and Mrs F. W. Cochran), and a son, C. Jules Brulatour. After Jules divorced Dorothy, he married actress, Hope Hampton. He died in Mount Sinai Hospital in New York on October 26, 1946, the same year Dorothy died. Information from Encyclopedia Titanica and obituary of Jules Brulatour in *Variety*, 23rd October, 1946.
33. *New York Review* 30 Aug 1919. From Robinson Locke collection, Scrapbook series 3, vol 407, op cit.
34. This account of Dorothy Gibson has relied heavily on her Encyclopedia Titanica web-site entry, which cites the Last Will And Testament of Dorothy Gibson Brulatour, *People Magazine*, 16 March, 1998. Contributors are listed as George Behe, Phillip Gowan, Marley Elizabeth Greiner, Heather Leser, Jacob Walter Shober, Hans J. Wollstein.
35. *Licht-Bild-Bühne* (LBB) 27 April 1912, p.7; and issues of *LBB* for 1 June p.3; 8 June p.3; 4 May pp.20, 22; 15 June p.4; 22 June p.2-3. *Der Kinematograph* 1 May 1912 and 15 May 1912.
36. For release by Flam. Rigo & C.i in Trento. See *La Cine-Fono et la Rivista Fono-Cinematografica* 6 July 1912, p.6; the same journal of 3 Aug 1912, p.4 notes that it is a German production. Thanks to Livio Jacob and Piera Patat for loaning me the microfilm of this rare journal.
37. Ad for the film in *Der Kinematograph* 12 June 1912.
38. *LBB*, no. 23, 8 June 1912.
39. Interview with Emil Schünemann by Gerhard Lamprecht, 6 Jan 1956. Kindly sent to me by Regina Hoffmann of Stiftung Deutsche Kinemathek.
40. There is a good internet site on the Berlin studios at: http://www.cinegraph.de/etc/ateliers/bioskop.html.
41. Much of the following account of the Misu film comes via Michael Wedel, **Jüngst wiederaufgetaucht – damals untergegangen. Anmerkungen zur Wiederentdeckung des Titanic-Films** *In Nacht und Eis* **(Deutschland, 1912),** *Filmblatt* no.6, Winter 1997, pp.41-45 **[Recently Discovered, and Once Again Sunk: Remarks on the Rediscovery of the Titanic film** *In Nacht und Eis*

(Germany, 1912)] Wedel's article is followed on pp.45-48 by an essay about the director of the film, Mime Misu. These two articles would have been but little use to me had Deac Rossell not translated them: many thanks to a kind friend and colleague.
42. Quoted in Wedel op cit, from **Besuche in Berliner Kino-Ateliers**, *LBB*, Nr. 24, 15 June 1912.
43. This account of the film's production appear in Mills p.19-21, from a description in a newspaper, *Das Berliner Tageblatt* quoted in Michael Hanisch, *Auf den Spuren der Filmgeschichte. Berliner Schauplätze* (Berlin: Henschel Verlag, 1991) p.142.
44. The difficulties of making the film were described by Emil Schünemann in the interview with Gerhard Lamprecht cited above: in particular, the re-creation through models of the *Titanic* striking the iceberg.
45. This was suggested by Michael Hanisch and following him Austilat. See Michael Hanisch, op cit, pp.140-144. This retells the legend of the film's initial failure, reproducing a censor card for *In Nacht* and a poster for *Eccentric-Club*. He also discusses Misu's career. Much of Hanisch's discussion has been overtaken by Michael Wedel's article.
46. Ads appeared in *Lichtbild-Bühne*, *Der Kinematogaph*, and *Lichtbildtheater-Besitzer* notably between 8 June and 26 July. A final advertisement appeared 31 August in the *Lichtbild-Bühne*. I am almost entirely reliant on Wedel (via Rossell's translation) for these sections.
47. **Der Untergang der** *Titanic*, *LBB*, no. 28, 13 July 1912.
48. *LBB*, no. 25, 22 June 1912.
49. Hanisch p.140. A detailed list of scenes was reproduced in the trade journal *Der Kinematograph* no. 288, 3 July 1912.
50. Sources for the date of the public premiere on 17 August 1912: LBB, no. 28, 1912, p. 1 (ad); no. 30, 1912, p.2 (ad); **Der Untergang der** *Titanic*, *LBB*, no. 28, 13 July 1912, pp. 18-19. This article also offers the information about the July press screening: 'The film TITANIC ODER IN NACHT UND EIS was shown to a large group of critics these days.'
51. Attested to by a letter of endorsement from a cinema owner in Pirmasens.
52. Desmet advertised a print of *Titanic* in *De Komeet*, 1 November 1912. In the same issue of *De Komeet* the Groningen based cinema owner R. Uges also offered *Titanic* for rent, and P. Silvius, another film renter, claimed to possess 4 copies of the film, 2 with German and 2 with Dutch intertitles. All this information on the Netherlands comes courtesy of Ivo Blom.
53. Frank van der Maden, *Welte Komt...*(Arnhem: n.p., 1989)
54. Advertisements in *Nieuws van de Dag*: 28 September (Grand Theatre), 1 October (Witte Bioscoop), 4 October (Parisien), 7 October (Witte), 14 October (Witte). Also see issue of 16 September.
55. *In Nacht und Eis*, M8. Copyrighted by A.J. Danziger of New York City for the Continental Kunstfilm Co. of Germany. The registration included 11 'prints' and one 'sheet print' – presumably meaning frames from the film, and a 7-page synopsis, printed in German, and illustrated with two frame stills of the ship striking the iceberg and sinking. See US Copyright Office, Register of 'Motion Pictures not Photoplays', Class 'M', and microfilm of associated documents,1912-1929, microfilm 92/100, at the Library of Congress.
56. **Parisian notes**, *Bios* 17 Oct 1912, p.195.
57. Daniel Deshayes, **95 ans de cinéma forain et en salle à Lisieux**, *Bulletin de la Société Historique de Lisieux*, no.33, 1991-1993, p.104.
58. See **The Moving Picture Lecturer**, issue no.22 of *Iris* (Autumn 1996) p.153.
59. Andreas Austilat, **The** *Titanic* **sufaces again**, *Berliner Tagesspiegel*, 18 February 1998. Cited in Wedel, op cit. The two collectors were Horst Lange and Jan Gildemeister.
60. *Der Kinematograph*, no. 281, 15 May 1912. The film was passed by the censors in Berlin 19 June 1912.
61. See Mills p.21.
62. Kirsten Lehmann and Lydia Wiehring von Wendrin, **Mime Misu – Der Regisseur des Titanic-Films** *In Nacht und Eis*, *Filmblatt* no. 6, Winter 1997, pp. 41-8 (again partially translated for me by Deac Rossell). There is a note that this article is on the Net, and the authors hope to have further

news contributed; it might be that more has turned up. See: http://www.bibl.hff-potsdam.de/misc/mime1.html
63. Ron Mottram, *The Danish Cinema Before Dreyer* (Metuchen: Scarecrow Press, 1988), pp.167-69.
64. Two or three scenes were lost in the US version. My discussion of this film is based on: Ron Mottram, **August Blom**, in *Schiave Bianche allo Specchio*... (Pordenone: Studio Tosi, 1986) – copies of an English manuscript version of this paper were distributed at the time. The film was originally planned as 9 reels.
65. Gifford, *Books and Plays in Films*, op cit, p.71. Interestingly, *The Miracle*, the film version of which was supposedly lost on the Titanic (see my chapter about film people on the *Titanic*), was also taken from a fictional work by Hauptmann.
66. Quoted by Daniel J. Leab in *Film History* vol.9,1, 1997, p.62.
67. Hauptmann's *'Atlantis'*, *MPW* 6 Sep 1913, p.1074. Unthan is not to be confused with Kobelkoff, the 'artiste tronc', who ran a film show in France in the early years. See Pierre d'Hughes, *Almanach du Cinéma des Origines à 1945* (Paris: Encyclopaedia Universalis, 1992).
68. Hauptmann's *'Atlantis'*, op cit.
69. *MPW* 6 June 1914, pp.1358-1359.
70. **The greatest art industry in the world**, *T.P.'s Weekly* 19 Sep 1913; **Ship sunk for the cinema**, *The Times* 13 July 1914, p.5, the film had its London premiere in July; *MPW* 4 April 1914, p.58.
71. Mr. Hansen kindly sent me a photograph of a few frames of the strip. He is unsure of the exact date, but it would probably have been manufactured by either Bing, Carette, or Plank. Letters to me from Mr. Hansen, a former cameraman, of 18 June 1999 and 1 August 1999, enclosing his own photographs. The Library of Congress has just received another copy of this nitrate film loop of the shipwreck, among a group of such 'animated' films in little cardboard boxes labelled 'Kurze Films fur Kinematographen in Farben'. The loops are mainly short, though the shipwreck is longer than the others and more complex, according to George R. Willeman. Message on AMIA-L, 21 April 2000, forwarded to me by Jeanpaul Goergen.
72. Based on Kostov's 1958 interview with Engov, and on a 1929 article in the Bulgarian press.
73. See *AFI Index* for 1911-1920. An Italian film released 17April 1915 entitled *Titanic*, directed by Pier Angelo Mazzolotti, and produced by Bonnard Films of Torino has no connection with the famous ship: the 'Titanic' referred to is a new kind of mineral. See Aldo Bernardini, *Archivio del Cinema Italiano* (Roma: ANICA, 1991) p.657. Thanks to Vittorio Martinelli for explaining that this film was not to do with the *Titanic* ship.
74. Though the ship in this film only has two funnels, whereas the *Titanic* had four.
75. Photographs of the production can be found in Archibald Gracie, *Sanningen om Titanics Untergang* (Stockholm, 1930), held in the BFI library. Proposals by the Chamber of Shipping over the making of a film of the disaster (*Atlantis*?) can be found in Britain's Public Record Office at MT9/2922.
76. Produced at the Hochschule für bildende Kunste, 1998, and broadcast on ARTE in February 2000. Thanks to Jean-Jacques Meusy for this information.
77. Alex Budd Francis (1867-1934), Harry Raver (d. 1941: apparently beaten to death by a burglar).

Notes and References: Helping the Victims

1. Dave Bryceson op cit, pp.132, 233, 297, 302. One of the biggest contributors to this fund, of £500, was the Gaekwar of Baroda, who had recently been disgraced when cinema films seemed to show his inadequate obeisance to the British royal family at the Delhi Durbar. See *Daily Sketch* 22 Apr 1912, p.6.
2. Mark Bown, *R.M.S. 'Titanic' – a Portrait in Old Picture Postcards*, op cit p.53, who says the fund exceeded £413,200.
3. For example, in early 1911 Oldham picture halls collected money for the Colliery Disaster Fund. *KLW* 19 Jan 1911, p.691.
4. *The Cinema*, May 1912: p.4.

5. *Bios* 25 Apr 1912, p.245.
6. The opening was to have taken place on the 15 April but it was delayed, and this is what allowed the first show to include *Titanic* films. See Maurice Thornton, **The Cinema in Clevedon**, *Mercia Bioscope*, no.72, August 1999, pp.4-5, 10. Thanks to Curzon Community Cinema in Clevedon, and to Nicholas Hiley for drawing this to my attention.
7. *Bios* 2 May 1912, p.321; 9 May 1912, pp.395, 397, 409, 417, 429; 16 May 1912, pp.471, 473, 481, 487, 495; 23 May 1912, pp.547, 563; 30 May 1912, pp.623, 639.
8. *KLW* 9 May 1912, p.150.
9. Ken George, *'Two Sixpennies Please': Lewisham's Early Cinemas* (London: Lewisham Local History Society, 1987) p.13.
10. *Bios* 25 April 1912.
11. *KLW* 6 June 1912, p.421.
12. **A lady in the case**, *KLW* 30 May 1912, p.347.
13. *KLW* 9 May 1912, p.150; 2 May 1912, p.68; *Bios* 9 May 1912: pp.391, 393.
14. **What the theatres are doing**, *KLW* 25 April 1912, p.7.
15. *KLW* 9 May 1912, p.151.
16. **What the Trade is doing for the 'Titanic' sufferers**, *KLW* 25 April 1912, pp.6-7.
17. **What the Trade is doing for the 'Titanic' sufferers**, *KLW* 2 May 1912, pp.68-69; 9 May 1912, pp.150-151; 16 May 1912, p.209; 6 June 1912, p.395.
18. Bryceson op cit p.297.
19. *Daily Mail* 17 April 1912.
20. *Bios* 2 May 1912, p.372.
21. See the chapter Film people on the *Titanic*.
22. *Bios* 2 May 1912, p.333; 2 May 1912, pp.307/309.
23. *Bios* 9 May 1912, pp.383/385; 16 May 1912, p.461; 23 May 1912, p.547.
24. My own calculation based on the listings in Michael Open, *Fading Lights, Silver Screens* (Antrim: Greystoke Books, 1985). This useful and well researched book is unavailable at either the British Library or British Film Institute. To Mr. Open's list of 9 film venues open at this date in Belfast I have added one other: the Alhambra, which as we see from newspaper listings of *Titanic* shows, was also showing films at this time.
25. *Belfast Evening Telegraph* 2 May 1912, p.1. This and the following references were kindly sent me by Linda Greenwood of the Belfast Public Libraries, for which I am most grateful.
26. **Picture House, Royal Avenue, Belfast**, *KLW* 9 May 1912, p.151.
27. *Belfast Evening Telegraph*, 6 May 1912, p.1. Incidentally, typical prices of the various classes of seats within a Belfast picture palace were 2d., 4d., and 6d.
28. *Belfast Evening Telegraph*, 9 May and 10 May 1912, p.1.
29. **Belfast Alhambra**, *Belfast Evening Telegraph*, 7 May 1912.
30. *Irish News*, 7 May 1912.
31. Michael Davie, *Titanic: the Death and Life of a Legend* (NY: Henry Holt, 1986) pp.xviii-xix.
32. *The Cinema* 18 June 1914, p.19.
33. *Bios* 1 Aug 1912, p.331.
34. **France and the Pictures**, *KLW* 2 May 1912, p.131. See also **Pour les victimes du 'Titanic'**, *CJ* 27 April 1912, p.21. At this point he'd already collected more than 500 Francs.
35. *Courrier cinématographique* 8 June 1912, p.27. This detailed article on Willy, with accompanying photograph, claims he'd collected nearly 800 Francs in this way. *Bios* 18 July 1912, p.191; 1 May 1913, p.313; *KLW* 2 May 1912, p.69.
36. **France and the Pictures**, *KLW* 27 June 1912, p.603.
37. **In the Mississippi Valley**, *MPW* 25 May 1912, p.744.
38. Study of cinema exhibition is still a poor relation in film history, and I hope that my chapter here will help to show that the sources are available for detailed study of early picture palace exhibition, a fascinating area for further research.

Notes and References: The *Titanic* and Silent Cinema: Conclusion

1. *Bios* 20 Feb 1913, p.550.
2. *Bios* 26 Mar 1914, p.1396.
3. **The days of the nickel movie**, *Baltimore Sun Magazine* 25 Nov 1956, p.2. Cited in: Kathryn H. Fuller, *At the Picture Show: Small-Town Audiences and the Creation of Movie Fan Culture* (Washington/ London: Smithsonian Institution Press, 1996) p.59.
4. A *Titanic* spoof is apparently to be released, entitled *Gigantic*.

Notes and References: Appendix 1: Extant *Titanic* films

1. Thanks to Luke McKernan, formerly of the NFTVA, for his characteristically clear description of this and other *Titanic* films in the archive, and also for his thoughts on 'genuine' films.
2. *The Lost Film of the Titanic*: a 30-minute VHS available from Kingfisher, with the Gaumont newsreel footage incorporated into a documentary, including interviews. This version of the Gaumont newsreel was discovered by a woman in her garden shed in 1998, and was sold at auction.
3. Note that in the television documentary series, *Liner* (Channel 4, October 1997) it was claimed that a German company filmed the construction of the *Titanic*, and the footage was screened. But this is another misidentification of the *Olympic* for the *Titanic*.
4. Catalogued as *Zur entsetzlichen Katastrophe der "Titanic" der 1600 Menschen zum Opfer fielen*. Thanks to Jeanpaul Goergen for the information.
5. Thanks to Anne Simon at Lobster Films, Paris, for this information.
6. *Journal of Film Preservation*, nos. 58-59, 1999, p.95.

Notes and References: Appendix 2: *Lusitania*

1. *OLCJ* July 1906, p.170.
2. *KLW* 26 Sep 1907, p.351.
3. See *KLW* 19 Sep 1907, p.325. McDowell had recently left Warwick to join Walturdaw.
4. *Bios* 7 Oct 1909, p.9.
5. American Film Institute catalogue, *Film Beginnings, 1893-1910* (Los Angeles: American Film Institute, 1993).
6. The first mentioned is: *The American Liner 'Lusitania' entering New York Harbour* (Pathé frères, 1911), NFTVA 31 feet: shows two shots of the liner being assisted by tugs.
7. A cameraman on a German U-Boat really did this during one sinking, claimed a French newspaper. See *The Cinema* (*TC*) 27 May 1915, p.7.
8. The display had opened as 'The Evolution of the Dreadnought' and was retitled to reflect the current war. Frank Martin Todd, *The Story of the Exposition* (New York: Knickerbocker Press, 1921) volume 2, p.364. The exposition was to celebrate the discovery of the Pacific Ocean and the recent completion of the Panama Canal. Interestingly, quite a large number of exhibitors used film for demonstration and publicity purposes.
9. In Mary Evans picture library, London.
10. National Archive microfilm roll M580-197, frames 455, 506. Incidentally, the ship had been painted war grey within days of the outbreak of war. See *The Illustrated War News* 12 May 1915, p.7.
11. PRO, FO 372/773, frames 432-441. This and the previous reference are cited in Thomas A. Bailey, Paul B. Ryan, *The Lusitania Disaster...* (New York: The Free Press, 1975) pp.16-19. The film was distributed in Britain by the M.P. Sales Agency: see *TC* 27 May 1915, p.9.
12. Archive Films and the Producer's Library Service distribute versions of this material, showing the Lusitania departing New York. Strangely, their descriptions suggest footage is included of soldiers on the ship and passengers scrambling in panic on the deck.

13. **Over the border**, *TC* 20 May 1915, p.vii.
14. *TC* 20 May 1915, p.37. The man was Frank L. Cooper of the Grand Cinema, Liverpool.
15. **Cinema audience's fury**, *TC* 20 May 1915, p.xv. This was said to have occurred on 'Monday night', which would be 17 May.
16. Vittorio Martinelli, 'Joli...Jolivet', *Immagine*, nuova serie no.35, Summer 1996, p. 19-29. Kindly translated for me by Ivo Blom.
17. **Lasky star saved in 'Lusitania' disaster**, (The Cinema *TC*) 13 May 1915, p.13.
18. Interview with Jolivet in the *Daily News*, partly reprinted in **Editorial Chat**, *TC* 13 May 1915, p.3.
19. These details are from Des Hickey and Gus Smith, *Seven Days to Disaster: the Sinking of the Lusitania* (London: Collins, 1981) pp.95, 199, 231, 249, 259, 313. Rita's sister committed suicide two months after her husband George Vernon had drowned.
20. From *Apollon* April 1916. The film was directed by Gino Zaccaria, and was 1,250 meters in length. See Vittorio Martinelli's 1916 Italian filmography, p.35.
21. *MPN* 18 Mar 1916, p.1633; *MPW* 26 Feb 1916, p.1257. See also *MPW* 11 Aug 1917, p.923.
22. See the entry for *Lest We Forget* in the *AFI catalogue, Feature Films, 1911-1920*. The film also featured Hamilton Revelle, L. Rogers Lytton, and Kate Blancke. Lescaboura's *Behind the Motion Picture Screen* (Scientific American/Munn, 1919) has three nice stills of a *Lusitania* film set under construction.
23. **A real cinema drama**, *The Times* 7 June 1917, p.5, col. c. British actor Poluski was on a sinking ship returning from South Africa, Tony Fletcher tells me.
24. **Editorial Chat**, *TC* 13 May 1915, p.3 and see also p.ix about concerns for his safety; **Mr. Edgar Hounsell**, *TC* 13 May 1915, p.61. Thanks to Tony Fletcher for these references.
25. **Round the trade in Birmingham**, *TC* 20 May 1915, p.71.
26. **Round the trade in Birmingham**, op cit.
27. There were plans to film the salvage of the *Lusitania* in the 1930s. John D. Craig and a team of underwater cameramen planned to film in colour, using lights, and also to record sound! See *Motion Picture Herald* 13 June 1936, p.70.
28. Clyde Jeavons, **In the Picture: Sunken Treasure**, *Sight and Sound* 52,1 (Winter 1982/83); *BFI News* no.54, November 1982; *British Journal of Photography*, vol.130, 1983, p.154. See also *American Classic Screen* Jan/Feb 1983, p.8 for Kevin Brownlow's comments.
29. *Bios* 9 Dec 1915, p.1166.
30. Thanks to Robert Monks in Ireland for this information. See also *MPW* 2 Oct 1914, p.67; and **Irish History on the Screen**, *MPW* 29 Aug 1914, p.1245 (an interview with Macnamara).
31. *TC* 17 June 1915, p.4. Taken from an account in *MPW*.
32. Vittorio Martinelli 1917 Italian filmography, p.271 – the film was 1,808 meters.
33. See James D. Scott, **American film propaganda in revolutionary Russia**, *Prologue*, vol. 30, Fall 1998, pp.173-4. In *The War, The West and The Wilderness* (Secker & Warburg, 1979), Kevin Brownlow states that the print of *Ireland, A Nation* was in the baggage of Edward Hounsell.
34. *The Cinema* 27 Mar 1919, p.74 and pp.4-5. Thanks to Tony Fletcher for these references.
35. See Donald Crafton, *Before Mickey: the Animated Film 1898-1928* (Cambridge, Mass.: The MIT Press, 1982) pp.116-118. For a more theoretical analysis of the titles see Giaime Alonge, **La parola scritta nei film di animazione di propaganda negli anni della Grande Guerra**, in the conference proceedings, Francesco Pitassio and Leonardo Quaresima, *Scrittura e Immagine* (Udine: Forum, 1997) pp.266-7. An American poster for the McCay film is reproduced in Renzo Renzi, ed., *Il Cinematografo al Campo: l'arma nouva del primo conflitto mondiale* (Ancona: Transeuropa, 1993).
36. The story appeared in Fanny Hurst, *Humoresque* (New York: Harper, 1919).

INDEX of main text and Appendices

A Fool There Was 127
A Message to Garcia 160
Abbott, Stacey 105
Across the Ocean on the Lusitania 150
Adler, Bert 77
Alaska 36
Alaska (Panoramic Views of) 37
Alaska-Yukon-Pacific Exposition 33
Albany Ward cinemas 134
Alhambra, Belfast 136-137
Alliance Corporation 157
Ambrosia 24
Ambrosio (Co., and Arturo) 153-156, 160
America, benefit shows 138
American Express Company 24
American Feature Film Company 81
American Mutoscope and Biograph Company 14
American Press Association 51, 57, 60
American Slide Company 53
American Standard Company 113
Anglo-American Film Distributing Comany 156
Animated Weekly 70, 72, 74-77, 80-81, 86, 89, 91, 97
Anti-German Riots in Liverpool Following the Loss of "Lusitania" 162
Argus Weekly newsreel 39
Arnaud, Etienne 111
Arrival of the Lusitania 150
Assassination of the Grand Duke Sergius 107
Astor, John Jacob 57
Atkinson Collection, extant film 146
Atlantic 127, 140
Atlantis 124, 126
Australia, Titanic films shown 98
Australia's National Film & Sound Archive 32
Authors Film Company 155
Avenue film theatre Kentucky 60

Baltimore, memorial 139
Bamforth
 postcards 61
 slides 61
Bara, Theda 127
Barker, fund contributor 134
Barry, Edward 156, 157
Beesley, Lawrence 41

Belfast shipyards 135
Belfast, *Titanic* in
 extant film 147
Belye Stolby Festival 146
Berger, Fred 98
Bernstein, I 88
Beulah 157
Binns, Jack 74, 76, 81, 107
 extant film 142-143
Biograph, Clapham Junction 133
Bioskop-Atelier 116
Blackenburg, Mayor 95
Blom, August 124
Bolton, benefit show 132, 139
Bool, Mr 100
Boston, film ban 96
Bought 127
Bowen, Frederick S. slides 61
Branly, Herr/Mons, extant film 145
Bride, Harold 57
Britannic 9
British and Colonial Kinematograph Co. 24
 benefit fund 134
British Columbia, 30-36
British Movietone, extant film 143
British Pathé 9 (*see also* Pathé)
 extant film 143
Broadway Cinema, Hammersmith, *Lusitania* 153
Brown, Simon 105
Brownlow, Kevin 160
Brulatour, Jules A. 115
Buckwalter, H.H. 28
Bull, E. H. 24

C.Q.D. or Saved by Wireless 107, 127
Cabinet of Dr. Caligari, The 115
Cameron, James 9, 106, 122
Camperdown 65
Canadian Pacific Railway 30-35
Card, James 57
Carluccio, Leopoldo 156
Carpathia 17, 52-53, 57, 74-76, 81, 84, 88, 98, 103, 109, 139
 extant film 142-143, 145-146
 Myriorama 65
Carpet from Baghdad, The 157

185

Carson, Sir Edward 137
Carson, Kit 33
Catastrofe del Titanic, La (In Nacht und Eis) 115
Catastrophe du Titanic, La (In Nacht Und Eis?) 121-122
Central Film Service Company 81
Central News Syndicate 55
Central Palace, North Shields 134
Chaplin, Syd 161
Cinema Parisien, Amsterdam 119
Clapham, A. J., Company 55
Clapton Cine Theatre 100
Clements, C.B. 46
Clevedon Picture House 130
Collett, Rev. Stuart, extant film 146
Colorado 27-29
Comique Theatre, Boston 97
Continental Kunstfilm/Film Studio 115-116, 121
Continental Screen Company (Continental Kunstfilm) 121
Cottam 74
Coufal, Mr 56
Crangle, Richard, postcards 62
Crashing Through to Berlin 161
Crystal Theater, Louisville 97
Crystal Theater, Illinois 138
Cullingford, A.G. 133
Cunard (*see also* White Star) 7
 offices, extant film 146
Curtiz, Michael 124
Czech people, *Lusitania* 162

Dante's Inferno slides 56
Das Gespenst von Clyde 123
Day, Will 35, 39-40, 45
de Boer, J. 120
De Camp, Horace 17
de Cippico, Count Giuseppe 153-155
De Commerce, J. 53
de Jong, G. 120
de Mille, Cecil B. 153
De Ramp Der Titanic 119
Dennis, J.S. 33
Dentler, *see* Martin Dentler Co.
Der Excentric-Club 124
dernière sortie du Titanic, La 103
Desmet 119
Disaster of the Titanic (In Nacht und Eis) 119
Doolan, Thomas, poem 105
Dover-street studios 14-15
Drama paa Havet , et 124
Dublin,
 benefit show 132
 Titanic films shown 100

Dupont, E. A. 127

Eagle's Eye, The 161
early cinema 10
Easter Bonnet, The 109
Eclair film company/Moving Picture Company and *The Diamond Master* 20
 head of 22
 and Dorothy Gibson 108-109, 111
 and Little Willie 137-138
 rush production 140
 studio fire 114
Eden Musee 36-37
Edison Company 160
Eine alt Legende, das Marienwunder 124
Elge-Gaumont 98
EMI-Pathé library, extant film 146
Emmett, Robert 160
Empire music hall, London, *Lusitania* screening 150
Empire Palace, Ripley (Myriorama) 65
Empire Theatre, Southampton 134
Empire, West Hartlepool 132
Encyclopedia Titanica website 147
 extant film 147
Engov, Jurden 126
Essanay
 fund contributors 134
 et Drama paa Havet 124
European xxx Company 24
Excelsior Slide Company 51
Excentric-Club, Der 124

Fahlström, Arne
 family 22-24
 intended career, *Titanic* voyage 23
 memorial lifeboats 24
Falmouth, benefit show 132
Famous Players Film Company 154
Famous Players Lasky 124
Farquarson, Mary G.C. (Mrs Marvin) 14-15, 17
Fate of the Titanic, The 135
Feature Film Company 57
films length of, running time 11
Films Limited 77, 89
Fisher, Harrison 107
Flaherty 47
Fönss, Olaf 124
Fool There Was, A 127
Forman, Justus Miles 160
France,
 benefit performances 137
 Titanic films shown 102, 103
Francis, David slides 61

Frohman, Charles 154
From the Bottom of the Sea 90
Fuller, Miss 133
Futrelle, Jacques
  career 19
  during *Titanic* disaster 20
Futrelle, Mary 19

Garai, Bert 69
Garden Theatre, New York 80
Gaumont *(see also Titanic* News Films)
  cameraman 52, 75
  extant film versions 142-143
  Fate of the Titanic, The 135
  fund contributor 134
  Lusitania film 153
  Titanic Wreck Special (see *Titanic* News Films)
Gaumont Actualités 102, 103
Gaumont Animated Weekly 72
Gaumont Newsreel/Weekly Newsreel 72, 89, 98, 102
  extant versions 142-143
  Lusitania film 153
Gazette Pictures (cinema) Ireland 102
Gem Picturedrome, Bolton 139
Genina, Augusto 160
George Eastman House 57
George, Katherine 45
Germany, *Titanic* films shown 98
Gespenst von Clyde, Das 123
Gibson, Dorothy 11, 14, 107-108, 111-112, 115
  film complaints 114
  filmography 129
Gibson, Mrs Leonard 109
Gigantic 127
Giglio, Mr 42
Glasgow, benefit show 132
Globe Film Company 84-88, 96-97, 135, 145-146
  (see also Titanic News Films)
  extant film 145-146
  Fate of the Titanic, The 135
Gordon, W. Lyndsay 56
Gosfilmofond Festival
  extant film 146
Grand Theatre, Amsterdam 119
Grand Truck Steamship Company 36
Great Northern Company 24
Great Ocean Disaster, The 124
Great Titanic Disaster (slides) 52
Griffith, David Wark 14
Guggenheim, Benjamin 42
  companion 42
Guggenheim interests, 36-38

Hale's Tours 29-31
Halifax Photographic Company 25
Hamburger, Aron 14
Hameister, Willy 115
Hamilton, Count Arthur 123
Hamilton, George H 46
Hansen, Hans-Danklev 126
Harbeck, Brownie 41, 45
Harbeck, Mrs (Stetter, Catherine L. (Katie) 27, 40, 43
Harbeck, William 11
  cameras 39
  companion 40-45
  family 27, 42, 45
  films of 25-39, 44
  life, career of 27 ff
  importance of 46-47, 141
  loss of films 46
Hardy, Thomas, poem 5
Harland & Wolff 7, 135, 137
Harris, Henry Birkhardt 25
Harris, Irene 25
'Harry Lauder Leaves for America' 150
Hauptmann, Gerhart 124
Havas news agency 69
Heads (story) 161
Hearst-Selig News Pictorial 160
Hepworth Cinema Interviews 160
Hepworth Company, fund contributors 134
Her Redemption (See *La mano di Fatma*)
Hinton-Fell-Elliott Inc 57
Hirthe, Rasmus 127
Hitchcock, Alfred 105-106, 127
Hitchens, Robert (Hutchins/Hitchins) 76, 84,
  extant film 142-143
Hodden, Dr. J. Stuart 19
Hogue, Father 84
  extant film 145
Holliday, Frank E. 72
Hounsell, Edgar 156, 157
Hoxton cinema, benefit performances 134
Hubbard, Elbert 160
Hubsch, fund contributors 134
Hudson Fulton 150
Hull, benefit show 132
Hurst, Fanny 161
Hutchins, *see* Hitchens

icebergs 80, 100
Il Siluramento dell'Oceana 160
In Nacht und Eis 115-123, 127
  credits 128
  extant versions 142
Incidents Connected with the Titanic Disaster 136

International News Association 53
Inverclyde, Lady Mary 149
Ireland a Nation 160
Irish politics 137

Jack Chanty 157
Jackson, Mrs Winifred 62
Jeavons, Clyde 157
Jeffrey, C. T. 160
Jeffries-Johnson fight 95
Jerwan, Mrs. Marie 21
Jewel Productions 161
Jewell, Peter (Myriorama) 66
Joe (dog) 130
Jolivet, Rita 153-156, 160
Jones, Patrick L. 160
Jourgeon, M. 22
Jury's Kine Supplies 39
  slides 61

Kaiser, the Beast of Berlin, The 161
Kaiser Wilhelm II 149
Kaiserin Auguste Victoria 115
Katrina 154
Kerry and Toft's (cinema) Roscommon 102
Kertész, Mihaly 124
Key to Yesterday, The 157
Kine Weekly, fund contributors 134
Kinemacolor 9, 77, 80, 85
Kinematograph Exchange, slides 61
Kingfisher Productions, video, 143
Kismet play 153
Kleine Collection, extant film 146
Kleine, George 153
Klondike gold rush 36
Kostov, Kostadin 126
Kronprinz Wilhelm 149

La mano di Fatma 154-155
La Rediviva (see *Lest We Forget*)
Lacania 149
Lapland, extant film 146
Last Chapter, The 157
Last Stand of the Paris Motor Bandits 102
Lest We Forget 155-156
Levi Company (slides) 51
Lévy, René 21
Library of Congress 85
  extant film 146
'Lieutenant Daring' 24
Lifeboat, The slides 60
'Little Willie' , 'Little Willy' 137
Liverpool, benefit show 132
Lobster Films, Paris, extant film 145

London, benefit shows 132, 134
Lord Mayor's Fund, contributors 134, 136
Loss of the Titanic, The Myriorama 65
Lost Film of the Titanic, The 143
Lost in Mid-Ocean 126
Lubin 107
Lumber Industry 38
Lusitania
  extant films 162
  film of departure 152
  film recovered from 25, 157
  filmed by Walturdaw 149
  filmed by Warwick 149
  films on board 157
  Gaumont Graphic 150
  Harbeck on 35
  memorial cards 150
  Pathé film 150
  postcard 62
  screened at Empire, London 150
  shown as *Titanic* 90
  sinking 149-150
  status 151
Lusitania Day 162
Lusitania Survivors' Appeal 162
Lusitania Tragedy (Warwick) 162
Lyric film theatre, Champaign, Illinois 138

Mackay-Bennett 42-43, 74, 84
  extant film 142, 145
MacNamara, Walter 160
magic lantern
  importance of 49
  types of slides 49
Maine 102
Malachard, Delphine 20
Malachard, Noel
  career 20
  Titanic voyage 21-22, 41
mano di Fatma, La 154-155
Marconi 76, 77, 84
  extant film 142, 145
Marechal, Pierre 109
Marion, Louise M. 60, 61
Marshall Collection, extant film 146
Martin Dentler Company 98
Martinelli, Vittorio 161
Marvin, Daniel Warner 14-15, 17, 41
Marvin, Henry Norton 14
Marvin, Peggy 17
Marvin, Mrs 14-15, 17, 41
Mary Scully 74, 76, 81
  extant film 142-143
Mauritania 57, 81

shown as *Titanic* 91
McCay, Winsor 161
McDowell, J. 149
Memphis, film ban 95
Message to Garcia, A 160
Metro 155
Metropolitan 124
Midland Exclusive Film Company 156
Miles Brothers 27, 150
Miracle, The 25
Miss Masquerader 108
Mississippi Flood 55
Misu, Mime 115, 117-124
Misugraph Film Company 124
Money God, The 124
Motion Picture Distributing and Sales Company 72
Mountain Climbing in the State of Washington 38
Moving Picture and Projecting Machine Operators' Union 42-43
Mullens, Albert 119
Museum of the Moving Image, *In Nacht und Eis* 123
music halls, benefit collections 134
Myriorama, *see* Poole's

Nachmann, Herr 124
Nanook of the North 47
NFTVA (National Film and Television Archive) 9, 88, 123,
extant film 142-143, 145, 146
film from *Lusitania* 157
Lusitania films 150, 162
screening 105
National Press Association 55
New Gem Theater, Baltimore 139
New York Motion Picture Company 24
news slides 48-62
newspapers, illustrated 69-70
Night to Remember, A 106, 140
Norddeutscher-Lloyd 7
Nordisk 124
North, Wilfred 161
Northcliffe, Lord 35
Norwegian Lifeboat Association 24
Novelty Slide Company 55-56

Oceania 160
Olympic
construction 7
extant film 145, 147
film of 84-86, 88
launch 9, 80
mislabelled *Titanic* 84-86, 89-91, 145, 147

postcards (as *Titanic*) 85
slides 61
O'Neill, Barry 127
Orrell, George 139
Ostriche, Muriel 115
Our Lifeboatmen slides 61
Over the Top 161

Palais de Luxe, Liverpool 132
Panama Pacific International Exposition 150
Panopticon, Belfast 136
Paradise Lost slides 56
Parkhurst Theatre, London 133
Patents Company of America 14, 72
Paterson, film ban 96
Pathé 9, 88, 102, 107
Pathé (Animated) Gazette 70, 146 ,162
Lusitania film 150
Pathé-Journal
and Malachard 20
Pathé Weekly
and Malachard 21
Pathé's Animated Gazette 70, 146, 162
Peril of Fire 124
Perret, Léonce 155
Persson, Ernst Ulrik 98
Peter Pan 154
Philadelphia, film ban 95
Phoenix cinema, London 132
Picture House, Belfast 135
Pinchot, Gifford N. 38
Plymouth
Lapland arrives, extant film 146
Poole
Charles William 65
family 65
John R. 65, 66
Poole's Myriorama 65-68
Pordenone Film Festival, *In Nacht und Eis* 123
postcards, memorial 62
Pretoria 65
Price of Applause, The 161
Prince George 36
Prince Rupert 36
Proszynski camera 35
Provincial Cinematograph Theatres, fund contributors 134
Pryor, Charles A. (Pryor and Claire) 52-53, 55, 75
Pye, Mrs 162
Pyke Cinematograph Theatres 134

Quello che videro i miei Occhi (see *Lest We Forget*)

Raise the Titanic 140

Ramp der Titanic, De 119
Rank Organisation 106
Rediviva, La (see *Lest We Forget*)
Reinhardt, Max 25
Renowned Pictures Corporation 161
Republic 74, 107
Republic Company 88
Rescue Ship Carpathia 139
Rhodesia, benefit performances 137
Richard, C.B. 24
Rink cinema, Lewisham 132
Rita Jolivet Film Corporation 155
Robey, George 162
Robinson, M.M. 52, 75
Roland 124
Rookery Road Picture House, Birmingham 157
Roosevelt, Theodore 162
Rosso, Antonio 155
Rostron, Captain A. H. 52, 57, 76, 84, 103, 139
  extant film 142, 146
Round-Up 38, 46
Russia, extant film in 146

St. George's Hall, Belfast 136
St. Paul's Cathedral, memorial service 72
Sales Company 24
San Francisco
  earthquake 27
  Exposition 38
Sanders, William 137-138
Saunders, Alfred H. 19, 46
Saved from the Titanic 109, 114-115, 127-128, 140
  credits 128
Savoy Moving Picture Theatre, New York 92
Scala Theatre 9
Schubert Film Corp 127
Schünemann, Emil 115
Selig Polyscope Company 27, 29, 157
  (*see also* Hearst-Selig)
Seward, Frederick K. 109
Shipwreck, The slides 60
Shipwrecked in Icebergs (*In Nacht und Eis*) 121
Siege of the Paris Motor Bandits 102
Siluramento dell'Oceana, Il 160
Sinking of the Lusitania, The 161
Slocum, Dr. L.M. 45
Sloper, William Thomson 109
Smith, E.J. Captain
  extant film 142-143, 145-147
  film of 76, 81, 84, 86, 88
  friend of 24
  Kinemacolor 80, 85
  slides of 51, 57, 61
Smith, Lester, slides 61

Southampton
  stricken areas 134
Southend, benefit show 134
Spiers, Morris 152
Stead, William Thomas
  and Biofix portrait 17
  career, death 17-19
SDK, (Stiftung Deutsche Kinemathek) Berlin 98, 122
  extant film 143
Strong Man of USA 162
Submarine Pirate, A 161
Sullivan, Arthur 62
Survivante du Titanic, La 113
Survivor of the Titanic, A 113
Swiss cinema 103
Swissair 'flight 111' 69
Synod Hall, Edinburgh 65
Syracuse New York Company 81

Taft, President 37
Teodoro 156
Terne Palace Cinema, Paris 121
Thompson, Frank 88, 114
Thompson, John 57
Tietgen 125
Titanic
  1943 film 140
  1953 film 140
  1997 film 140
  1998 film 127
  benefit shows 130-138
  extant films 142-148
  film ban 95-96
  filming of, Harbeck 39
  filming on board 41
  films on board 24-25
  genuine films of 89, 105
  importance in Bulgaria 126
  memorial painting 139
  scam shows 90-96
  secondhand films 100-103
  size of 7
  slides 50-62
  toy filmloop 126
  unknown producer, extant film 146
Titanic Disaster (see *Titanic* News Films)
Titanic Disaster Heroes 136
Titanic Disaster, The slides 55
Titanic News Films
  Animated Weekly/Gaumont newsreel/*Titanic Disaster*/*Titanic Wreck Special* 70-81, 89, 97-98
  Animated Weekly/Gaumont, film in Europe 81-85, 89, 98, 102, 135, 142-144, 148
  genuine films of the *Titanic* 89

190

Globe/Warner, *Titanic Disaster* 84-88, 96-97, 135, 145-146
Pathé Gazette, *Titanic* newsreel/*Titanic Disaster* 70, 146
Titanic avant le grand depart, le 145
Topical Budget/Film Company/*Titanic* films 50, 70-72, 89
Titanic oder In Nacht und Eis (*In Nacht und Eis*) 118
Titanic Wreck Special (see *Titanic* News Films)
Titanic's Fate 136
Topical Budget 70, 72, 89
  Britannic 9
  Lusitania 162
Topical Film Company 50 (*see* Topical Budget)
Topical Press Agency 61
Tottenham, London, benefit show 134
Touraine 65
Tracked by Bloodhounds 28
Traffic in Souls 160
Tragedy of the Lusitania (Pathé's Animated Gazette) 162
Triangle Film Corporation 161
Trip over Cripple Creek Short Line 29
Truth Wagon, The 157
Tverdovskii, Ivan 146
Tyler Apparatus Company 61
Tyler, Walter Co. 61
  fund contributor 134

U-20, U-Boat 150
U-Boat attack on Danes 156
Unafraid, The 153
Underwood and Underwood 57
Universal 161
Universal-Jewel Productions 161
Untergang der Titanic, Der 115
Unthan, Charles 124
Unwritten Law, The 107
Urban, Charles 7
Uttley, Commissioner 95

Vanderbilt, Alfred Gwynne 154, 162
Vernon, George 154
Victoria, British Columbia 31, 33
Vitagraph 107, 126, 161
  fund contributors 134

Walter Tyler company (*see* Tyler)
Walturdaw Company, filming *Lusitania* 149
Warner Theater Film Company/Warner's Features 88, 96
  extant film 146
Warner's Features (*see* Warner Theater Film Company)
Warwick Bioscope Chronicle
  Lusitania 150, 162
Warwick Trading Company
  filming *Lacania* 149
  Lusitania 149-150
Was die Titanic sie lehrte 113
Watson, J. Fred 24
Wavertree Picturedrome, Liverpool 100
Weber's Theatre, New York 76-77, 97
wedding film, Marvin 15
Wedel, Michael 123
Welsh, Mr 85
West, Eugene 94
Western State Illustrating Company 35
White Slave Traffic slides 56
White Star 7
  Cunard offices, extant film 146
  Harbeck contract 39
  London Office 70
  New York Offices 17, 76, 84,
  New York Offices extant film 142, 145
Whitely, Thomas 57
Wills, Archie 36
Wilson, President 151
Winchester, Bishop of 5
Winnipeg Exposition 38
Witte Bioscoop, Amsterdam 119-120
Wolverhampton, benefit show 132
'World Wars' (*Lusitania* exhibit) 150
Wreck of the Titanic (slides) 51
Wynard, Charles 46

Yakovleva, Natalia 146
Yellowstone Park, Scenes in 28
Yermak 100
Yorkshire, *Titanic* films shown 100
Yvois, Henriette 40-41, 43

Zukor, Eugen 124
Zvani 155